PATTERN CUTTING
for MEN'S COSTUME

ELIZABETH FRIENDSHIP

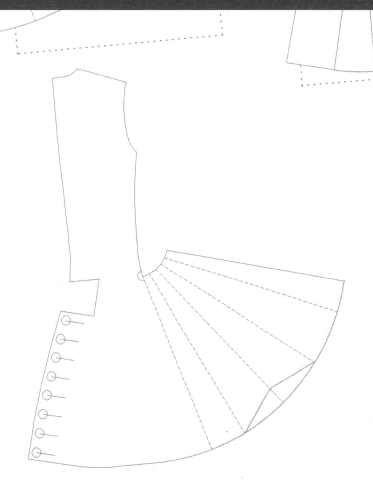

methuen | drama

To the Design students of the Royal Welsh College of Music and Drama, past, present and future, with gratitude and affection

Acknowledgements

My grateful thanks go to the following for their encouragement, help and support:

The staff and students of the Royal Welsh College of Music and Drama, Cardiff

The staff and students of the National College of the Arts, Seychelles

Karen Thomas, Betty Palmer, Jill Salen, Sean Crowley, Nigel Hook, James North

Althea MacKenzie of the Hereford Museum; Estelle Gilbert of the Somerset Rural Life Museum, Glastonbury; Mr Exton of Exton's, Gentlemen's Outfitters, Raglan

Jenny Ridout of A&C Black; Nicky Thompson, Margaret Brain and Susannah Jayes

First published 2008
A&C Black Publishers Ltd
36 Soho Square
London W1D 3QY

© 2008 Elizabeth Friendship

ISBN 978-1-4081-0006-6

A CIP record for this book is available from the British Library.

This book is produced using paper that is made from wood grown in managed, sustainable forests. It is natural, renewable and recyclable. The logging and manufacturing processes conform to the environmental regulations of the country of origin.

Typeset in 11pt/15pt Frutiger Light

Printed and bound in Malta by Gutenberg Ltd.

Contents

Introduction

The two most commonly used methods of cutting patterns for theatrical costumes are flat pattern cutting and cutting on the stand. Although many beautiful costumes can be made on the stand, the former method is much more versatile. Students are often daunted by the mathematics involved in flat pattern cutting but they look more complicated than they are. Once the basic principles are understood the rewards are considerable. This book was written for theatre design students as a foundation which will enable them to follow careers in any branch of costume.

When we look at paintings of fashionable people of the past, it would seem that the human body has changed over the years; fashionable men in the late Middle Ages appear to have had broad shoulders and narrow waists, mid-16th-century men were tall and powerfully built, Elizabethan men had long slender legs and so forth. In fact, the human body has not changed shape significantly in millennia. There are racial differences certainly: some African races such as the Maasai and Samburu have long slender bodies, southern Europeans are generally short and stocky, as are South American Indians, and most Orientals are small and delicately built; but they have always had these characteristics. It is the cut and construction of their clothes that has made fashionable people appear to change shape.

The peasants that Pieter Bruegel the Elder painted in the mid-16th century look well nourished and of normal proportions, but fashionable men of the same period might almost be from a different species. In fact, their bodies would not have been very different: it is the cut of their clothes which gives the impression of fundamentally different proportions. Attention is focused on specific parts of the body and emphasises them giving the appearance of exaggerated proportions as fashion dictates: the shoulders look wide and consequently the waist narrow; the legs look long and the body slight. When analysing costume, look at the overall impression and note where the proportions deviate from the norm and how this has been achieved. Within reason, any body can give the desired impression by the cut and construction of the garments, the position of the seams and the use of padding and stiffening.

There are very few original early garments still in existence and they all belonged to the rich; there are no peasant costumes. One should not think that all early garments were exactly like the few existing examples; there would have been as many variations as tailors to make them and customers to assert their preferences. The patterns in this book are not faithful reconstructions of existing garments, but they will give the correct shapes of the most common garments for each period.

The period patterns in Chapters 6–9 of this book cover both fashionable and non-fashionable garments from the middle of the 16th century to the end of the 18th and non-fashionable garments to the mid-19th century. During the second half of the 18th century, as fine tailoring developed in England, the concept of 'fit' as opposed to 'shape' became the hallmark of the trade. The aim of fine tailoring is to make a man look good no matter what his shape and all men do look good in a well-cut suit. This book does not enter the realms of fine tailoring which employs very specific skills. The method given here is more akin to dressmaking which is better suited to most period costume. Even non-fashionable 19th-century suits can be made from these instructions, but fashionable coats from the late 18th century onwards are best left to tailors.

There are many occasions when costumes are required to give the feeling of a period without absolute fidelity and sometimes they are required to incorporate elements from several periods. An understanding of the rich variety of period styles and the ways they can be achieved will enable the cutter to draft patterns for any wearable costume. The method in this book is designed so that the cutter will be able to draft a faithful pattern from any costume sketch or illustration whether or not it is for conventional period costume.

HOW TO USE THIS BOOK

Chapter 1 includes a section on equipment; only the first eight items are essential and none of these is very expensive, so it is worth getting good tools some of which will last a lifetime.

The next section lists necessary measurements and a diagram of where they should be taken. There are also charts of 'average' measurements which should be used in preference to doubtful measurements which may have been supplied.

Chapter 2 gives advice on drafting patterns, cutting out the garment and constructing a toile. There are also some brief notes on construction and some useful techniques for making theatrical costumes.

Chapter 3 deals with basic patterns using 'average' measurements. This is the core of the book: it is important that these patterns are mastered before attempting those that follow. The basic patterns are for the upper body, straight sleeve, two-piece sleeve and trousers. They should be regarded as the norm. There is very little ease on the upper body pattern, the waist is in the natural position, the neck lies at the base of the neck, the shoulder seam lies along the top of the shoulder and is not exaggerated. Waist suppression (i.e. the amount that has to be deducted to make the garment fit at the waist) is deducted from the pattern in the most usual positions. The sleeves and trousers are cut without exaggeration. All these patterns would make simple, rather dull garments without any special features, but experience in cutting these patterns will give an understanding of how pattern pieces should look.

The use of .25cm, .5cm, and .75cm may seem over-precise and something of an anomaly but it is easier to see a fraction of a centimetre than individual millimetres.

Chapter 4 deals with altering the basic patterns for individual measurements, a process which should be carried out before the patterns are modified.

Chapter 5 explains the basic principles of modifying patterns.

Chapters 6–9 deal with the ways of adapting patterns for period costumes. The patterns are in chronological order rather than order of complexity; some are very easy, a few more challenging. If the basic patterns have been understood, the period patterns should not be a problem. Each chapter has a brief introductory account of the costume of that period. This is by no means comprehensive and cannot take the place of a good history of costume; a list of standard works is included in the bibliography.

Chapter 10 includes patterns which belong to many periods – cloaks and simple trousers.

1

Getting started

EQUIPMENT

The equipment for cutting patterns is not extensive; only the first eight on the list are absolutely necessary and it is worth while getting the best quality. The only expensive item is the tailor's dummy which, although not essential, is very useful.

Scissors – a large pair of sharp scissors is essential for good work. It is possible to cut patterns on newspaper or wallpaper but not possible to make good patterns without good scissors. You must have separate scissors for cutting paper and fabric. Scissors do not last a lifetime and should be replaced as soon as they become blunt and start to slow down the work. It is not worth while having them sharpened.

Cutting paper – despite the note about scissors, it is much easier and more pleasant to use good cutting paper. Flat sheets of brown wrapping paper are best for patterns which are to last. Otherwise use plain white pattern cutting paper. This is thin enough for the lines to be seen through to the back which is often useful. Paper printed with lines or 'dot and cross' is not accurate enough for careful patterns. Pattern card is used for really durable patterns.

Tape measures – good quality tapes that do not stretch and can be stood on edge to measure curves should always be used.

Adhesive tape – clear tape or masking tape is suitable; the latter is easier to use as it tears easily and it is possible to draw on it. If a lot of tape is to be used, a tape dispenser saves sore fingers and is not expensive.

Rulers and straightedges – clear plastic rulers, as long as possible, are best for general use but an opaque ruler is necessary when marking dark materials. Wooden metre/yard sticks are not accurate enough for

cutting patterns. Straightedges need to be at least two metres/yards long. It is possible to buy rulers of this length but the strips of aluminium framing used by sign writers are ideal as they are light enough to handle and do not bend. Plastic window framing is also suitable but a little heavier. Either type of framing can be marked with a felt pen which is useful when cutting long garments such as cloaks. The marks can be wiped off with a damp cloth when no longer needed.

Pencils and pens – most people have a preference for a particular grade of pencil (the harder the pencil the cleaner the lines), others would rather use a non-smudging pen. Coloured pens and crayons are useful. Tailor's chalk, wax chalk and soap are traditionally used for marking woollen fabrics.

Tracing wheel and carbon paper – the best kind of tracing wheel has needle points and a thumb rest. Carbon paper is sometimes sold as tracing paper.

Dressmaking pins and pattern weights – long, fine steel pins are best. Pins are most often used to keep sections of pattern in place when tracing lines etc. Weights serve the same purpose and are in many ways preferable. Special weights are sold for the purpose but the weights from old-fashioned kitchen scales will do perfectly well or even small food tins.

Tailor's dummy – this is an expensive item not essential for flat pattern cutting but very useful.

Fashion ruler and French curves – these are useful for drawing armholes, necklines and general curves.

Calculator – to make sure that your calculations and measurements are accurate and not rough and ready!

MEASUREMENTS

There is a general misconception that people used to be smaller than they are now and we are gradually getting bigger. In fact, the average height of the men on the *Mary Rose*, Henry VIII's warship that sank in the Solent in 1545, was 171cm (5'7") and some were 180cm (5'11") – much the same as the average height of men in Britain today. Malnutrition and disease are the chief causes of stunted growth and the reason why people in the 19th century were generally smaller than they are now. The appalling living and working conditions of the poor, who had moved from the country to the cities to work in mills and factories, and the deterioration of their diet, had a detrimental effect which was to last into the 20th century. As a result, the minimum height for a man entering the army for the Boer War had to be reduced from 5'6" (167.5cm) to 5'4" (162.5cm).

No table of measurements can ever hope to be definitive, but those that British tailors used in the early 20th century had more chance of accuracy than is possible now. Most if not all of their clients would have been middle-class Caucasians. Even so the 'Apollo', or preferred figure, seems rather small by present-day standards, very small compared to people of African origin but quite large compared with the small-framed Oriental races. Physical differences between different races persist: some races are short and stocky, others long and lean; but improved diets, changed lifestyles and increased racial intermixing have led to much greater diversity in physical build.

When a client is measured by his tailor he wears a suit. The jacket measurements are taken over his suit jacket which will then be removed so that the waistcoat and trouser measurements can be taken. The tailor keeps suit patterns for all his clients which will be updated as necessary. He aims to give his clients the appearance of perfect proportions; that is why a man will always look good in a well-cut suit no matter what size he may be.

According to tailoring books of the early 20th century, ideal proportions are:

Height	5'8"	(approximately 1.725m)
Weight	135lb	(approximately 60.75kg)
Chest	36"	(approximately 91cm)
Waist	32"	(approximately 81cm)

Although these measurements are still valid, the measurements tailors take are not usually appropriate for costume makers (in any case, few men now have bespoke suits and many young men do not have one of any description). Period costumes before the end of the 18th century did not use modern tailoring techniques and many costumes bear no resemblance to a modern suit, so a different system is necessary. The measurements on the charts in this book bear more resemblance to dressmaking than tailoring, although the proportion of chest, waist and seat has been retained (i.e. the chest is 10cm (4") larger than the waist and the seat is 5cm (2") larger than the waist).

The measurement charts

The measurements have been collated from many sources: individual measurements of professional and amateur performers, clothing factories, medical charts and tailors' measurements. The Basic Patterns in Chapter 3 are drafted from the charts and they will be found to be satisfactory for 'average' proportions.

Adapting the charts for individual measurements

Many men will conform to the charts but many will not. Instructions are given in Chapter 4 for adapting the chart measurements to individual requirements. Sometimes the deviation from the chart will be found to be considerable; you should not be afraid of making dramatic alterations when making for exceptional sizes; there *are* men with 150cm (59") waists.

Taking measurements

The person being measured must not wear clothes that distort his shape such as thick pullovers, belts or bulging pockets. He should stand naturally and not wear shoes. It is important to establish the precise points for taking measurements and it is easy to over-measure. The waist line is one problem area as it not necessarily where the trouser waist band is worn. (Tailors say that trousers only hang correctly if worn with braces, the male waist line being insufficiently defined to provide adequate support.) A piece of elastic should be tied round at the desired position (usually about 4cm (1½") above the hip bone) and measurements for nape to waist and outside leg taken from or to this level. A short necklace of small beads or chain that fits snugly round the base of the neck also provides useful anchor points.

TAKING MEASUREMENTS	
1 HEIGHT	Taken against a wall with a set square on top of the head and no shoes
2 CHEST	Taken round the widest part
3 WAIST	Taken round the elastic floor (usually taken as 4cm (1½") above the hip bone)
4 SEAT	Taken round the fullest part
5 CROSS CHEST	Measured from where the arms join the chest
6 NECK POINT TO SHOULDER	From the neck point to the bone the end of the shoulder
7 NECK POINT TO ELBOW	From the neck point – to the shoulder point – to the elbow
8 NECK POINT TO WRIST	From neck point – to end of shoulder – to elbow – to wrist with arm slightly bent
9 TOP ARM	Measured round the fullest part
10 ELBOW	Measured round the elbow with the arm slightly bent
11 WRIST	Measured round the wrist bones
12 OUTSIDE LEG	Measured from the elastic to the floor
13 INSIDE LEG	Measured from the fork to the floor
14 NAPE TO WAIST (at back)	Measured from the prominent bone at the base of the neck to the elastic
15 CROSS BACK	Measured from where the arms join the body
16 NAPE TO FLOOR	Measured from the prominent bone at the base of the neck to the floor

Note. The shoulder and arm measurements are taken continuously to avoid over-measuring. The length of arm measurement is the total neck point to wrist measurement less the shoulder length.

The numbers on the diagram opposite refer to the measurements above. The red lines indicate where a piece of elastic should be tied to establish the waist line.

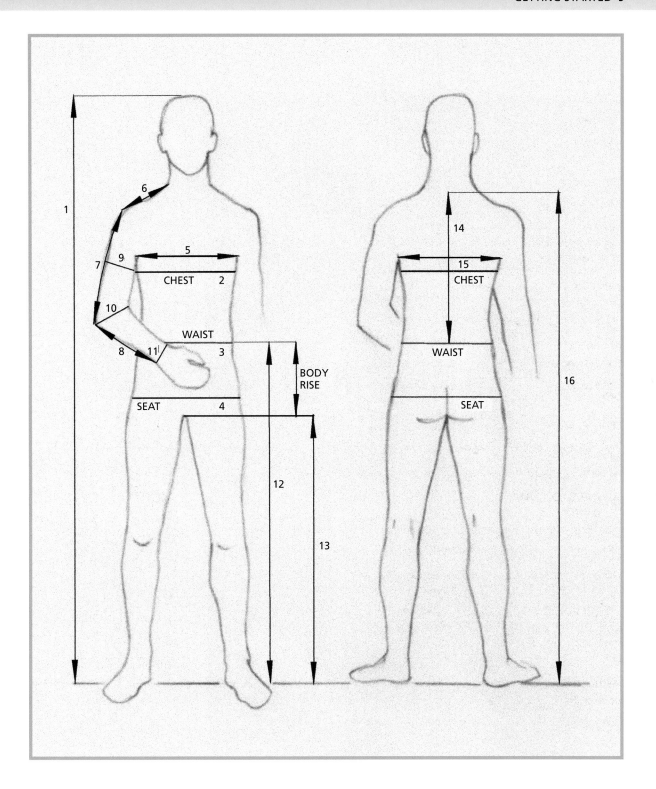

METRIC MEASUREMENTS FOR CUTTING BASIC PATTERNS

MEASUREMENTS FOR UPPER BODY PATTERN										
CHEST SIZE	80	85	90	95	100	105	110	115	120	125
NAPE TO WAIST	See following chart									
BACK NECK WIDTH	12	12.5	13	13.5	14	14.5	15	15.5	16	16.5
BACK NECK RISE	1	1.25	1.5	1.75	2	2.25	2.5	2.75	3	3.25
BACK SHOULDER SLOPE	4.5	4.5	4.5	5	5	5	5.5	5.5	5.5	6
SHOULDER LENGTH	12	13	14	15	16	17	18	19	20	21
ARMHOLE DEPTH	18	18.5	19	19.5	20	20.5	21	21.5	22	22.5
CENTRE FRONT LENGTH = NAPE TO WAIST MEASUREMENT MINUS –	6	6.5	7	7.5	8	8.5	9	9.5	10	10.5
FRONT DART WIDTH	3	3.5	4	4.5	5	5.5	6	6.5	7	7.5
FRONT DART LENGTH	15	16	17	18	19	20	21	22	23	24
LEVEL OF CROSS CHEST ABOVE CHEST LINE	5	5	6	6	6.5	6.5	7	7	7.5	8
CROSS CHEST	34	36	38	40	42	44	46	48	50	52
WAIST	70	75	80	85	90	95	100	105	110	115
FRONT LENGTH ADDITION	1	1	1.5	1.5	2	2	2.5	2.5	3	3

NAPE TO WAIST MEASUREMENTS					
HEIGHT	1.65m (5'5")	1.7m (5'7")	1.75m (5'9")	1.8m (5'11")	1.85m (6'1")
NAPE TO WAIST	40	42	44	46	48

MEASUREMENTS FOR BASIC SLEEVES									
CHEST SIZE	80	85	90	95	100	105	110	115	120	125
WIDTH OF SLEEVE	34	35	36	37	38	39	40	41	42	43
LENGTH OF SLEEVE	Nape to waist measurement plus depth of sleeve head measurement								
DEPTH OF SLEEVE HEAD	13.5	14	14.5	15	15.5	16	16.5	17	17.5	18
FRONT PITCH	½ Depth of sleeve head measurement								
BACK PITCH	⅓ Depth of sleeve head measurement								
LEVEL OF ELBOW	Midway between front pitch and wrist								

EXTRA MEASUREMENTS FOR SIMPLE TWO-PIECE SLEEVES									
CHEST SIZE	80	85	90	95	100	105	110	115	120	125
SLASH WIDTH	1.5	2	2	2.5	2.5	3	3	3.5	3.5	4
AVERAGE WRIST MEASUREMENT	28	28	30	30	30	32	32	32	34	34

MEASUREMENTS FOR BASIC TROUSERS									
Three inside leg measurements are given in the following chart for short, medium and tall men									
CHEST SIZE	80	85	90	95	100	105	110	115	120	125
SEAT	85	90	95	100	105	110	115	120	125	130
OUTSIDE LEG	98	99	100	101	102	103	104	105	106	107
INSIDE LEG	75cm for all sizes								
OUTSIDE LEG	103	104	105	106	107	108	109	110	111	112
INSIDE LEG	80cm for all sizes								
OUTSIDE LEG	108	109	110	111	112	113	114	115	116	117
INSIDE LEG	85cm for all sizes								
BODY RISE	23	24	25	26	27	28	29	30	31	32
FRONT CRUTCH WIDTH	5.5	5.75	6	6.25	6.5	6.75	7	7.25	7.5	7.75
WAIST	70	75	80	85	90	95	100	105	110	115
KNEE	42	44	46	48	50	52	54	56	58	60
TROUSER BOTTOMS	40	40	42	42	44	44	46	46	48	48

IMPERIAL MEASUREMENTS FOR CUTTING BASIC PATTERNS

MEASUREMENTS FOR UPPER BODY PATTERN

CHEST SIZE	32"	34"	36"	38"	40"	42"	44"	46"	48"	50"
NAPE TO WAIST	See following chart									
BACK NECK WIDTH	4¾	5	5¼	5½	5¾	6	6¼	6½	6¾	7
BACK NECK RISE	⅜	½	⅝	¾	⅞	1	1⅛	1¼	1⅜	1½
BACK SHOULDER SLOPE	1¾	1¾	1¾	2	2	2	2¼	2¼	2⅜	2⅜
SHOULDER LENGTH	4¾	5	5¼	6	6¼	6½	6¾	7	7¼	7½
ARMHOLE DEPTH	7	7¼	7½	7¾	8	8¼	8½	8¾	9	9¼
CENTRE FRONT LENGTH = NAPE TO WAIST MEASUREMENT MINUS –	2⅜	2½	2¾	3	3¼	3½	3½	3¾	4	4¼
FRONT DART WIDTH	1¼	1½	1½	1¾	2	2¼	2½	2¾	3	3¼
FRONT DART LENGTH	6	6¼	6½	6¾	7	7¼	7½	7¾	8	8¼
LEVEL OF CROSS CHEST ABOVE CHEST LINE	2	2	2½	2½	2¾	2¾	3	3	3¼	3¼
CROSS CHEST	13½	14¼	15	15¾	16½	17¼	18	18¾	19½	20
WAIST	28	30	32	34	36	38	40	42	44	46
FRONT LENGTH ADDITION	½	⅝	¾	⅞	1	1⅛	1¼	1⅜	1½	1⅝

NAPE TO WAIST MEASUREMENTS

HEIGHT	5'5" (1.65m)	5'7" (1.7m)	5'9" (1.75m)	5'11" (1.8m)	6'1" (1.85m)
NAPE TO WAIST	15¾"	16½"	17¼"	18"	19"

MEASUREMENTS FOR BASIC SLEEVES

CHEST SIZE	32"	34"	36"	38"	40"	42"	44"	46"	48"	50"
WIDTH OF SLEEVE	13½	13¾	14	14½	15	15¼	15¾	16¼	16½	17
LENGTH OF SLEEVE	Nape to waist measurement plus depth of sleeve head measurement									
DEPTH OF SLEEVE HEAD	5¼	5½	5¾	6	6¼	6½	6¾	7	7¼	7½
FRONT PITCH	½ Depth of sleeve head measurement									
BACK PITCH	⅓ Depth of sleeve head measurement									
LEVEL OF ELBOW	Midway between front pitch and wrist									

EXTRA MEASUREMENTS FOR SIMPLE TWO-PIECE SLEEVES

CHEST SIZE	32"	34"	36"	38"	40"	42"	44"	46"	48"	50"
SLASH WIDTH	½	¾	¾	1	1	1⅛	1¼	1⅜	1½	1⅝
AVERAGE WRIST MEASUREMENT	11	11¼	11½	11¾	12	12¼	12½	12¾	13	13¼

MEASUREMENTS FOR BASIC TROUSERS

Three inside leg measurements are given in the following chart for short, medium and tall men

CHEST SIZE	32"	34"	36"	38"	40"	42"	44"	46"	48"	50"
SEAT	34	36	38	40	42	44	46	48	50	52
OUTSIDE LEG	38⅝	39	39⅜	39¾	40⅛	40½	40⅞	41¼	41⅝	42
INSIDE LEG	29½" for all sizes									
OUTSIDE LEG	40⅝	41	41⅜	41¾	42⅛	42½	42⅞	43½	43⅝	44
INSIDE LEG	31½" for all sizes									
OUTSIDE LEG	42⅝	43	43⅜	43¾	44⅛	44½	44⅞	45¼	45⅝	46
INSIDE LEG	33½" for all sizes									
BODY RISE	9⅛	9½	9⅞	10¼	10⅝	11	11⅜	11¾	12⅛	12½
FRONT CRUTCH WIDTH	2	2¼	2¼	2½	2½	2¾	2¾	3	3	3¼
WAIST	28	30	32	34	36	38	40	42	44	46
KNEE	16¾	17½	18¼	19	19¾	20½	21¼	22	22¾	23½
TROUSER BOTTOMS	16	16¾	17½	18¼	19	19¾	20½	21¼	22	22¾

2

Cutting techniques

DRAFTING THE PATTERN

- Good scissors are essential; it is impossible to cut good patterns with poor scissors.
- Paper patterns should be cut for all but the very simplest garments. Cloaks, early shirts and simple trousers are exceptions.
- If the cutting paper has one side smooth and one rough, decide which side you are going to mark and keep to it. Some pattern pieces can be difficult to identify after a period of time so always keeping one side of the paper uppermost is helpful.
- The patterns should be drawn with fine, clear elegant lines, the angles should be sharp and the curves smooth.
- The patterns in the book are drawn with the centre back on the left-hand side of the page and the centre front on the right.
- The patterns are drafted without seam allowance unless otherwise stated.
- Always check the pattern pieces by fitting them together and ensuring the seam lines match and the curves are smooth.
- Mark each piece of pattern carefully with the size and the name of the intended wearer and pin them all together.
- Sometimes it is useful to keep patterns for future use such as average-size hose or 18th-century coats, both of which are time-consuming to make but easy to adapt for different sizes. Keep patterns when you are regularly making costumes for the same person. A good basic pattern can be kept and copies adapted as required. As a general rule, however, it is better to start afresh and cut new patterns rather than accumulate quantities of cut paper.
- **If the pattern is not cut properly, no amount of fiddling with the fabric will ever make a good garment.**

CUTTING OUT THE GARMENT

- When fabric is bought it is rarely cut along the grain. It may be possible to rectify this by cutting along the weft threads if they are clearly visible; otherwise a thread should be pulled leaving a row of small holes and the fabric cut along these. It is possible to tear many fabrics along the grain but this is not a good practice as the edge becomes distorted.

- When cutting out a garment the fabric is usually cut double. It should be laid out with the selvedges and cut edges matching making a perfect rectangle. In practice, fabric is often twisted but this can usually be corrected by pulling the fabric firmly until it is straight. If it is very twisted do not be tempted to cut it straight as this will cause part of the garment to be off the grain. Tack round the double fabric matching the selvedges and the cut edges, and then press with a damp cloth until the two layers lie flat. This is admittedly a counsel of perfection but it should always be followed when making important garments in expensive fabric.

- If the fabric has a pattern which must be matched exactly, it can be cut as a single layer. One side of the garment should be marked out with the pattern face up then the pattern must be turned over to mark the second side or the garment will have two left sides. This method is also used when the fabric is very difficult to mark.

- Place the pattern on the fabric with the grain running as indicated on the diagrams leaving enough space for 2.5cm (1″) seam allowances on all the pieces; 5cm (2″) should be left down the front of a jacket, for example, where there is to be an opening.

- Either pin the pattern to the fabric or weight it down.

- Draw accurately around the pattern making sure all the angles where seams meet are sharp and not rounded off.

- Always take care to mark the position of pockets, buttons and buttonholes accurately.

- When the pattern has been marked out on the upper layer of the fabric remove the pattern. Pin the two layers together, place tracing paper underneath and mark the lines through with a tracing wheel.

- Cut out the pieces leaving 2.5cm (1″) seam allowances (5cm (2″) where there is an opening). Generous seam allowances enable small alterations to be made to the garment and the seams can be trimmed and finished neatly.

- Many theatrical garments are cut with a backing fabric such as calico which gives the garment more body and improves the appearance of cheap fabric. The backing should be cut out as above and the pieces laid on the outer fabric. The two layers are tacked together, avoiding the marked lines and then treated as a single layer.

CONSTRUCTING THE TOILE

- It is good practice to cut and make up all but the simplest patterns as toiles and to fit them before cutting the intended fabric. Ideally, if the intended fabric is very thick the toile should be made in fabric of similar weight. If a backing is to be used this can be made up instead of making a separate toile.
- The toile is cut out as the above instructions leaving generous seam allowances.
- Match the seams pinning first the two ends, then the middle, then pinning in the middle between the pins until they are about 10cm (4") apart. This is to avoid stretching the top fabric and is particularly important when pinning long seams or when joining a seam cut on the bias to one cut on the straight. Tack each seam as it is pinned making sure the marked lines match.
- The whole toile can be sewn by hand, tacked and machined or pinned (with the pins at right angles to the seam) and machined, depending on the time available and value of the garment.
- Each seam should be carefully pressed.
- Tack round the edges of the garment, i.e. neck, openings, hems, wrists etc.
- Some people fit the toile right side out, others find it easier to have it inside out: it is a matter of personal preference. Make any necessary alterations and mark them with pencil. When the toile has been fitted redraw the alterations neatly. If there are alterations on both sides of the garment, average the amount and make both sides equal.
- Transfer the alterations to the pattern and mark it so that the alterations are not accidentally duplicated.

This may seem over-fastidious and indeed there are many occasions when short cuts must be made but if it is to be an important garment time spent on these preliminaries will pay dividends.

BRIEF NOTES ON CONSTRUCTION

- If a toile has been made and fitted or the pattern is known to be correct, it is possible to make up the garment almost to completion without further fittings.
- Always make up the most intricate parts first: i.e. complete the flies or other trouser openings before sewing the side seams; attach the cuffs before inserting the sleeves into the armholes; collars can be attached before the side seams are sewn and the sleeves inserted; buttonholes and pockets can be completed on coat fronts and so on. It is easier to sew these important parts when working on a flat area and it avoids dragging the garment about unnecessarily.
- Sew on any decoration whilst the garment is flat. Ease on and tack onto the fabric before machining. If time is short, braid can be machined without tacking provided care is taken not to stretch it.
- When possible press each seam as soon as it is sewn to keep the seam allowances flat.
- When the garment is not being worked on, hang it on a coat hanger and do not leave it in a heap on the worktable.

SOME BASIC CUTTING TECHNIQUES

Increasing and decreasing patterns

This technique is most often used for cutting skirts for doublets and coats but the same principle can also be used to flare parts of garments such as sleeves, collars, cuffs etc.

> *Sheet of paper for the basic strips:*
> Width at top of the panel x required length

Diagram 1

1 Mark the corners of the paper A, B, C, D as diagram.

2 Divide the paper equally into strips and mark them E–F, G–H and I–J as diagram.

Note. The diagram has four strips for clarity; a wider panel may need more or may divide more easily into different proportions e.g. 5 or 10.

Diagram 2

3 Put the strips on another piece of paper and spread evenly to the required hem width. The gaps between F–F, H–H and J–J are equal.

4 C–K and D–L each = half the measurement of the gaps.

5 A–K, B–L and the dashed lines in the gaps all = the length of the original strips. Redraw the top edge and hem in smooth curves.

Diagrams 3 & 3a

If the panels are to hang evenly like a bell they should be cut with the centre of each panel on the straight grain of the fabric. If the fabric can be used in either direction, the panels can be reversed as in Diagram 3a otherwise they must all be cut as Diagram 3.

Diagram 4

To widen the pattern at the top, gaps can be left between the strips remembering to add half the gap width at either end. If the panels are cut as in Diagram 5 with one side on the straight grain and the other on the bias, they must be sewn straight to bias as in Diagram 6 which will cause them to move in the direction of the arrow when being worn. This is desirable when making a long gown with a train but not when the garment has to hang evenly as with a short Tudor gown for example, where the panels must be cut with the centre on the straight grain.

CUTTING FLARES

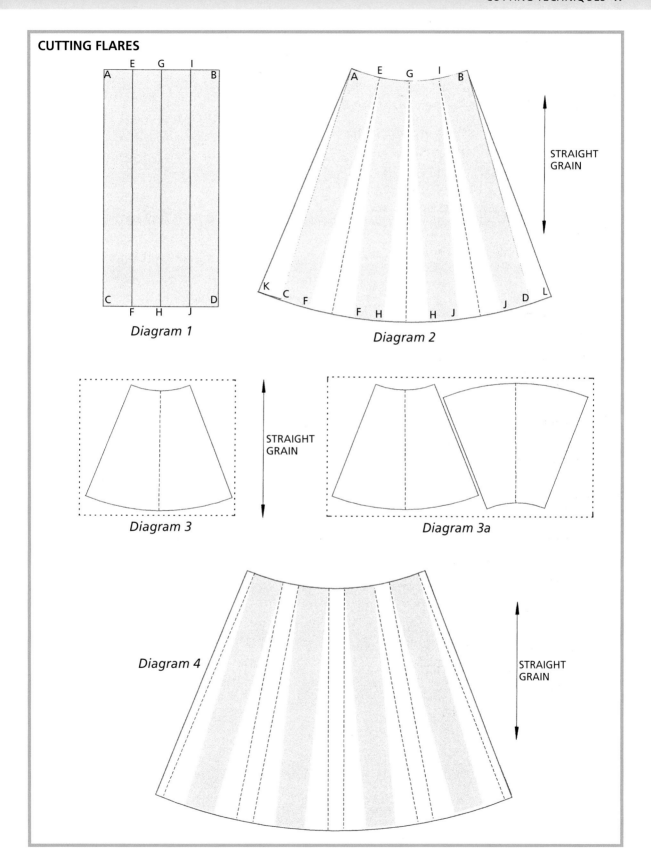

Diagram 1

Diagram 2

STRAIGHT GRAIN

Diagram 3

STRAIGHT GRAIN

Diagram 3a

Diagram 4

STRAIGHT GRAIN

Decreasing the width

This technique is most useful for collars and cuffs. In the diagrams the pattern is divided into four strips for clarity but as with the instructions for increasing the width, more strips may be preferable.

> *Sheet of paper:*
> Maximum width of the pattern
> x
> Required length

Diagrams 7 & 7a

6 Divide the paper into strips as diagram.

7 Mark the strips 1, 2, 3, 4 as diagram.

8 Deduct the required reduced width from the total width of the pattern and divide the remainder by 4 (or the number of strips). This is the amount each strip is to be overlapped.

Diagram 8

9 Overlap strip 1 with strip 2, strip 2 with strip 3 etc.

10 Deduct half the overlap measurement from each end of the pattern as diagram.

11 Redraw the top and bottom edges with smooth lines.

12 Cut off surplus paper to complete the pattern.

Cutting curved seams for waist suppression on the upper body pattern

Diagram 1

The broken lines drawn on the back section are some of the most usual positions for the back seam where waist suppression will be deducted.

Diagram 2

If a more extreme position like line A is used, a second seam such as line D will be necessary to give a good fit. In this case the centre back can be cut on the fold. If more than one seam is used the suppression should be divided between them but whether there are one or more seams the suppression should always be taken towards the side seam as Diagram 3.

Diagrams 4 & 4a

When waist suppression is taken out on a curved seam one side will always be longer than the other. The seams should be matched at the armhole end and corrections made at the waist. The waist line is then redrawn in a smooth curve. If the armhole has become distorted it should also be redrawn.

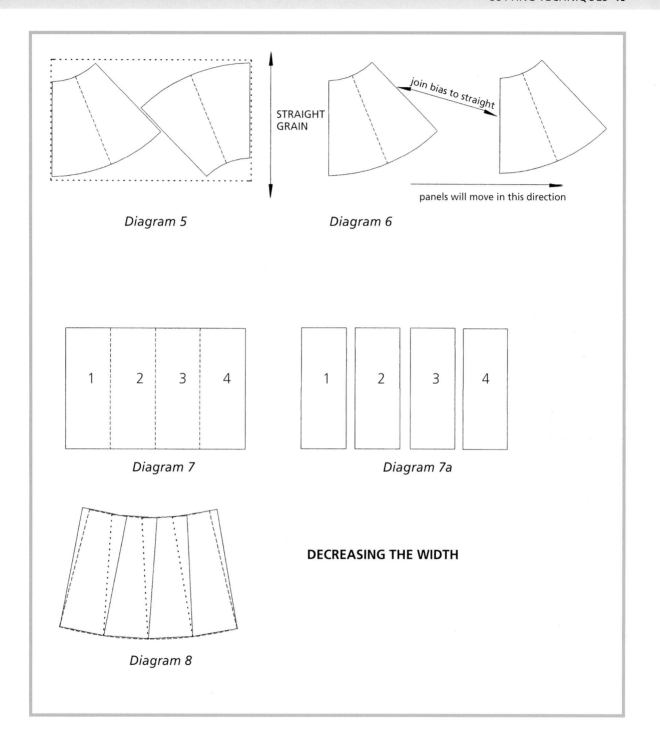

Diagram 5

STRAIGHT
GRAIN

join bias to straight

panels will move in this direction

Diagram 6

| 1 | 2 | 3 | 4 |

Diagram 7

| 1 | 2 | 3 | 4 |

Diagram 7a

Diagram 8

DECREASING THE WIDTH

Cutting curved seams for waist suppression on the upper body pattern

Diagram 1

The broken lines drawn on the back section are some of the most usual positions for the back seam where waist suppression will be deducted.

Diagram 2

If a more extreme position like line A is used, a second seam such as line D will be necessary to give a good fit. In this case the centre back can be cut on the fold. If more than one seam is used, the suppression should be divided between them but whether there are one or more seams the suppression should always be taken towards the side seam as Diagram 3.

Diagrams 4 & 4a

When waist suppression is taken out on a curved seam one side will always be longer than the other. The seams should be matched at the armhole end and corrections made at the waist. The waist line is then redrawn in a smooth curve. If the armhole has become distorted it should also be redrawn.

CUTTING CURVED SEAMS ON THE UPPER BODY PATTERN

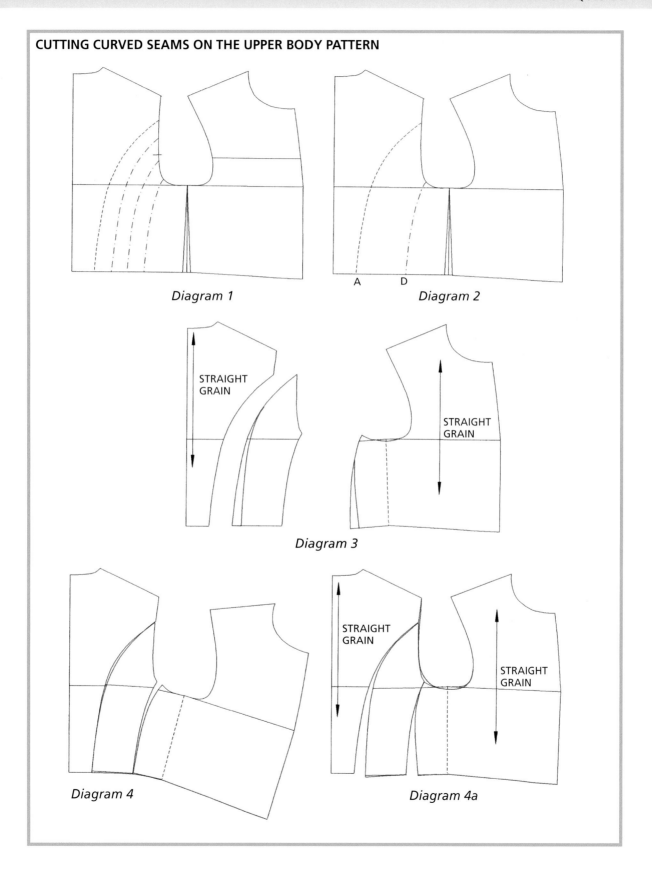

Diagram 1

Diagram 2

Diagram 3

Diagram 4

Diagram 4a

CALCULATING CIRCLES AND SLEEVE HEADS

Circles – to calculate the circumference and diameter

If the diameter of a circle is known, the circumference can be calculated. Likewise, if the circumference is known, the diameter can be calculated. The formulas are as follows:

> For calculating the circumference:
> diameter x 3.14
> For calculating the diameter:
> circumference ÷ 3.14

For pattern cutting purposes, the answer should be rounded up or down as appropriate. For example, in metric:

> If the diameter is 21cm, the circumference is 21 x 3.14 = 65.94
> which would be rounded up to 66cm.

> If the circumference is 66cm, the diameter is 66 ÷ 3.14 = 21.019
> which would be rounded down to 21cm.

Or in Imperial measurements:

> If the diameter is 8", the circumference is 8 x 3.14 = 25.12"
> which would be rounded down to 25".

> If the circumference is 25", the diameter is 25 ÷ 3.14 = 7.96"
> which would be rounded up to 8".

A quick way to make a rough calculation is to use a ruler and tape measure. If the diameter is known, place the ruler on the table and stand the tape measure on edge in a circle as shown in the photograph.

If the circumference is known, make the tape measure into a circle of that dimension and measure across the widest part.

Check that the answers are reasonably accurate by taking a measurement at right angles to the first. This method does not give perfect results but is very useful as a guide.

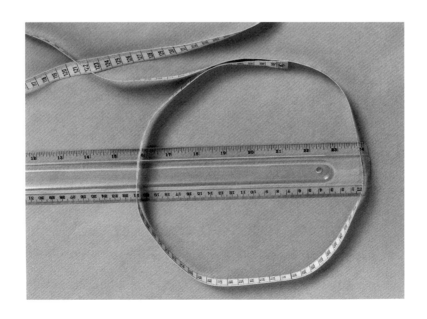

Sleeve heads – to calculate the sleeve width and depth of head

1 Measure the armhole.
2 Find this measurement on a tape measure.
3 Place a ruler on the table.
4 Flip the tape measure along the ruler in the rough shape of a sleeve head as shown in the photograph.
5 Measure the distance across the ruler to establish the sleeve width.

6 Place a second ruler at right angles to the first to establish the height of the sleeve head.
7 Adjust the tape measure to widen the sleeve and lower the depth of head or narrow the sleeve and raise the depth of head.

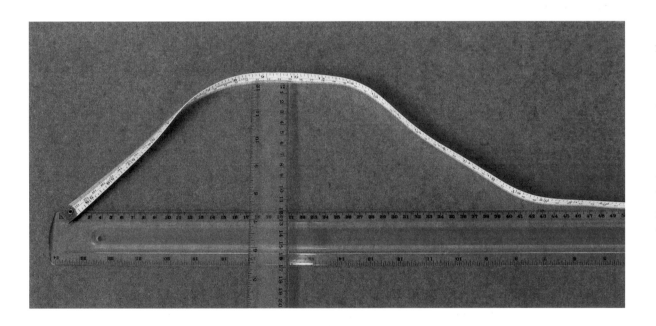

3

Basic patterns

BASIC PATTERN FOR UPPER BODY

Sheet of paper:
½ chest measurement + 3cm (1¼")
x
Nape to waist measurement + 10cm (4")

Diagram 1

On the left-hand side of the paper

1 Measure down 5cm (2"), A.

2 From A square out A–B right across the paper.

3 Measure down A–C = nape to waist measurement. A–C is the centre back of the pattern.

4 Square out C–D right across the paper. C–D is the waist line.

5 Square out A–E = **half** back neck width.

6 Square up E–F = back neck rise.

7 Measure down A–G = back shoulder slope.

8 Square out G–H right across the paper.

9 Draw shoulder length from F to meet G–H at I.

10 Measure down G–J = armhole depth.

11 Square out J–K right across the paper. J–K is the chest line.

On the right-hand side of the paper

12 Measure up D–L = centre front length.

13 Square out L–M = **half** front dart width.

14 Measure down L–N = front dart length.

15 Join M–N in a smooth, shallow curve.

M–N–D is the centre front of the pattern.

16 Measure out B–O = half back neck width **plus** 5.5cm (2¼").

17 Square up O–P = back neck rise **minus** .5cm (¼").

18 Draw shoulder length from P to meet G–H at Q.

To draw the armhole

Diagram 2

19 Mark R midway between J–K.

20 Measure up K–S = level of cross chest above chest line.

21 From S square out construction line 1 parallel to K–R.

22 Construction line 1 cuts the centre front line at SS.

23 SS–T = **half** cross chest measurement.

24 On the back pattern, I–U = .5cm (¼").

25 From U square down construction line 2 to meet J–R at UU.

26 V is approximately ⅓ up construction line 2 from UU.

27 Draw the armhole by joining in Q–T–R–V–I in a smooth, continuous curve.

28 Square down from R to meet C–D at W. R–W is the side seam.

29 Cut along R–W and separate the back pattern from the front.

30 Cut along the back shoulder line, F–I.

BASIC PATTERN FOR UPPER BODY

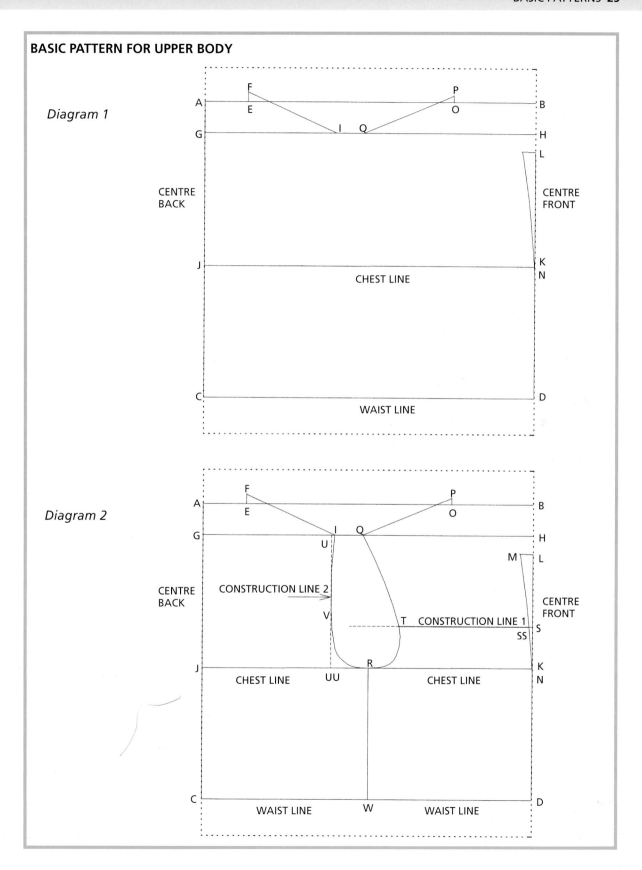

Diagram 1

Diagram 2

To draw the neckline

Diagram 3

31 Join shoulder lines F–I and Q–P with adhesive tape.

32 Draw the neckline through A–F/P–M making a curve as near a semi-circle as possible.

The total measurement for the finished neckline should measure approximately:

CHEST SIZE	80–85–90 32"–34"–36"	95–100–105 38"–40"–42"	110–115 44"– 46"	120–125 48"–50"
BETWEEN	39–43cm 15⅜"–17"	44–48cm 17⅜"–19"	49–51cm 19⅜"–19¾"	52–54cm 20½"–21¼"

33 Cut round the neckline. Whilst the pattern is in this position check that the armhole forms a smooth line at the shoulder; adjust if necessary.

34 Cut along the shoulder line.

35 Mark the armhole and neckline measurements on the pattern for future reference.

Waist suppression

Diagram 4

The pattern is based on half the chest measurement plus an extra 3cm (1¼") for ease. Only 1.5cm (½") need be added for ease on the waist of this close-fitting pattern so there is a surplus of 8cm (2¾") which may be suppressed as follows:

1cm (½") at the centre back tapering to nothing midway between G–J.
1cm (¼") each side of W tapering to nothing at R.

The remaining 4cm (1¾") should be taken out in a seam at the back of the pattern as follows:

X is midway between C–W.
Join V–X with a straight line.
X–Y = 4cm (1¾").
Join V–Y with a straight line.

Diagram 5

36 Cut out the suppression and rejoin the pattern with adhesive tape. V–X will be found to be longer than V–Y.

37 Rejoin the pattern so that it meets at V. Check the armhole curve and correct if necessary.

38 From D measure down D–Z = front waist addition.

39 Redraw the waist line as diagram.

40 Cut off surplus paper.

41 Cut along V–X to complete the pattern.

Diagram 6

When cutting out the basic upper body pattern, the centre back can be placed on the fold of the material this will mean that there will be no seams except on the shoulder. Otherwise the pattern can be cut down the side seam R–W and/or down the back seam V–X as required. If there are no side seams and the garment is to have sleeves, the underarm point, R, should be marked.

Note. If the pattern is to be divided along V–X it is advisable to curve the line as drawn in red to avoid the sharp point which would be difficult to sew.

BASIC PATTERN FOR UPPER BODY – continued

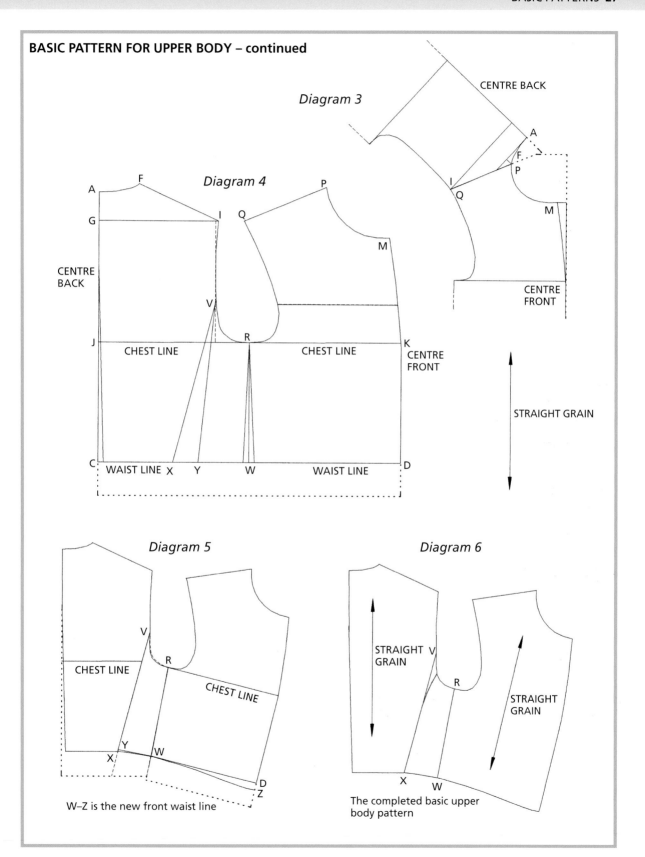

Diagram 3

CENTRE BACK

Diagram 4

CENTRE BACK

CHEST LINE

CHEST LINE

CENTRE FRONT

WAIST LINE

WAIST LINE

CENTRE FRONT

STRAIGHT GRAIN

Diagram 5

CHEST LINE

CHEST LINE

W–Z is the new front waist line

Diagram 6

STRAIGHT GRAIN

STRAIGHT GRAIN

The completed basic upper body pattern

BASIC STRAIGHT SLEEVE

Sheet of paper:
Width of sleeve
x
Length of sleeve + 2cm (¾")

Diagram 1
1 Mark A 1cm down left-hand side of paper.
2 Square out A–B right across the paper.
3 Measure down A–C = length of sleeve.
4 Square out C–D right across the paper.
5 Measure down A–E = depth of sleeve head.
6 Square out E–F right across the paper.
7 Divide the paper in four down its length by folding it in half and then the sides into the middle. Press the folds firmly. Unfold the paper.
8 On A–B mark the creases from left to right G–H–I.
9 On C–D mark the creases from left to right J–K–L.

To draw the sleeve head

Diagram 2
10 From G measure down G–M = depth of sleeve head. M is the back pitch.
11 From I measure down I–N = ½ depth of sleeve head. N is the front pitch.
12 Join E–M, M–H, H–N, N–F with straight lines.
13 Draw the sleeve head in a smooth continuous curve as Diagram 3.

The line should curve approximately:

1cm (⅜") below E–M
1.5cm (⅝") above M–H
1.5cm (⅝") above H–N
2cm (¾") below N–F

These measurements are only a guide and should be adjusted when necessary to ensure that the sleeve head is always nicely rounded.

To establish the elbow line

The level of the elbow line is midway between N–L.
14 Square out from this point right across the paper.
15 Mark O at the intersection the elbow line and M–J. O is the elbow point.

Diagram 3
16 Turn the pattern over and fold the sides to the middle to check the underarm curve at F/E.
17 From L measure up 2cm (¾") to P.
18 Join J–P in a straight line and redraw in a gentle curve as drawn in red on diagram.
19 Unfold and cut off surplus paper round the sleeve head to complete the pattern as in Diagram 4.

Note. The sleeve head must always be larger than the armhole, the amount depending on the thickness of the fabric to be used but never less than 1cm (⅜"). The shaping at the wrist may be ignored for very simple sleeves.

BASIC TWO-PIECE SLEEVE

Sheet of paper:
Width of sleeve measurement + 2cm (¾")
x
Length of sleeve +1cm (⅜")
Extra paper as instructions

Diagram 1
Follow the instructions for the basic straight sleeve without shaping the wrist.
1 Mark the elbow line with a tracing wheel.

Diagram 2
2 With the pattern right side up fold F–D and E–C to meet along H–K.

BASIC STRAIGHT SLEEVE

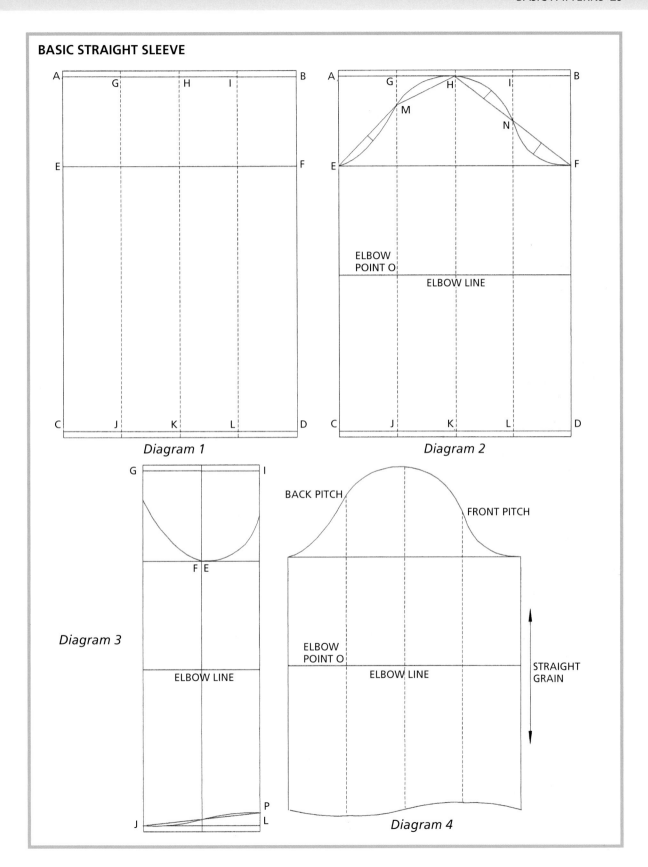

Diagram 1

Diagram 2

Diagram 3

Diagram 4

3 Draw round the underarm part of the armhole N–F/E–M. E/F is the underarm point.

4 Unfold the pattern and cut along M–J and N–L.

5 Discard the two top pieces of pattern. The remaining piece will be the upper section of the sleeve.

Diagram 3

The upper section of the pattern

6 Mark O on the elbow line .75cm from the left-hand edge of the paper as diagram.

7 Mark P on the elbow line .5cm from the right-hand edge of the paper as diagram.

8 Join N–P–L in a gentle curve. Cut along this line.

9 Join O–M with a straight line.

Diagram 4

10 From O cut along the elbow line almost to P and open the slash width measurement as following chart:

SIZES		SLASH WIDTH	
80	32″	1.5cm	⅝″
85	34″	2cm	¾″
90	36″	2cm	¾″
95	38″	2.5cm	1″
100	40″	2.5cm	1″
105	42″	3cm	1¼″
110	44″	3cm	1¼″
115	46″	3.5cm	1⅜″
120	48″	3.5cm	1½″
125	50″	4cm	1⅝″

11 Secure a piece of paper under the slash.

12 L–Q = ½ wrist measurement for two-piece sleeve as following chart:

SIZES		TOTAL WRIST	
80	32″	26cm	10¼″
85	34″	26cm	10¼″
90	36″	27cm	10⅝″
95	38″	27cm	10⅝″

SIZES		WRIST	
100	40″	28cm	11″
105	42″	28cm	11″
110	44″	29cm	11⅜″
115	46″	30cm	11¾″
120	48″	31cm	12¼″
125	50″	32cm	12⅝″

13 Join O–Q in a gentle curve and cut along M–O–Q to complete the upper section.

Diagram 5

The completed upper section with the underarm curve marked.

Diagram 6

The under section of the pattern

14 Place the upper section of the pattern on another piece of paper, weight it down to prevent it from moving and draw carefully round M–O–Q–L–P–N.

15 Mark round the underarm curve with a tracing wheel and mark the underarm point. Remove the upper section. Cut off surplus paper from the under section.

Diagram 7a

15 Match the back seams of each section to check the sleeve head is a smooth continuous curve.

Diagram 7b

16 Match the front seams of each section to check the sleeve head is a smooth continuous curve.

17 Cut off surplus paper from the lower section to complete the pattern.

Note. When cutting this pattern always ensure that the points where the side seams meet the sleeve head at M and N on the upper section are clear and not rounded.

BASIC TWO-PIECE SLEEVE

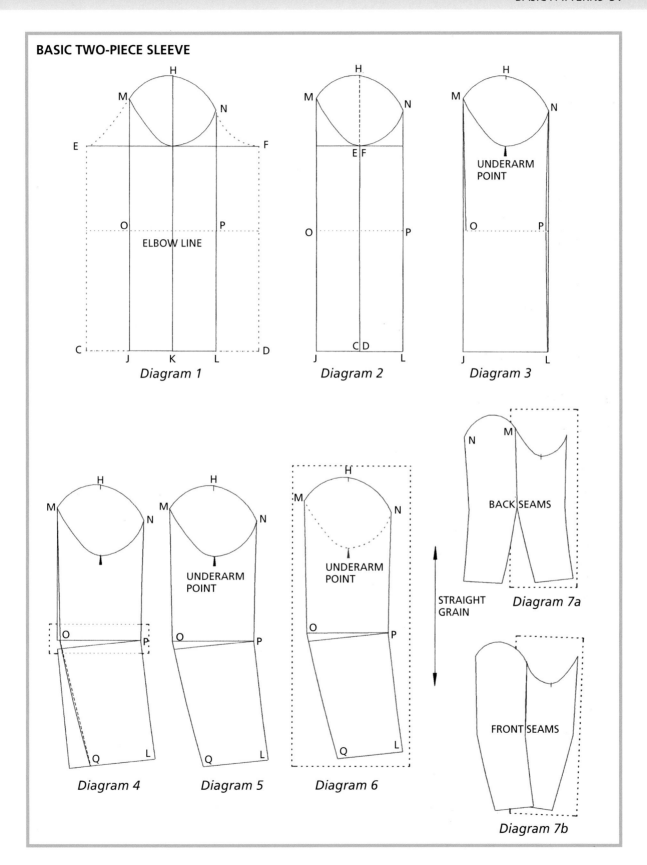

Diagram 1

Diagram 2

Diagram 3

Diagram 4

Diagram 5

Diagram 6

Diagram 7a

Diagram 7b

BASIC TROUSERS PATTERN

For the front section
Sheet of paper:
¼ seat measurement + front crutch width

x

Outside leg measurement

The front section

Diagram 1

1 Mark the paper A, B, C, D as diagram.

2 From C measure up C–E = inside leg measurement.

3 Square E–F right across the paper.

4 From C measure up C–G = ½ inside leg measurement + 5cm (2").

5 Square G–H right across the paper. G–H is the knee level.

Diagram 2

6 From F measure out F–I = front crutch width.

7 From I square up to meet A–B at J.

8 From I measure up I–K = front crutch width + 2cm (⅝").

9 Shape the front crutch J–K–F as diagram.

10 From J measure out J–L = ¼ waist measurement.

11 Join L–E in a straight line then redraw in a gentle curve as diagram.

12 Mark M midway between E–F.

13 From M square down to meet G–H at N and C–D at O.

14 N–P = ¼ knee measurement, N–Q = ¼ knee measurement.

15 Join E–P and F–Q with straight lines. Round off the point at E.

16 O–R = ¼ bottom of leg measurement, O–S = ¼ bottom of leg measurement.

17 Join P–R and Q–S with straight lines.

18 Cut off surplus paper to complete the front section of the pattern.

Fly-front fastening

Diagram 2a

19 From J draw the width of the facing = 4cm (1½") towards L.

20 Draw the facing as diagram making it about 4cm (1½") shorter than the measurement J–K.

21 Trace the facing onto another piece of paper and cut off the surplus.

Diagram 2b

22 Cut a placket 4cm (1½") wide and the same length as the facing.

Note. If making up trousers from these instructions a waist band will be necessary. Cut a straight strip the waist measurement + an overlap of 5cm x about 3.5cm (2" x about 1⅜"). This will need backing with firm fabric such as canvas or strong cotton. The waist band should be cut with a seam at the centre back as this is where any alteration will be made.

BASIC TROUSERS PATTERN

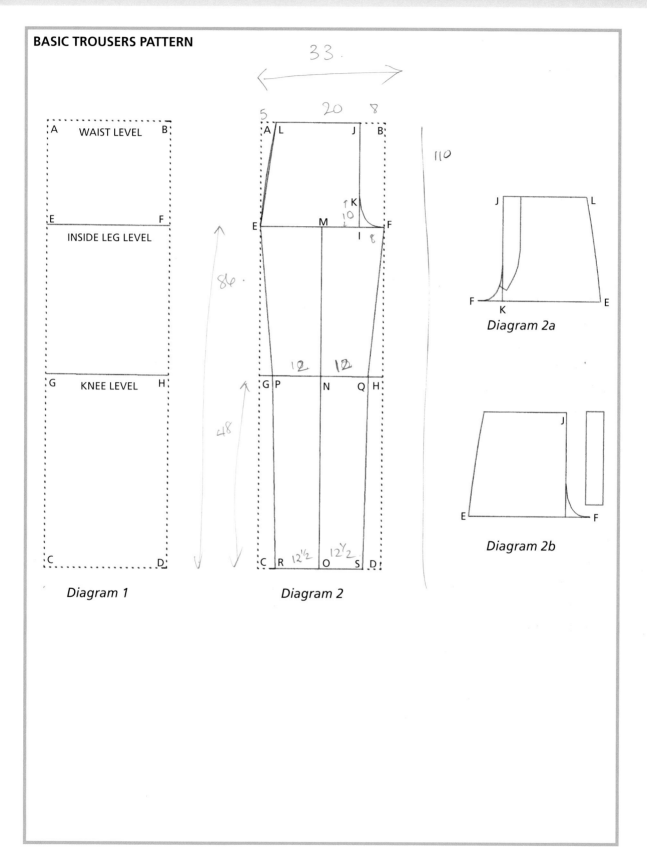

Diagram 1

Diagram 2

Diagram 2a

Diagram 2b

For the back section

Sheet of paper:

¼ seat measurement + following additions:

25 + 10

SEAT MEASUREMENT		¼ SEAT MEASUREMENT +	
85–90	34"–36"	20cm	8"
95–100	38"–40"	22cm	8¾"
105–110	42"–44"	24cm	9½"
115–120	46"–48"	26cm	10¼"
125–130	50"–52"	28cm	11"

Outside leg measurement + 5cm (2") for all sizes

112

Diagram 3

23 From the bottom of the paper measure up knee level (C–G on Diagram 1) and square out construction line 1 right across the paper.

24 From the bottom of the paper measure up inside leg level (C–E on Diagram 1) and square out construction line 2 right across the paper.

25 From the bottom of the paper measure up outside leg level (C–A , waist level, on Diagram 1) and square out construction line 3 right across the paper.

26 Mark T where construction line 2 meets the right-hand side of the paper.

27 From T measure out T–U = front crutch width.

28 Place the front section of the pattern so that E–F lies along construction line 2 and F meets U.

Diagram 4

29 From K slash almost to E. Open the slash 5cm (2").

30 Place weights on the front pattern and from J draw the back waist line = ¼ seat

measurement + 1cm (⅜") to meet construction line 3 at V.

31 Join V–P in a straight line.

32 Trace P–R onto the back section to complete the back outside leg line.

33 Draw back crutch line J–T as diagram.

34 On construction line 1 measure out Q–W = 2.5cm (1").

35 On bottom edge of the paper measure out S–X = 2.5cm (1").

36 Join T–W and W–X with straight lines.

37 The front inside leg measurement on the front pattern will be shorter than on the back; adjust by shortening the back length at T as diagram.

38 Remove the front section and rejoin the slash.

Waist suppression

39 Measure the total waist line of both front and back sections and deduct ½ the required waist measurement + 1cm (⅜"); the remainder is the amount to be suppressed.

40 From V measure V–Y = approximately ⅓ the waist measurement of the back section.

41 Square down Y–Z = 10cm (4").

42 Mark ½ the suppression each side of Y and join to Z.

43 Cut off surplus paper to complete the pattern as Diagram 5.

BASIC TROUSERS PATTERN – continued

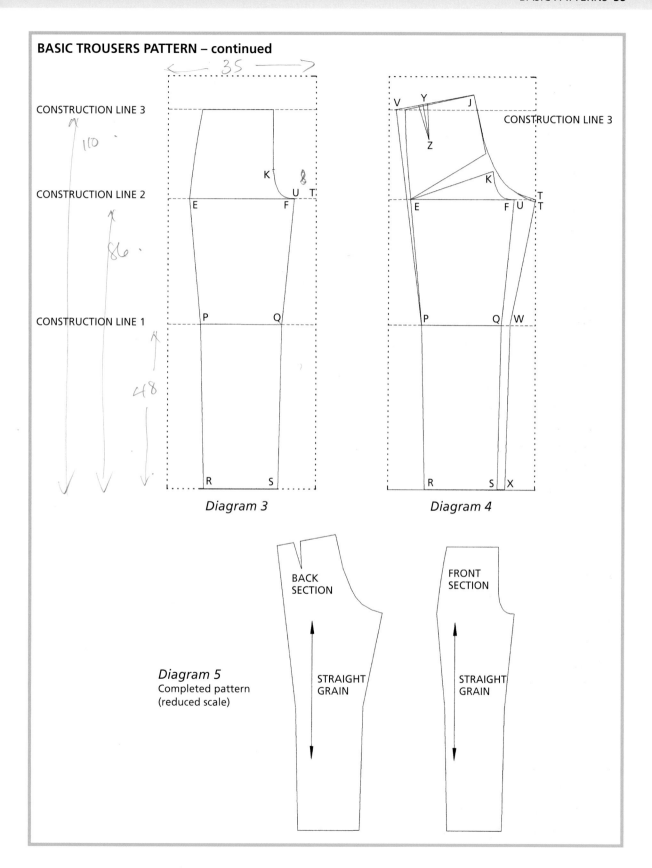

Diagram 3

Diagram 4

Diagram 5
Completed pattern
(reduced scale)

BACK
SECTION

STRAIGHT
GRAIN

FRONT
SECTION

STRAIGHT
GRAIN

4

Cutting basic patterns to individual measurements

The instructions for drafting patterns using basic measurements will be satisfactory in many circumstances, but there will be just as many when modification is needed. Whatever variations are necessary, always start with the correct chest size for upper body patterns and the correct seat size for trousers. The most usual differences are tall slim men who are much taller than the average for their horizontal measurements, or the reverse – stout men who are shorter than average for their bulk.

If the chest measurement is small and the man tall, he is likely to have thin arms and neck and narrow shoulders so the measurements on the chart for neck, shoulders, armhole depth and probably waist will conform to his chest size. The necessary alteration will be to lengthen the nape to waist and centre front length measurements.

If the chest measurement is large but the man short, he is likely to have big arms and neck and broad shoulders, so only the nape to waist and centre front length measurements should be shortened and the other measurements left unchanged.

There are many other variations such as tall men with large bodies and relatively short legs. This is a figure type very common amongst opera singers. The opposite, small bodies and long, well-developed legs, is often found amongst dancers. Tall thin men may have a pronounced 'beer belly'. Instructions are given to accommodate this more difficult figure. The arm length is usually proportionate to the nape to waist measurement but this is not always the case. The variations are endless. It is helpful if any pronounced deviations from the 'average' are noted when measurements are taken.

ALTERING SIMPLE UPPER BODY PATTERNS

Very simple patterns can be altered by cutting, as Diagram 1, and spreading or overlapping the pieces; too much manipulation will cause distortion.

Cutting along A–B widens the pattern, as Diagram 2. The pattern can be narrowed by overlapping the pieces.

Cutting along C–D, as Diagram 3, increases the nape to waist/centre front length measurements, they can be shortened by overlapping the pieces.

Cutting along C–D and E–F, as Diagram 4, can lengthen or shorten the nape to waist/centre front length and the armhole.

All the lines can be cut and the pieces spread or overlapped but it is more satisfactory to cut a new pattern.

Diagram 5

To alter a pattern for a corpulent figure, cut along the front section A–B, spread the pieces and redraw the pattern as diagram. Make sure that the new shoulder line matches the back.

The pattern pieces can be put on a sheet of paper and redrawn or simply pinned onto the fabric, drawn round and marked through with carbon paper and a tracing wheel. The second method is satisfactory for a simple one-off garment.

ALTERING SIMPLE UPPER BODY PATTERNS

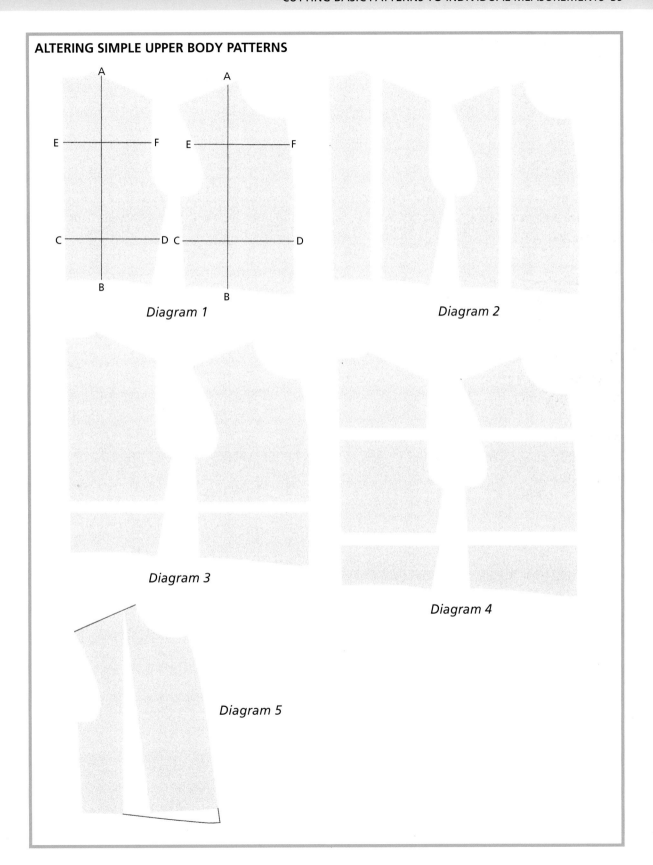

Diagram 1

Diagram 2

Diagram 3

Diagram 4

Diagram 5

MAKING MINOR ALTERATIONS WHEN DRAFTING THE BASIC BLOCK

When the alterations are minor, the basic upper body pattern can be drafted incorporating the new measurements in the following way.

Tall and short men

The only necessary modifications are the nape to waist and front waist to neck measurements. Take these on the body remembering to fasten a strong piece of elastic around the natural waist. Once the nape to waist measurement has been marked on the pattern it can be cut in the usual way remembering to adjust the front waist measurement to compensate.

Small and large waists

If the required waist measurement is only a little smaller than shown on the chart, the suppression can be adjusted on the back section when the pattern is drafted as Diagram 1.

Similarly, if the required waist measurement is only a little larger than shown on the chart, the adjustment can be made on the back section when the pattern is drafted as Diagram 2.

If there is a little extra on the stomach, the pattern should be modified as Diagram 3.

ADAPTING PATTERNS TO INDIVIDUAL MEASUREMENTS

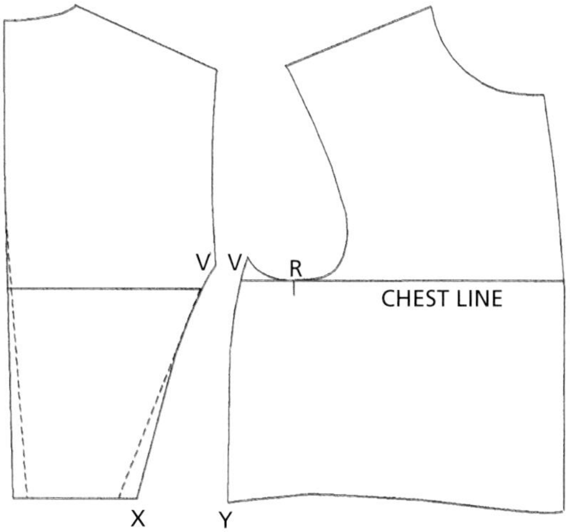

V V R CHEST LINE

X Y

Diagram 1

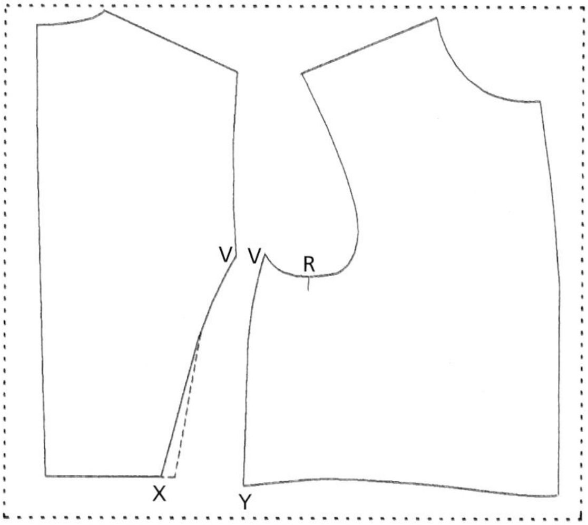

V V R

X Y

Diagram 2

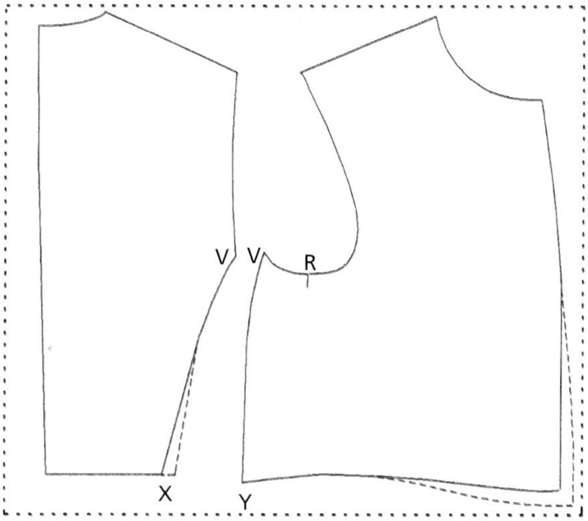

V V R

X Y

Diagram 3

STRAIGHT
GRAIN

Diagram 4

1 Mark A where chest line meets the centre back.

To lengthen the pattern

Diagrams 5 & 5a

2 B is midway between A and the bottom of the pattern.

3 From B draw a line parallel to the chest line right across both sections of the pattern.

4 Cut along this line.

5 Place the pattern on another sheet of paper leaving a gap to increase the nape to waist measurement the required amount.

6 Rejoin the seam lines as diagram.

To shorten the pattern

Diagrams 6 & 6a

7 Mark A as for lengthening the pattern and cut along the line.

8 Overlap the pieces as diagram.

9 Redraw the seam lines as diagram.

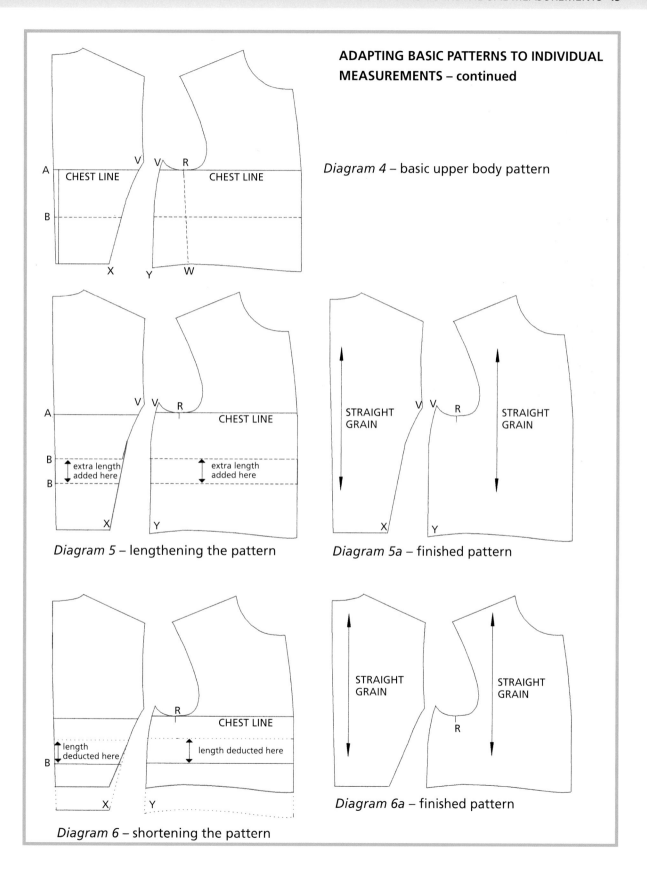

ADAPTING BASIC PATTERNS TO INDIVIDUAL MEASUREMENTS – continued

Diagram 4 – basic upper body pattern

Diagram 5 – lengthening the pattern

Diagram 5a – finished pattern

Diagram 6 – shortening the pattern

Diagram 6a – finished pattern

Pattern for a large beer belly

The easiest way to cut a pattern for someone with a large stomach is to start with a basic pattern for the correct chest size then cut and spread the front section.

Diagram 7

R–W is the position of the original side seam.

10 R-A = half the front chest line.

11 Square down A–B to meet the waist line.

12 A–C = approximately ⅓ A–B.

13 Square across to meet R–W at D.

14 Join A to S where the cross chest line meets the centre front.

Diagram 8

15 Cut along the red lines:

R–W, A–B, A–S, D–C

The pieces will look like Diagram 8.

Diagram 9

Spread the pieces as diagram:

16 The gap at A–A = 3cm (1¼").

17 The gap at R–R = 2cm (¾"). The underarm point is midway between R–R.

18 W–W meet.

These measurements are only a guide (they will increase the waist line by approximately 8cm (3⅛") on the half pattern).

19 Redraw the centre front line in a gentle curve, as drawn in red on the diagram, making it the individual measurement centre front length.

20 Redraw the waist line as drawn in red on the diagram.

Diagram 9a is the finished pattern with the back section unaltered.

Diagram 10

The pieces of pattern have been spread to increase the waist at the underarm and make the armhole wider than in Diagram 9. Diagram 10a is the finished pattern again without any alteration to the back section. The back pattern could be adapted as in Diagrams 2 and 3 if greater width was needed. The principles of modifying the pattern for enlarged waist lines remain the same but they can be adapted as appropriate for the figure.

Note. Sometimes there is extra bulk at the side waist line in which case more length will be required in this area. In the diagrams the waist line is lengthened in the centre front and tapers to the position of the underarm seam. If extra length is required, redraw the waist line from the centre front and taper it to the back seam.

ADAPTING BASIC PATTERNS TO INDIVIDUAL MEASUREMENTS
Alterations for a beer belly

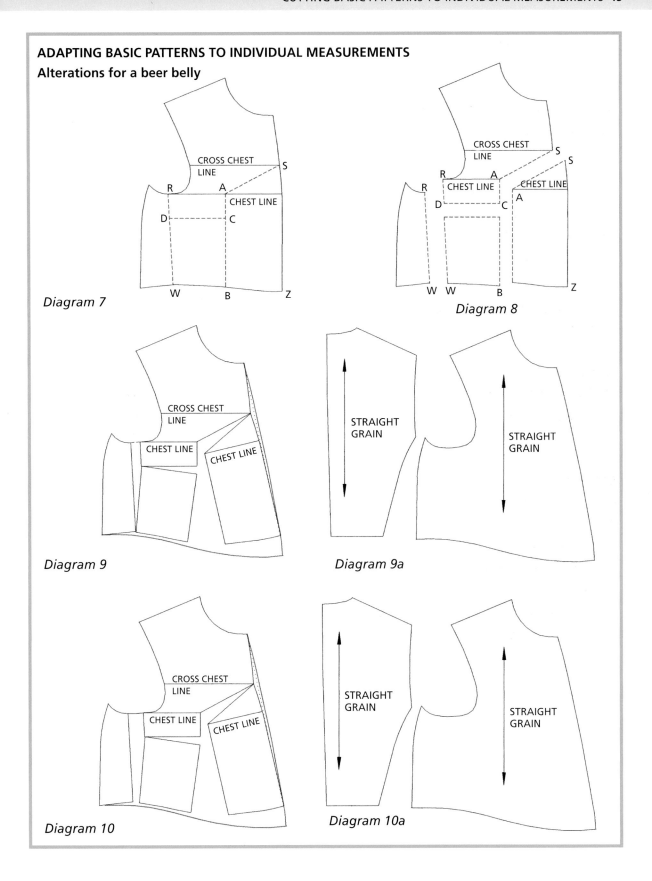

Diagram 7

Diagram 8

Diagram 9

Diagram 9a

Diagram 10

Diagram 10a

LENGTHENING AND SHORTENING SLEEVES

Straight sleeves

Straight sleeves are so easy to cut it is better to start from scratch if the upper body pattern has been cut to individual measurements. If the arm-hole has not been altered from chart measurements and a straight sleeve pattern exists it can easily be altered as follows.

Diagram 1

Straight sleeve lengthened and shortened following the shaped line. The sleeve head remains untouched.

Two-piece sleeves

The length can be adjusted as follows but if more alteration is needed it is better to start from scratch and draft a new pattern.

Diagram 2

It is necessary to make the alterations both above and below the elbow line to keep the balance of the sleeve.

1 On the upper section mark A on the back seam line midway between the sleeve head and the elbow line. Draw A–B parallel to the elbow line.

2 From A square straight across to B.

3 C–D is midway between the elbow line and the wrist.

4 On the under section mark E midway between the sleeve head and the elbow line. G is midway between the elbow line and the wrist.

5 Cut along A–B, C–D, E–F and G–H.

Diagram 3

6 Pin the pieces of pattern on another sheet of paper dividing the required extra length between the two gaps.

7 Redraw the side seams as diagram.

8 Cut off surplus paper to complete the pattern.

Diagram 4

9 Overlap the pieces by the same amount at each slash and secure with adhesive tape.

10 Redraw the seam lines as diagram.

11 Cut off surplus paper to complete the pattern.

Note. Always check that the new seam lines match after alterations have been made.

ADAPTING BASIC PATTERNS TO INDIVIDUAL MEASUREMENTS – SLEEVES

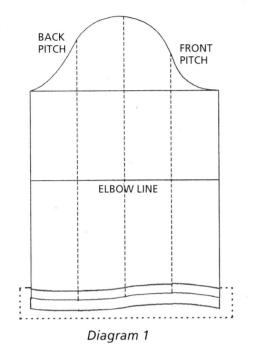

Diagram 1

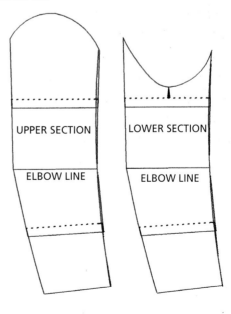

Diagram 2 – basic two-piece jacket sleeve

Diagram 3 – two-piece jacket sleeve lengthened

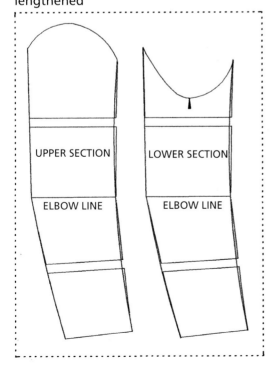

Diagram 4 – two-piece jacket sleeve shortened

CUTTING PATTERNS TO INDIVIDUAL MEASUREMENTS – TROUSERS

Incorporating individual measurements in the basic pattern

Most deviations from the basic measurements for trousers are for longer or shorter bodies, longer or shorter legs or larger or smaller waist sizes. There are always exceptions e.g. a large 'beer belly' or trousers to go over a huge amount of padding but in most cases the pattern can be drafted in the same way as the instructions for the basic trouser pattern using the correct seat size from the basic chart and corresponding front crutch width, knee and trouser bottom measurements. The individual waist, inside leg and outside leg measurements should be substituted as appropriate. To avoid confusion it is helpful to make a new chart as below:

SEAT	As chart
OUTSIDE LEG	Individual measurement if necessary
INSIDE LEG	Individual measurement if necessary
FRONT CRUTCH WIDTH	As chart
WAIST	Individual measurement if necessary
KNEE	As chart
TROUSER BOTTOMS	As chart

Adapting an existing pattern – altering the length

Diagram 1
Shows where the pattern should be cut to make alterations.

On the front section

1 Mark A at the centre front waist.

2 B is midway between A and the inside leg level.

3 Square across B–C.

4 I–J is midway between the inside leg level and knee level.

5 M–N is midway between the knee level and bottom of the trousers.

On the back section

6 D–E = A–B.

7 Draw E–F parallel to the back waist line.

8 G–H is midway between the inside leg level and the knee level.

9 K–L is midway between the knee level and the bottom of the trousers.

Lengthening the pattern

Diagram 2
The pattern can be lengthened in the body, the whole leg or just the thigh by spreading the pieces as diagram. If lengthening the whole leg, it is more satisfactory to insert pieces above and below the knee.

Shortening the pattern

Diagram 3
The pattern can be shortened by overlapping the pieces as appropriate.

When lengthening or shortening the pattern the seams should be redrawn in smooth lines and checked to make sure they match. The legs of basic trousers can be adjusted by lengthening or shortening the bottom of the legs.

CUTTING PATTERNS TO INDIVIDUAL MEASUREMENTS – TROUSERS
Simple alterations to an existing pattern

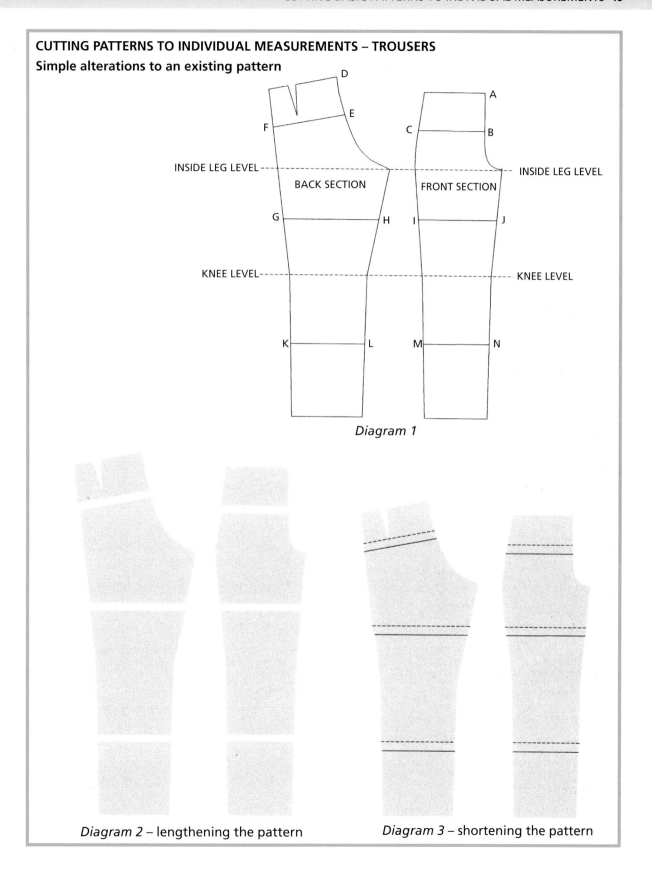

Diagram 1

Diagram 2 – lengthening the pattern

Diagram 3 – shortening the pattern

ALTERATIONS FOR PROMINENT AND FLAT SEATS

When cutting patterns for prominent or flat seats only the back pattern is altered. This is one occasion when cutting a pattern for the correct seat size is inappropriate as the figure is disproportionate. It is better to start with the measurements listed under the correct chest size in the tables in the measurement section.

1 Take the new through crutch measurement (i.e. from waist at front through the legs to the waist at back) remembering to tie a piece of elastic round the waist.

2 Cut a pattern for basic trousers using the measurements listed under the correct chest size. Mark E, F, K, J as Diagram 1.

3 Measure the front and back crutch on the pattern and deduct this measurement from the new measurement. The difference will be the amount of alteration necessary for the new pattern.

Prominent seat

Diagram 2

4 On the front section cut along E–K and place the pattern on another sheet of paper as for basic trouser pattern.

5 Open the slash 5cm (2") **plus** ⅔ the extra measurement.

6 Weight down the pattern.

7 From F measure out F–T = front crutch width **plus** ⅓ the extra measurement.

8 Complete the pattern as for basic trousers.

Flat seat

Diagram 3

9 On the front section cut along E–K and place the pattern on another sheet of paper as for basic trousers.

10 Open the slash 5cm (2") **minus** ⅓ the reduced measurement.

11 Weight down the pattern.

12 From F measure out F–T = front crutch width **minus** ⅓ the reduced measurement.

13 Complete the pattern in the usual way.

Diagram 3a
Back section as instructions for basic trousers.

Diagram 3b
Back section for prominent seat.

Diagram 3c
Back section for flat seat.

Note. The front section remains unchanged for prominent and flat seats. The basic trouser pattern allows for a waistband of 3.5cm (1½") to be added. This must be taken into account and added when measuring the through crutch measurement on the basic pattern.

CUTTING PATTERNS TO INDIVIDUAL MEASUREMENTS – TROUSERS
Alterations for prominent and flat seats

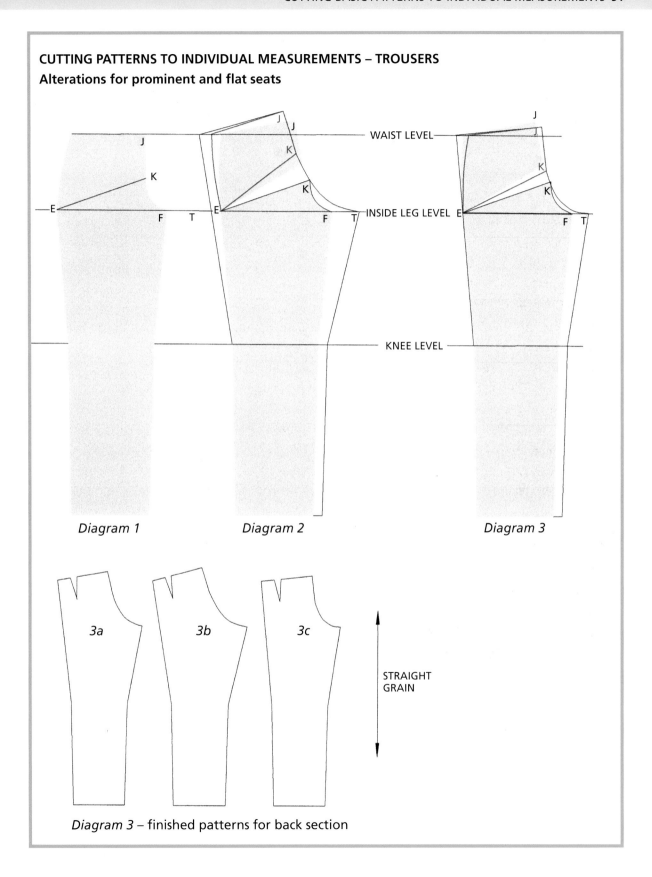

Diagram 1 Diagram 2 Diagram 3

3a 3b 3c

STRAIGHT GRAIN

Diagram 3 – finished patterns for back section

ALTERATIONS FOR A BEER BELLY

Alterations for a beer belly are only made on the front section of the basic trouser pattern as the extra girth will all be around the stomach. To establish the necessary amount, measure the complete waist and then measure the back from side seam to side seam. Deduct the back measurement from the total and divide the remainder by 2; this will be the waist measurement on the altered front pattern.

The through crutch measurement will also require adjustment, i.e. the measurement from the waist at the front, between the legs to the waist at the back. Deduct the measurement on the basic pattern from the new measurement. The remainder will be the extra amount needed to increase the front crutch line.

On the front section

Diagram 1

1 Cut a complete trouser pattern in the usual way using the correct seat size and corresponding measurements. Mark J and F.

2 Draw a line A–B 1cm (½") below the Inside leg level.

3 C is midway along A–B.

4 Square up to D.

5 Cut along A–B and C–D.

Diagram 2

6 Place a piece of paper under the pattern as and secure with adhesive tape.

7 Open the slash C–D the required amount for the altered waist line.

8 Weight down the pattern pieces.

Diagram 3

9 From J raise the front crutch line the required amount.

10 Measure the side seam on the back section of the pattern and check that it matches the side seam on the front section. Make any alteration at the waist.

11 Redraw the waist line in a gentle curve as diagram.

Diagram 4

If the waist line is particularly large, additional width can be added by leaving the side seam of the front section straight and not shaping it in the normal way. The side seams must be checked to make sure they match and corrected if necessary at the waist.

Diagram 5

Completed pattern with waist suppression.

Diagram 6

Completed pattern without waist suppression.

Note. The basic trouser pattern allows for a waistband of 3.5cm (1½") to be added. This must be taken into account and added when measuring the through crutch measurement on the basic pattern.

CUTTING PATTERNS TO INDIVIDUAL MEASUREMENTS – TROUSERS
Alterations for a beer belly

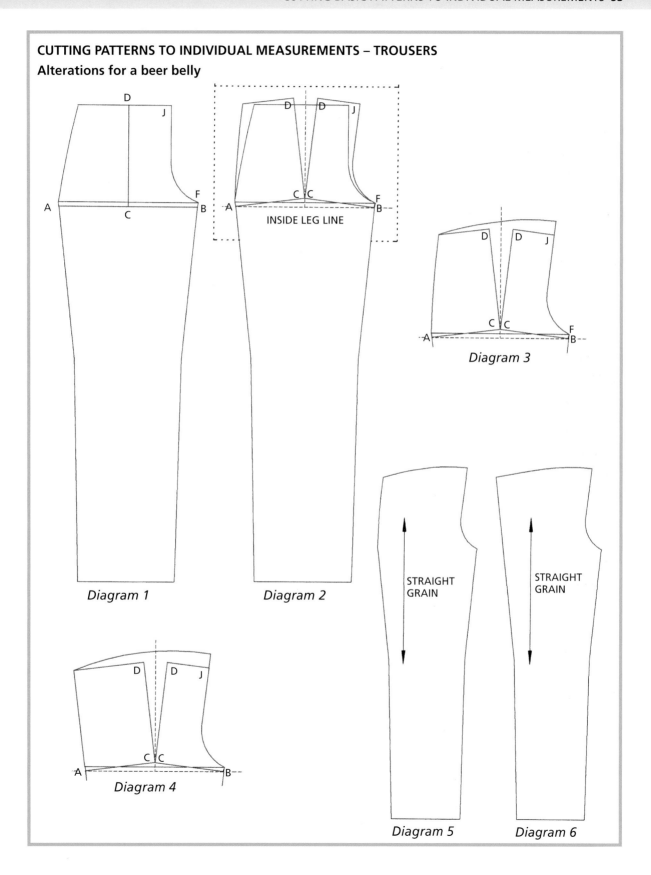

Diagram 1

Diagram 2

INSIDE LEG LINE

Diagram 3

Diagram 4

STRAIGHT GRAIN

STRAIGHT GRAIN

Diagram 5

Diagram 6

5

16th-century peasant costume

The clothing of the poor was always worn until it fell apart. If there was enough good fabric left, it would be cut down for children's clothing, if not it would be used for patching or cleaning cloths. Very few working men's clothes have survived from recent times, let alone the 16th century. Consequently resource material has to come very largely from paintings and sculpture. An invaluable source is the work of Pieter Bruegel the Elder. He was a Flemish painter born probably in Breda between 1525 and 1530 and died in 1569. He painted ordinary folk at work and play; he painted them front, back and side, indoors and out in all the seasons of the year and he painted them in meticulous detail. In *The Parable of the Blind* the seam on the lace fastening the fourth man's coat is clearly visible as is the stitching on his coif. This attention to detail is usual in most paintings of the period, but few show so many ordinary people and none as comprehensively as Bruegel. The patterns in this section are all based on Bruegel's work. Careful examination of the paintings will show a wealth of useful details such as the mittens lying beside the man fixing his skates in *The Census at Bethlehem*; the footless hose rolled to the knee in *The Procession to Calvary*; cloths tied round the legs of the men in *Hunters in the Snow*. It is clear that garments were lined with contrasting fabric; some were made of felt and a few from leather. Not only are the actual garments shown in great detail but also the different ways they could be worn. The men in *Harvest* work in their shirt sleeves; those in *The Parable of the Blind* wear layers of clothing. In *The Battle between Carnival and Lent* some people are wearing fancy dress. In *Children's Games* the children wear scaled-down versions of adult clothes in great variety; some of the boys are wearing short doublets and hose, others have long coats; one boy is wearing trousers and another has knee breeches. There is no other painter of the period so useful to costume designers and makers. Although Bruegel was painting in the Low Countries, it can be assumed that peasant costume would have been similar in shape throughout Western Europe.

The six men in Breugel's *The Parable of the Blind* are wearing layers of practical, undecorated garments with minimal fastenings. The coats worn by the two men on the extreme left are probably made of felt, as is the sleeveless coat on the man second from the right. Some of the men have additional layers to protect their legs.

MATERIALS AND SEWING TECHNIQUES FOR 16TH-CENTURY PEASANT COSTUME

Wool and linen were by far the most common fabrics used for the costume of all classes in the Middle Ages and continued to be so amongst the lower classes when the rich were wearing silk. The quality would have varied considerably; the wool for the lower classes would have been from ancient breeds of sheep that had harsh, kempy fleece, whereas the upper classes would have worn fabric woven from fleece of superior quality. The most common woollen fabric was kersey, a loosely woven flexible fabric believed to have got its name from the town of that name in Suffolk. It was cheap and durable and was used extensively for the clothing of peasants, commoners, priests and soldiers. By 1542 kersey was being exported as far as Hungary. It was woven in 12 yard lengths, a yard wide (rather less than 11 metres long, rather less than 91.5cm wide). It was the common lining fabric and also used to make hose until the development of knitting.

Linen was used for underclothes, coifs, hose, shirts and nightshirts. Its smooth texture would have protected the skin from contact with harsh wool. The cool, damp climate of Northern Europe was ideal for the

cultivation and manufacture of linen. For the most part, it was a domestic industry; peasants grew flax in their plots and processed it at home for their own use.

Felt was used for unlined coats and cloaks. It came in lengths of 4⅓ ells x 1⅓ ells (3.64 x 1.12 metres, rather less than 4 yards x 44 inches). As it was not woven and did not fray, it could be cut in any direction with minimal turnings and it did not need lining.

Bruegel's peasants are often depicted wearing bright red garments; whether or not this was common in the Low Countries it was highly improbable in Britain. The British dye industry was still in its infancy; the most common dye was woad, which gave shades of indigo blue. It could be used to over-dye fabric previously dyed yellow with weld, to give shades of green. Although there are a few plants which yield red dye in Britain, most red and purple fabric was imported and far beyond the reach of the lower classes. Most of the fabric worn by peasants in Britain would have been in its natural shades of white, grey or brown.

All outer wear was lined unless made of felt. In some cases it might have been interlined when stiffening was required but this would rarely be needed for peasant clothing as the fabrics would have been firm enough to support the collars and cuffs without additional stiffening. There were no facings, the outer fabric of the garment being joined to the lining edge to edge round the hem, sleeve ends and neck.

Laces were the most common form of fastening. They were made from lengths of fabric sewn into a narrow tube and finished with narrow metal tags so that they could be passed through eyelet holes easily. The fifth man from the left in *The Parable of the Blind* is wearing a sleeveless coat made of felt; the lace holes are short slits which must have been reinforced with some kind of glue to prevent tearing. Some garments were fastened with buttons and buttonholes, buttons and loops or hooks and loops, but in most cases the fastenings were minimal; often one lace and a leather belt are all that fasten a coat. Hose were always fastened to the doublet with laces but frequently some or all were left undone.

PEASANT DOUBLETS

The doublet was originally a close-fitting military garment padded and quilted to prevent armour from chafing the skin. If worn without armour, the padding was sufficiently thick to give some protection from sword cuts. Gradually it became a civilian garment worn over the shirt and under the tunic or cote. Hose were kept up with laces which passed through pairs of eyelets round the waist of the doublet. In hot weather workmen would remove their outer garments and work in their shirts, doublet and hose or sometimes just shirt and doublet.

In its 16th-century form it was common for the doublet to end at the waist or have skirts reaching any level to mid-thigh. Sometimes it had a small stand- or built-up collar. It usually met edge to edge down the centre front and had a small overlap or wrap over to fasten down the left side. The fastenings were probably hooks and loops, buttons and loops, buttons and buttonholes or laces. The sleeves were usually fitted into wide armholes and tapered towards the wrist or they were full and pleated into the armhole and cuffs. If the garment was sleeveless it was called a jerkin and could be worn over a regular doublet or simply over a shirt.

In Breugel's *The Wedding Dance in the Open Air*, the men are wearing a variety of garments for a village celebration. One man has a small amount of slashing at the top of his hose but, with the obvious exception of the wide sleeves and codpieces, the garments follow the natural lines of the body without distortion.

PEASANT DOUBLETS AND JERKINS

Basic upper body pattern with front length addition but no waist suppression

Sheet of paper:

7cm (2¾") wider than the pattern

x

2cm (¾") longer than the pattern

Diagram 1

Place the pattern so that the centre back is on the left-hand edge of the paper about 1.5cm (⅝") from the top, and a 2cm (¾") gap between the side seams as diagram.

Diagram 2

1 Mark A midway between the centre front and centre back.

2 Square down to B.

3 From A measure down ⅓ depth of side seam to C.

4 C–B is the new side seam.

5 Lower the back and front necklines 1.5cm (⅝").

6 Raise the shoulder lines 1cm (⅜") and redraw making them the original length, ending in D and E as diagram.

7 V is ⅔ of the way down the back armhole as on the basic upper body pattern.

8 Join D–V with a straight line.

9 Mark F on the same level as V.

10 Join E–F with a straight line.

11 Draw the underarm curve through F–C–V as diagram.

12 Cut along C–B.

13 Cut off surplus paper.

Diagram 3

14 Join the shoulder lines to check neckline and armhole. Adjust if necessary.

Diagram 4

The finished pattern.

The man is wearing a wide-sleeved short doublet to which his hose could be fastened although all the front laces are undone. The doublet is lined edge-to-edge and fastened with two laces. His collarless shirt is long enough to tuck well down inside his hose.

The musician is wearing a short red jerkin with a small built-up collar and short skirts, over a short wide-sleeved doublet.

(Both details from Breugel's *The Wedding Dance in the Open Air*.)

PEASANT DOUBLETS AND JERKINS

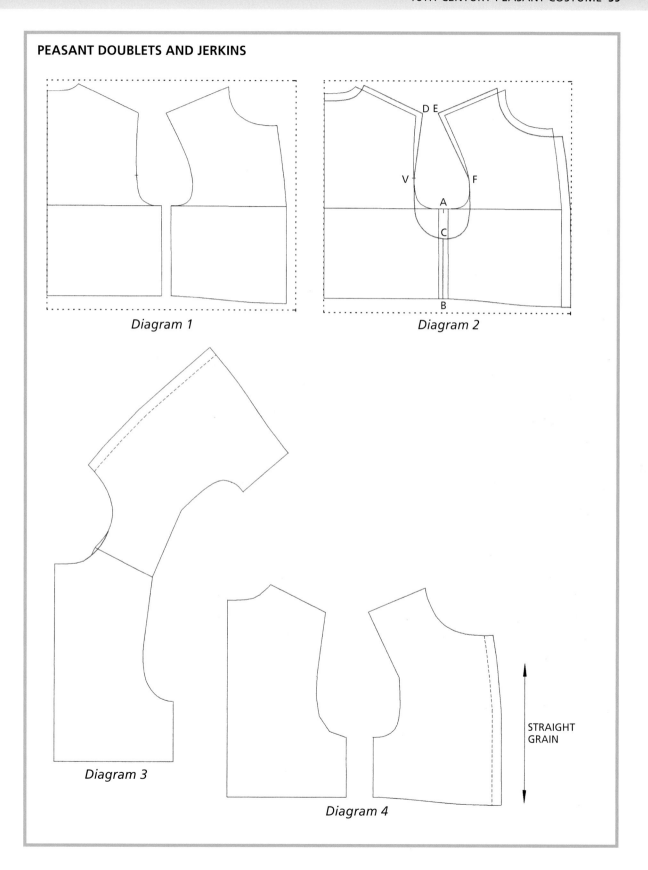

Diagram 1

Diagram 2

Diagram 3

Diagram 4

STRAIGHT
GRAIN

Skirts

If skirts are required they can be cut in the same way as the basic doublet pattern. Cut a strip of paper the same measurement as the doublet waist by the required depth of skirt. Cut and spread the paper as for the basic doublet pattern.

Sleeves

The armholes of these doublets are very deep which would restrict movement if joined to the hose; it is for this reason that most if not all the points are undone when the wearer is engaged in manual work or dancing in Bruegel's paintings. Any of the doublet sleeve patterns can be used.

Waist suppression

Diagram 5

15 I is midway along the bottom of the back pattern.

16 Join V–I.

17 I–J = the amount to be taken out.

18 Join V–J.

19 Cut out I–V–J and rejoin the pattern with the pieces meeting at V.

Diagram 6

20 Add a small piece of paper at I/J and correct the waist line as diagram.

Diagram 7
The finished pattern.
Note. The front section remains unaltered.

Doublet with raised neckline

On the back section of any doublet pattern.
Diagram 8

21 Secure a piece of paper under the pattern as diagram.

22 Measure A 1cm down the shoulder from the neckline.

23 Draw A–B = 2.5cm (1") parallel to the centre back.

24 A–C = 2.5cm (1").

25 Draw B–C in a smooth curve as diagram.

26 Square out B–D.

27 Cut off surplus paper.

On the front section of the pattern
Diagram 9

28 Secure a piece of paper under the front section of the pattern as diagram.

29 Turn the back section over and place it on the front section so that the shoulder lines match as diagram.

30 Trace round the curve B–C.

Diagram 10

31 Redraw the centre front in a straight line E–F as diagram.

32 Join F to the neck point of the shoulder line.

33 Cut off surplus paper.

Diagram 11
The finished pattern.

Note. The instructions are for a collar 2.5cm (1") high but this is only an illustration; it may be raised or lowered following the same instructions. The centre front can be extended and a button stand added as drawn in red.

PEASANT DOUBLETS AND JERKINS – continued

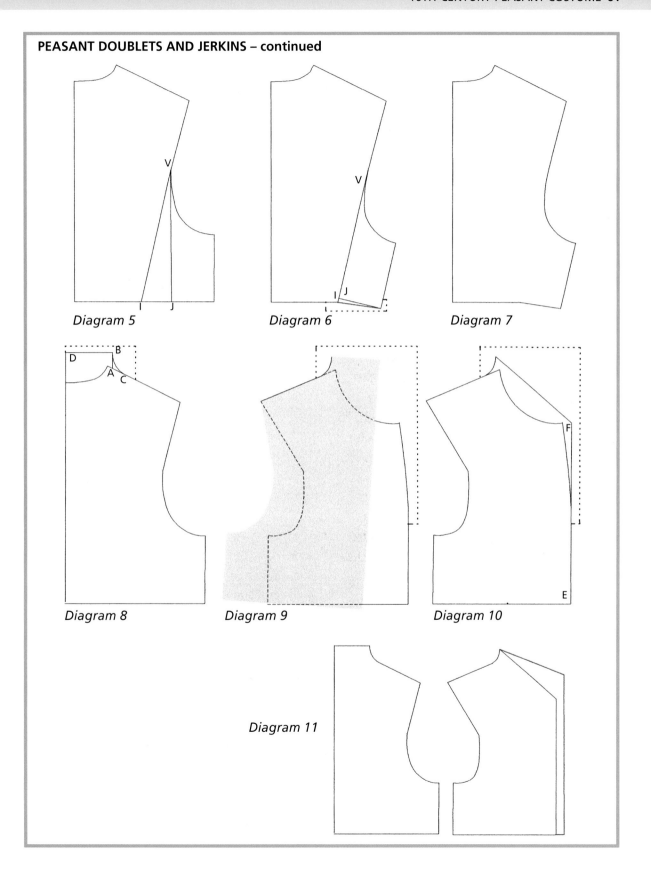

Diagram 5

Diagram 6

Diagram 7

Diagram 8

Diagram 9

Diagram 10

Diagram 11

SLEEVES FOR PEASANT DOUBLETS

Sheet of paper:
Circumference of the doublet armhole

x

Length of sleeve

Diagram 1

The simplest sleeve can be made from a rectangle without any shaping. Mark the paper A, B, C and D as diagram. A–B is the same measurement as the circumference of the armhole; A–C and B–D are the side seams. There would be plenty of movement in this sleeve but the width at the wrist might be impractical. To make it more practical, the wrist could be gathered into a cuff or the sleeve tapered as in the following variations.

Narrowing the wrist

Diagrams 2a & 2b

1 Fold the paper in half, A–C to B–D.

2 Measure round the hand loosely.

3 Measure half this measurement from the fold towards A–C.

4 Redraw the side seam with a straight line or curve it as Diagram 2b.

5 Pin the paper to stop it moving.

6 Cut off surplus paper to complete the pattern.

Widening the sleeve head

Diagram 3

7 Cut the paper down the middle from A–B to C–D.

8 Overlap the pieces until C–D measures the required wrist measurement and secure with adhesive tape.

9 Place the pattern on another sheet of paper and weight it down.

10 Rejoin A–B with a smooth curve as diagram.

11 Check the wrist measurement and adjust if necessary.

12 Trace round the pattern and cut off the surplus paper.

Diagrams 4a & 4b

The sleeves will be easier to fit into the armhole if they are cut with a shallow head as follows.

13 Fold the pattern in half as diagram.

14 From A measure down A–E = 5cm (2").

15 Curve the head as diagram.

16 The side seams can be left straight or curved as diagram.

17 Pin the paper to stop it moving and cut off surplus to complete the pattern.

Diagrams 5 & 6

If a wide sleeve is required, the pattern can be cut down the middle and spread as Diagram 5.

If width is required at the top only, spread the pattern as Diagram 6 in which case the wrist should be curved as diagram.

SLEEVES FOR PEASANT DOUBLETS

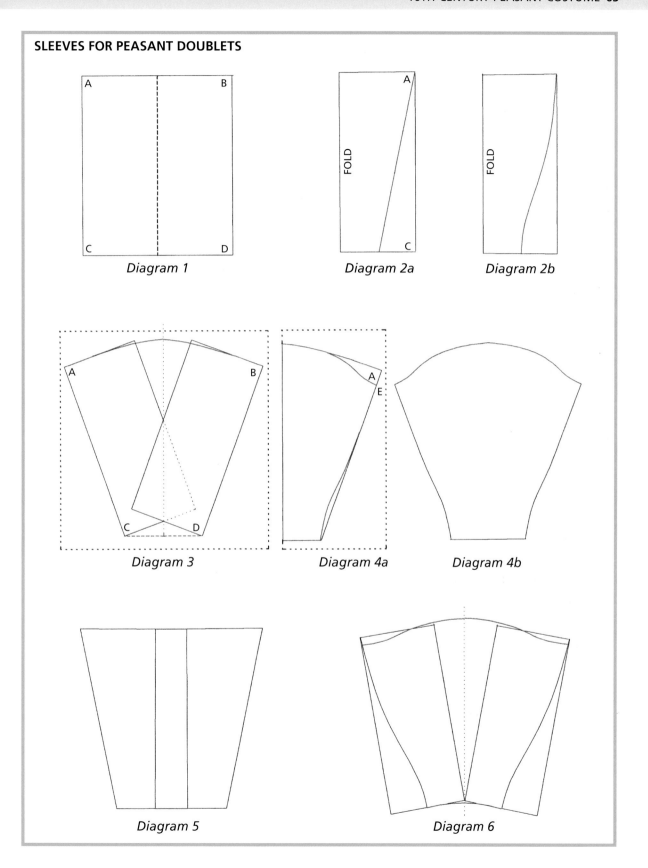

Diagram 1

Diagram 2a

Diagram 2b

Diagram 3

Diagram 4a

Diagram 4b

Diagram 5

Diagram 6

BASIC PEASANT COAT

The coat is based on the peasant doublet/jerkin pattern (see p. 58) with chest line marked but no button stand. If it is to be worn over a similar doublet, the coat should be cut a size larger.

For the basic pattern

Sheet of paper:

Total width of peasant doublet pattern + 10cm (4")

x

Required length of coat + 5cm (2")

Diagram 1

1 Mark the paper A, B, C, D as diagram.

2 Place the pattern on the paper as diagram and trace around it.

3 Mark the centre back neck point E.

4 Mark the centre front neck point F.

5 Mark the underarm point G.

6 From G square down to meet C–D at H.

7 I is midway along the back chest line.

8 From I square down to meet C–D at J.

9 K is on the armhole 3cm (1¼") above the chest line.

10 L is midway along the front chest line.

11 From L square down to meet C–D at M.

12 N is on the armhole 3cm (1¼") above the chest line.

13 From F square out to meet B–D at O.

14 Cut along G–H to separate the back and front sections of the pattern.

15 Cut off surplus paper around neck, armhole and shoulders.

16 Cut along K–I–J and N–L–M which are marked in red on the diagram.

Diagram 2

17 Mark the pattern sections 1, 2, 3, 4 as diagram.

Calculate the required hem measurement for the half pattern. Deduct the measurement of the pattern (i.e. the measurement C–D) from the required hem measurement; the remainder is the amount of flare to be distributed at the hem. This will be divided between the centre back, the slash in the back pattern, the side seam and the slash in the front pattern. Either place the patterns on another piece of paper or secure strips to accommodate the flare. The flare will be distributed as diagram i.e. the same amount in the front and back slashes and half as much at centre back and each side seam.

This knee-length coat is probably made of felt. It is a very basic shape fastened with a single lace. (Detail from Breugel's *The Parable of the Blind*.)

BASIC PEASANT COAT

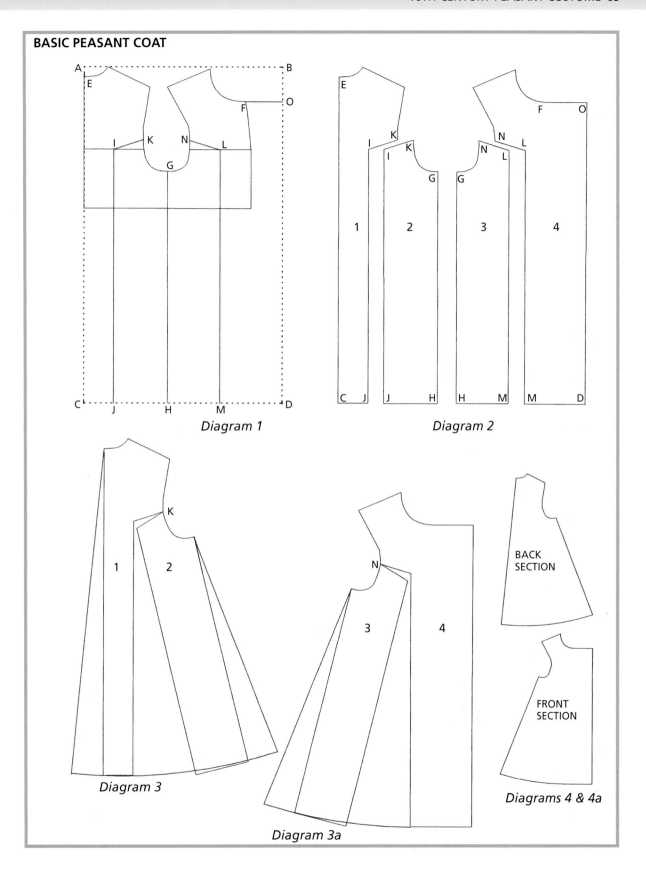

Diagram 1

Diagram 2

Diagram 3

Diagram 3a

Diagrams 4 & 4a

An addition of 70cm (35") would give a generous amount of flare. It should be distributed as follows:

> 10cm (5") at centre back.
> 20cm (10") in the back slash.
> 10cm (5") at each side seam.
> 20cm (10") at the front slash.

Diagrams 3 & 3a

18 From E on section 1 redraw the centre back line adding 10cm (5") at the hem.

19 From K pivot section 2 so that the gap at the hem measures 20cm (10").

20 From N pivot section 3, so that the gap at the hem measures 20cm (10").

Pivoting sections 2 and 3 will cause the armhole to distort slightly and become a little less deep. On such a simple coat this is not critical and need not be adjusted.

21 From G on section 2 redraw the side seam adding 10cm (5") at the hem.

22 From G on section 3 redraw the side seam adding 10cm (5") at the hem.

23 Section 4 remains unchanged.

24 Match the new front and back side seams and redraw the hemline in a smooth curve.

25 Cut off surplus paper.

Diagrams 4 & 4a

The completed pattern.

Sleeves

Any of the sleeve variations for peasant doublet can be used for coats.

Collars

A stand collar or raised neckline can be used.

The coat can be made to fit down the back by gathering the centre back waist into cartridge pleats. These are made just above and below the waist and held in place by sewing a piece of tape across the inside.

Note. If the coat is to go over a thick doublet, modify the pattern as follows:

> Raise the shoulders .5–1.5cm (¼ –⅝").
> Lengthen the shoulder 1–1.5cm (⅜"–⅝").

The length of peasants' coats is very variable but as a general guide, a modern overcoat is half the height of the wearer + 20cm (8").

PEASANT HOSE

Despite the fact that peasant hose were made from woven fabric they were quite close fitting. They must have been cut out roughly then fitted to the wearer as men's legs are by no means proportionate to body size and there are no standard measurements. Big men can have thin legs and many athletes and dancers have slender bodies and well-developed leg muscles. To get a good fit, cut the hose with ample seam allow-ance on the back leg seams. Join the crutch seam then pin the back seam on the wearer. Fit one leg carefully keeping the seam allowance even. Mark the pin lines with chalk. Copy the lines onto the other leg with a tracing wheel and carbon paper. Mark the alterations onto the pattern and if it is an average size it is worth keeping it for future use.

Note. The hose pattern is adapted from the basic trouser pattern without waist suppression.

The man's hose do not appear to be fastened to his doublet but are sufficiently tight fitting to stay in place whilst he is dancing. The opening is fastened with two laces; his ample shirt fills the gap. (Detail from Breugel's *The Wedding Dance in the Open Air*.)

On the front section of the pattern

Diagram 1 & 1a

1 Mark the waist level A–B.

2 Mark the inside leg level C–D.

3 Mark the knee level E–F.

4 Mark the centre line G–H (M–N–O on the basic pattern).

On the back section of the pattern

5 Mark the inside leg level J–K.

6 Mark the knee level L–M.

7 Mark N = front crutch width measurement from K.

Diagram 2

8 Place the front section of the pattern (drawn in blue on diagram) on top of the back section so that D meets N and the inside leg and knee levels are in line as diagram.

9 Weight down the patterns.

10 Trace H–G onto the back section with a tracing wheel and continue up to the back waist in a straight line to O.

11 Remove the front section of the pattern.

Diagram 3

12 From O on the back section cut along the traced line and mark the pieces section 1 and section 2 as diagram.

Diagram 4

13 Turn the front section over.

14 Join section 2 to the front section so that K–M meets D–E.

15 Join section 1 to the front section so that J–L meets C–F.

16 Place a piece of paper under the gap at A–C–I and secure with adhesive tape, cut off surplus.

17 Measure the waist of the pattern and deduct the required measurement.

18 Take out the suppression from O on section 1 as diagram.

Note. At this point the crutch seam can be sewn and the hose fitted down the back seams as described at the beginning of the instructions; otherwise the pattern can be modified as follows.

HOSE

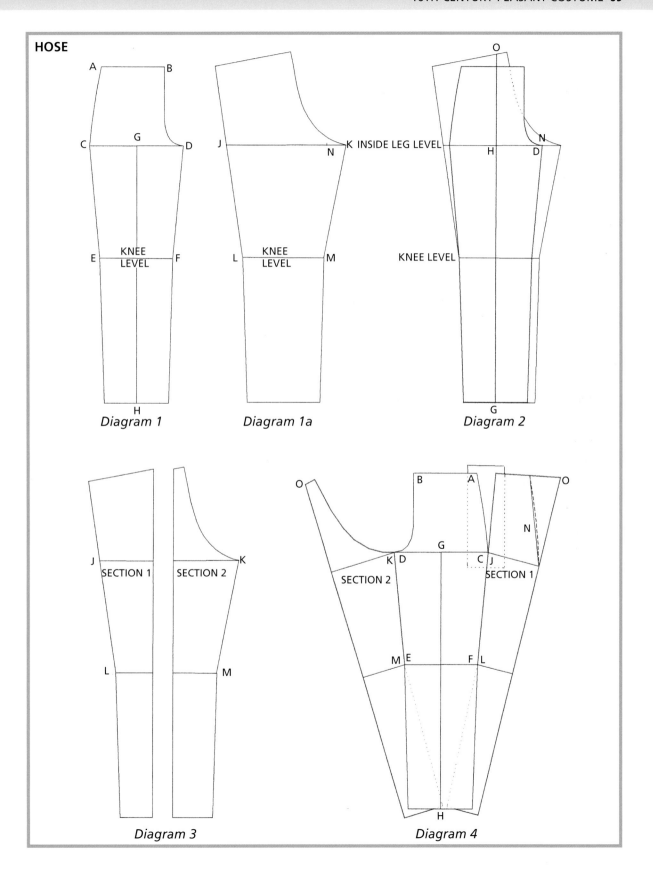

Diagram 1

Diagram 1a

INSIDE LEG LEVEL

KNEE LEVEL

Diagram 2

SECTION 1

SECTION 2

Diagram 3

SECTION 2

SECTION 1

Diagram 4

Shaping the back seam

The following measurements are necessary to shape the back seam:

TOP OF THIGH	8cm (3¼") below inside leg line
KNEE	The widest part at top of knee cap
SMALL KNEE	The narrowest part – average 7cm (2¾") below the knee level
CALF	The widest part – average 8cm (3") below small knee
ANKLE	Measure round the heel and instep with the foot pointed to ensure that the foot can get through

Diagram 5

19 Inside leg level to P = measurement to top of thigh level.

20 P–Q = top of thigh to knee level.

21 Q–R = knee to small knee level.

22 R–S = small knee to calf level.

23 S–T = calf to ankle level.

24 From P square out half the difference between actual top of thigh and pattern measurements.

25 From Q square out half the difference between actual knee and pattern measurements.

26 From R square out half the difference between the actual small knee and pattern measurements.

27 From S square out half the difference between the actual calf and pattern measurements.

28 From T square out half the difference between the actual ankle and pattern measurements.

29 Join the new points in a smooth line as diagram.

Diagram 5a

30 Pin the edges of the paper together from the inside leg level to the bottom and cut along the new line, drawn in red.

31 Unpin the pattern.

Note. If the hose are to end at the ankle, cut 8cm (3¼") from the bottom of the leg – this is an average measurement which should be adjusted as required. If they are to be footed hose or have a strap under the instep, shape the bottom of the leg as follows.

Diagram 6

32 Mark the ends of the seams U and V as diagram.

33 U–W = 7cm (2¾"), V–X = 7cm (2¾").

34 Join W–X with a straight line.

35 H–Y = 8cm (3¼") – height of instep, adjust if necessary.

36 Join W–Y and X–Y.

37 Draw W–Y–X in a smooth curve, approximately 2cm (¾") from the centre of W–Y and 1.5cm (⅝") from X–Y.

38 Cut round the curve W–Y–X.

Diagram 7
The finished pattern.

Note. This is a complicated pattern so it is worth while keeping a copy of the Diagram 4 stage so it can be adapted for individual measurements.

HOSE – continued

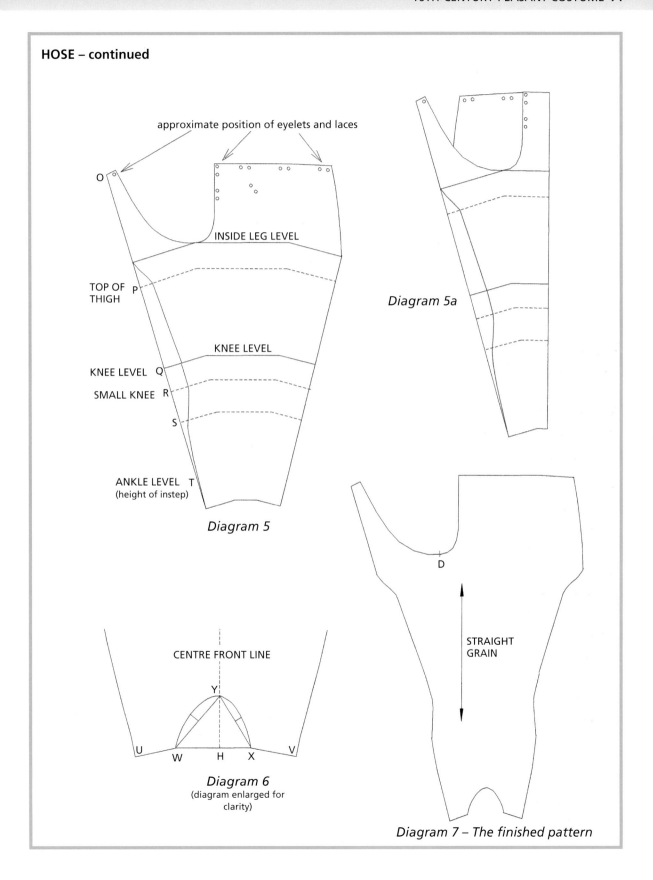

approximate position of eyelets and laces

INSIDE LEG LEVEL

TOP OF
THIGH   P

KNEE LEVEL

KNEE LEVEL   Q

SMALL KNEE   R

S

ANKLE LEVEL   T
(height of instep)

O

Diagram 5

Diagram 5a

CENTRE FRONT LINE

Y

U
W   H   X
V

Diagram 6
(diagram enlarged for
clarity)

D

STRAIGHT
GRAIN

Diagram 7 – The finished pattern

FOOTED HOSE

Cutting the sole pattern

Draw around the foot keeping the shape as smooth and simple as possible. This pattern can be reversed for left and right feet but in practice one symmetrical pattern can be used for both feet. Alternatively a good shape can be made using an insole which can be bought at most chemists; they come in one large size marked with smaller sizes so that they can be cut down.

The measurements for the upper foot pattern are as follows.

MEASUREMENT 1	Centre back of heel to B and C on the sole
MEASUREMENT 2	Measured over the highest point of the instep
MEASUREMENT 3	Front of foot from the highest point of the instep over toes

Diagram 1

1 Make two copies of the sole pattern – one to be used for the sole, the other modified for the upper.

2 Mark A at the centre back of the sole on both copies.

3 On one copy mark A–B and A–C = measurement 1 (average measurement of 7cm (2¾"))

Diagram 1a

4 Join B–C with a straight line.

5 Cut along B–C and discard the heel piece.

Diagrams 2 & 2a

6 D is midway between B–C, square up to the toe E.

7 From D cut almost to E.

8 Open the slash so that B–C = measurement 2.

9 Secure a piece of paper under the slash.

10 Redraw the toe in a smooth curve repositioning E as diagram.

11 E–F = measurement 3.

12 Draw B–F–C in a smooth curve.

13 Cut off surplus paper to complete the pattern as Diagram 2a.

Diagrams 3 & 3a

14 When making up footed hose, B–E–C is joined to W–Y–X then the sole attached matching A to the centre back leg seam U/V.

FOOTED HOSE

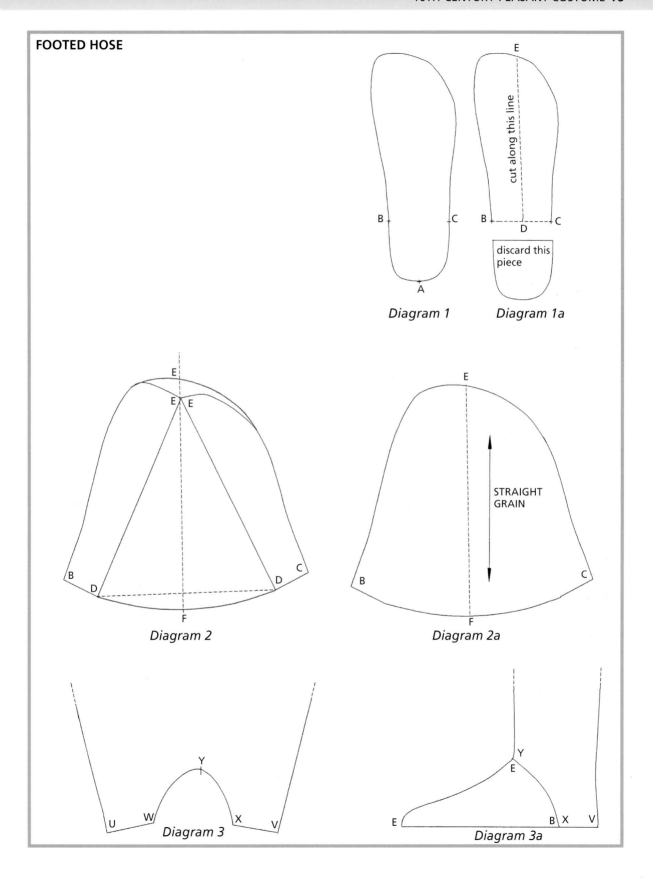

Diagram 1   *Diagram 1a*

Diagram 2   *Diagram 2a*

Diagram 3   *Diagram 3a*

BASIC CODPIECE

The codpiece began as a simple triangle of fabric which covered the front opening of joined hose. It gradually developed an exaggerated shape as is evident in Bruegel's paintings where they are worn even by the young boys in *Children's Games*. The protuberance would have been stuffed with straw, fleece or other padding and backed with a much flatter shape like the basic codpiece pattern.

Note. The measurements given are for an 'average' size: seat 100cm, 1.7m tall (seat 40", 5'9" tall).

> *Sheet of paper:*
> 14cm x 26cm (5½" x 10¼")

Diagram 1

1 Mark the paper A, B, C, D as diagram.

2 From A measure down A–E = 1.5cm (⅝").

3 From B measure down B–F = 1cm (⅜").

4 Join E–F in a smooth curve as diagram.

5 Measure down F–G = 6cm (2⅜").

6 From C measure out C–H = 5cm (2").

7 Join G–H with a straight line.

8 From G measure G–I = 10cm (4").

9 Square out I–J = 1.25cm (½").

10 Draw G–J in a gentle curve.

11 Join J–H with a straight line.

12 From G square out G–K = 8cm (3⅛").

13 Join E–K as diagram.

Note. The shape at E needs to be large enough to accommodate two eyelets comfortably.

14 From A measure down A–L = 17cm (6¾").

15 Square out L–M = 6cm (2⅜").

16 Join M–K with a straight line and redraw curving out .75cm (¼") from the centre as diagram.

17 Join M–H with a straight line.

18 Cut off surplus paper.

19 From M draw M–N to meet J–H at right angles.

20 Cut along M–N to complete the pattern as Diagram 2.

To make up the basic codpiece

1 Cut two pieces of the main part (marked section 1) on the straight grain as Diagram 2.

2 Cut section 2 on a bias fold as Diagram 3.

3 The two pieces of section 1 are sewn down the centre front, F–G–N.

4 M–N/N–M on section 1 is joined to M–N/N–M on section 2.

5 The point of section 2 is inserted into the front crutch of the hose matching point H on the codpiece with D on the hose and sewing as far as M.

Note. D is the top of the original inside leg seam.

6 The main part of the codpiece is attached to the hose by laces through eyelets at E.

Note. The basic codpiece will usually require lining but no padding. It can be used as a foundation for exaggerated styles as follows.

Exaggerated codpieces

Exuberant codpieces in the Bruegel paintings have a backing cut like the basic codpiece pattern but the front part has the central seam extended into a bag shape which is padded firmly causing folds to form round the base. The folds are stitched down to the lining which keeps the padding in place and retains the shape. The modifications are made between G and J as Diagram 4.

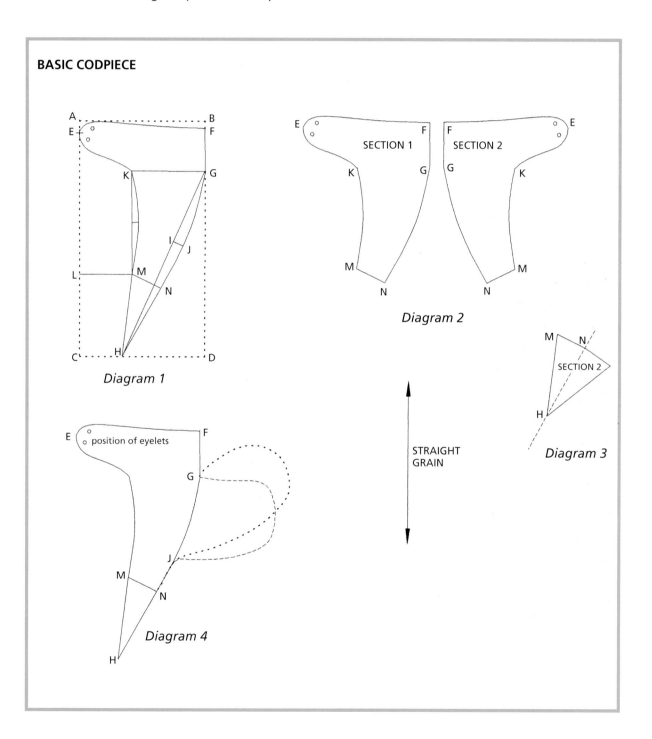

BASIC CODPIECE

Diagram 1

Diagram 2

Diagram 3

STRAIGHT GRAIN

SECTION 1

SECTION 2

o position of eyelets

Diagram 4

6

Fashionable costume 1530–1666

Costume in the period covered in this section begins with the powerful, square silhouette typified by Hans Holbein's portrait of Henry VIII and continues to the mid-17th century when the doublet ceased to be fashionable and was replaced by the coat.

The most obvious difference between costume of the fashionable and that of working people is the quality of the fabrics. As most of the materials for fashionable clothing had to be imported they were restricted to the very rich. The best silks, damask, satin, taffeta, velvets etc came from France and Italy, as did cloth of gold and cloth of silver. The British silk industry was largely restricted to ribbon manufacture until the late 17th century and never equalled that of the Continent or the Orient. The most popular furs – lynx, wolf and sable – were also imported as were most of the jewels which encrusted the most extravagant garments. British dye houses had not yet developed the excellence they were to achieve by the 18th century. Blue and yellow dyestuffs were the only ones produced in quantity in Britain and therefore available to the poor: all others had to be imported. That is why anyone wearing blue in a Tudor painting will be a servant.

Sumptuary laws dictated the cost and quality of materials that could be worn by different ranks. Only the most exalted people could wear the most costly furs and fabrics. The fact that these laws had to be made, and so many *were* made, implies that people did dress above their station and the laws were frequently broken by those who could afford luxuries.

The second major distinction between rich and poor was the cut of the garments and never more so than in the Tudor and early Stuart periods. The use of braid, particularly when it incorporated metal threads, helped to stiffen the garment, but canvas and buckram as well as padding were necessary to hold the fashionable shapes. This was also achieved with layers of linen and wool. A collar might have two layers of wool and two of linen pad-stitched together forming a substantial thickness. Bombast was used to bulk out doublets, sleeves and, in particular, trunk-hose: rags, flock, horsehair, wool, flax, cotton or bran were used. Bran was not popular as it leaked out if the stitching was loose or there was a break in the fabric. Philip Stubbs in his *Anatomie of Abuses* of 1583 wrote that padding could weigh as much as 5lb.

Most of the existing garments of the period have survived because they were so special or they have been taken from the tombs of important people. The clothing worn in most portraits was doubtless the most expensive the sitters owned. One can assume more simple and probably more comfortable clothes were worn on other occasions, although they would still have followed the current fashionable shape.

The term 'hose' at this period refers to all leg wear including breeches; it was not until the end of the period that it referred exclusively to stockings. The lower parts of hose were called nether stocks and were knitted from wool, cotton or silk. Delicate nether stocks required a good pair of legs if they were to look elegant, so various types of padding were invented to help the less fortunate.

Henry VIII was heavy and about 188cm/6' 2" in height by the time this portrait was painted. The fashionable costume gives the impression of great strength and power, which is emphasised by the pose and deliberate shortening of the distance between his waist and knee. He is wearing a short fur-lined gown over matching cote and doublet. The Spanish codpiece protrudes between the skirts of the cote although the breeches are hidden. The neck and wrists of the shirt are finished with small frills. (*Henry VIII* by Hans Eworth, after Holbein.)

Slashing was a popular form of decoration from c.1480–c.1650. There are several stories to account for its origin. The traditional one is that it was invented by the Swiss after their victory over the Duke of Burgundy's army at the Battle of Grandson in 1476 when they plundered a quantity of luxurious silk garments. The Swiss were bigger than the Burgundians so they slashed the clothes in order to wear them. The slashing was considered rather attractive so gradually it became a popular form of decoration. Diana de Marly in *Fashion for Men* puts forward another possibility: that the Swiss soldiers, who had defeated attempts by larger nations to end their independence, wore their battle-torn clothes as a badge of national pride. Whatever the origins, slashed clothes became popular throughout Europe.

MATERIALS AND SEWING TECHNIQUES FOR 16TH-CENTURY FASHIONABLE COSTUME

Many of the fabrics used for fashionable clothing are no longer available or prohibitively expensive. Furnishing fabrics are often used as an alternative, but they tend to be loosely woven and have a tendency to fray. The raw edges of some of the existing 16th-century garments have been sealed with glue or wax to stop them fraying; Fray Check or emulsion glue will serve the same purpose. Metallic fabrics are particularly prone to fraying and this can be avoided by painting the cutting line (not the sewing line) with Fray Check or emulsion glue and allowing it to dry before cutting.

Fashionable costumes, particularly doublets, require stiffening to maintain their shape. In the past this was achieved with layers of heavy linen or layers of felted wool pad-stitched together. Belly pieces were sometimes made even more rigid with whalebones. This time-consuming process can be replicated using industrial felt and either steel or plastic boning. Industrial felt is available in various thicknesses and degrees of stiffness and can be used for collars, panes of trunk-hose, wings and entire doublets. Felt can be cut in any direction without seam allowances. If used for doublets, the pieces can be zigzagged together, leaving the shoulder seams undone, and then covered with the outer fabric which should have been cut with generous seam allowances. The outer fabric is turned over the felt and sewn to the wrong side. The shoulder seams can then be joined and a lining stitched in place. It is helpful to put the felt layer on a stand when covering with the outer fabric so that it covers the felt smoothly and does not drag. Alternatively, the felt pieces can be covered separately and the seams overcast by hand.

Alçega in his *Libro de Geometrica, practica y traça* of 1589 advocates adding three finger breadths (4.25cm) to the length but very little in width when cutting a padded doublet. This will obviously vary with the thickness of the padding but is a good general guide. The lining should be made up with the padding, put on a stand and the outer fabric fitted over the top so as to avoid any pulling.

Obviously all 16th-century garments were made entirely by hand and parts are difficult if not impossible to machine satisfactorily. Cartridge pleating must always be done by hand as no other method will give the right effect. Heavy sleeves, particularly when fur lined, are easier to set into the armholes if hand stitched using double waxed thread. If braid is being used for decoration, as much as possible should be sewn onto the fabric before the garment is completed so that the ends can be stitched into the seams. It must always be eased on and never stretched or the fabric will pucker. A toile or the lining of the doublet should be made up and fitted before the outer fabric is cut to avoid alterations. If the braid is very narrow, for instance round buttonholes, the ends can be threaded through to the back of the material using a large needle or stiletto and the ends sewn down neatly.

GOWNS, COTES, DOUBLETS, JERKINS AND CLOAKS

In the early years of the period there was a marked difference between the clothing worn by men of means in Northern Europe and that worn in the south. The two French envoys in Holbein's painting *The Ambassadors*, c.1531, typify the northern style. The man on the right, Bishop Georges de Seive, is wearing a long-sleeved, fur-lined, damask gown of simple cut. This style was worn in the previous century and continued to be worn by clerics, scholars and older men until the end of the 16th century. In fact it is still worn on formal occasions, in much the same shape, by the learned professions and government officials of the present day. The man on the left, Jean de Dinteville, is wearing a short gown sometimes known as a half- or demi-gown with long

These fur-lined gowns provided warmth and added width and bulk to the wearers giving gravitas to these two young men. The man on the right, Georges de Selve, Bishop of Lavour wears a long, fur-lined brocade gown of simple cut suitable for a prince of the Church. Jean De Dinteville wears a short gown with hanging sleeves and segmented over-sleeves. Underneath, he has a black cote and pink satin doublet over a white shirt. The neck of the shirt is gathered to form a small stand collar with a tiny frill; there are small soft frills at the wrist. (*The Ambassadors* by Holbein.)

hanging sleeves. The whole garment is lined with fur including the pleated embellishments at the top of the sleeves. The fronts are turned back to show the fur lining and would be joined across the back to form a square collar. Underneath he is wearing a black velvet cote over a pink satin doublet which has no centre front opening so presumably is fastened at the side. Both these men were in their twenties but their clothes make them appear much older. The broad, bulky clothes of Jean de Dinteville give the impression of great strength and power which is even more impressive in Holbein's portrait of Henry VIII.

In Southern Europe the line was much more slender. Although the short gown was worn, it was not as bulky as in the north and the shoulders were sloping rather than square. It was worn over the doublet but without the cote, the extra layer being unnecessary in milder climates. Gradually the Spanish styles were adopted in the north. The gown and cote ceased to be worn by men of fashion and were replaced by cloaks and jerkins. The doublet developed a high Spanish collar and the tiny frill round the neck of the shirt was enlarged to become the ruff.

Fashionable doublets were always rather stiff, shapely garments lined with linen, usually interlined and often embellished with braid and embroidery. Early doublets were sometimes side-fastening, particularly when worn with the cote, but more generally they fastened down the front. In the early years the waist was in the natural position but the front started to curve downwards towards the middle of the 16th century and in the second half formed a distinct point, which was emphasised by a belly piece. The peascod-bellied doublet (c.1570–1600) had the point padded so that it swelled over the girdle. After 1600 the doublet became a simpler, fitted shape and gradually the waist was raised but the pointed front was retained.

In the early years the doublet skirts were 1–15 centimetres long (4"–6") and the centre fronts cut back to accommodate the codpiece, but when it ceased to be worn the skirts met down the centre front. The peascod-bellied doublet had narrow skirts usually cut in one piece or with separate sections at the centre back. When the waist was raised the skirts became longer and were cut in overlapping tabs.

Doublets had stand collars; sometimes the back was cut in one with the back of the doublet and separate pieces for the fronts. This is the method used in all Alçega's patterns, but a completely separate collar gives a better fit. The sleeves were fairly bulky in the early years but always of simple cut; as the 16th century progressed they became close fitting and in the second quarter of the 17th century the upper part was slashed to reveal the shirt. The armhole seam was covered by wings, originally to hide laces when the sleeves were detachable, but which became purely decorative. Another feature that was no longer functional was the laces which had once held up the hose. These started to be worn on the outside as can be seen on Charles I's doublet (see p. 124).

Jerkins were generally worn for warmth over the doublet. They were cut like doublets, sometimes with hanging sleeves but generally sleeveless. Sometimes they matched the doublet but could be contrasting as in the portrait of Sir Walter Raleigh (see p. 121).

Short cloaks were fashionable from the third quarter of the 16th century. They varied in length from just below the waist to mid-thigh and could be a complete circle, three-quarters of a circle or towards the end of the century, semi-circular. Sometimes they had hoods, sometimes stand collars, and they were frequently highly decorative. One interesting variant had side panels which could be removed, enabling the cloak to be worn like a tabard.

BASIC DOUBLET/JERKIN

Sheet of paper:
½ chest measurement + 5cm (2"), 7cm (2¾") if a button stand is required

x

Nape to waist measurement + 5cm (2")

The body pattern

Diagram 1

1 Draft a basic upper body pattern with front length addition but no waist suppression adding 5cm (2") ease (instead of the normal 3cm (1¼").

2 Mark V, R, W, X as diagram (using the same lettering as for the basic upper body pattern).

3 Join V–X with a straight line.

4 X–Y = the required waist suppression.

5 Join V–Y.

6 Cut along X–Y and V–Y.

7 Cut off surplus paper leaving the bottom strip.

Diagram 2

8 Rejoin the pattern so that the two sections meet at V.

9 Redraw the waist line.

10 Cut off surplus paper.

11 Cut along the new side seam.

12 Add a button stand of 2cm (¾") parallel to the centre front if required.

Diagram 3

The completed pattern.

The skirts

Diagram 4

13 Measure the waist line of the pattern and cut a strip of paper this length x the required skirt length.

14 Mark the paper A, B, C, D as diagram. A–B will be the waist, C–D will be the hem edge.

15 Fold the paper into eight.

Diagram 5

16 Cut along the creases from C–D almost to A–B.

17 Place the pattern on another piece of paper and spread the slashes as required.

Note. The flare on the skirts must be appropriate for the fullness of the hose.

18 Weight down the pattern and draw round it and discard.

19 A–C will be the centre back and B–D the centre front.

20 Check the waist measurement and adjust at the centre front if necessary.

21 Cut off surplus paper to complete the pattern.

BASIC DOUBLET/JERKIN

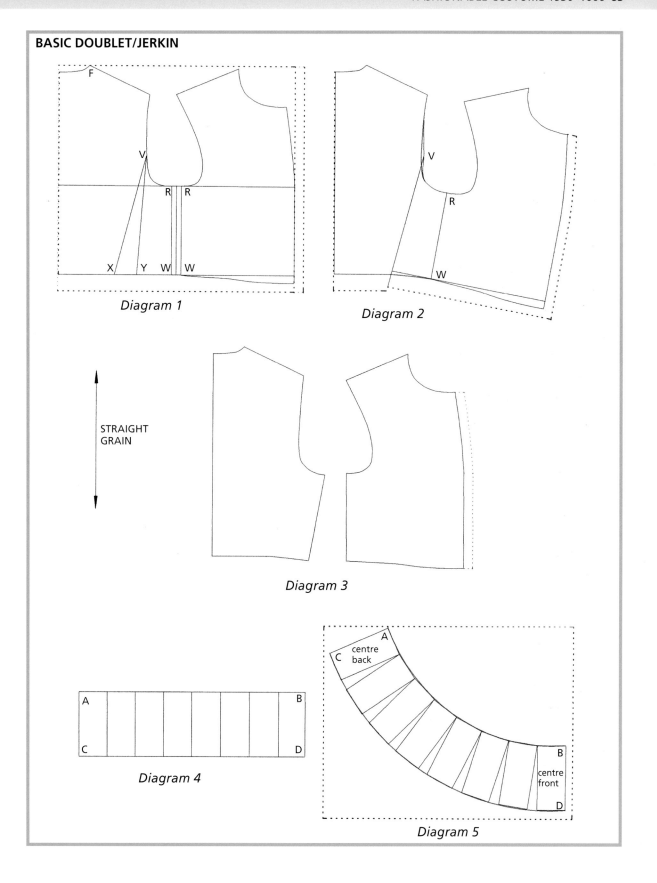

Diagram 1

Diagram 2

STRAIGHT
GRAIN

Diagram 3

Diagram 4

Diagram 5

BASIC PERIOD SLEEVE

Note. This pattern is the basic shape of most fashionable sleeves from the middle of the 16th century until the early years of the 19th; it is based on the simple two-piece sleeve pattern.

Simple two-piece sleeve pattern with the elbow line marked

Sheet of paper:

Sleeve length + 5cm (2")

x

Circumference of armhole + 5cm (2")

Diagram 1

1 With the pattern pieces as diagram, mark the upper section of the simple two-piece sleeve pattern A, B, C, D; B is the highest point on the sleeve head.

2 Mark the lower section E, F, G as diagram (the lower section needs to be turned over).

Diagram 2

3 Mark H 1cm (⅜") down the left-hand side of the paper and square across to I.

4 J is midway along H–I. Square down to K on the bottom of the paper.

5 J–L = ½ depth of sleeve head measurement.

6 From L square out L–M and L–N.

7 Place the upper section of the pattern on the paper so that B touches H–I and A meets M–N.

8 Place the under section of the pattern so that C and E meet and F touches MN as diagram.

9 J–O = ½ circumference of the armhole.

10 J–P = ½ circumference of the armhole.

11 Redraw the sleeve head curving 1–1.5cm (⅜"–⅝") under M–N on the lower section as diagram.

12 Join O–D with a straight line and redraw curving approximately 1cm (⅜") from the centre.

13 Join P–G with a straight line and redraw curving approximately 1cm (⅜") from the centre.

14 Cut off surplus paper to complete the pattern as Diagram 3.

Diagram 3

The sleeve can be made more elegant by curving the upper back seams approximately 1cm (⅜") as drawn in red. If the wrist needs to be narrower, it can be taken in down the lower back seam as drawn in red. If the wrist is narrower than the measurement round the palm of the hand, it will require an opening which is usually made in the back seam.

Note. Tailor's pattern books usually draw the sleeve pattern with the under section armhole superimposed on the upper section as Diagram 4.

BASIC PERIOD SLEEVE

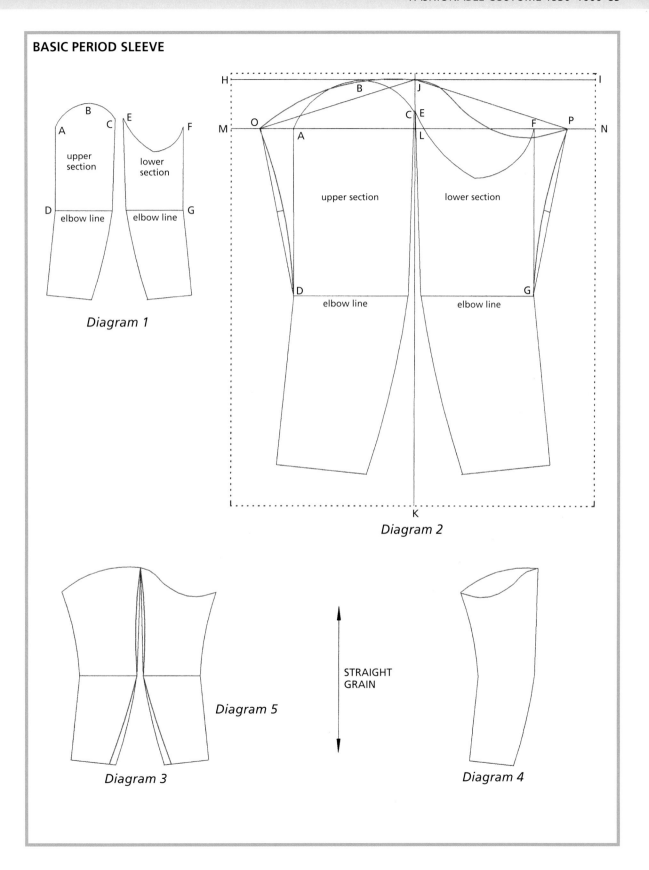

Diagram 1

Diagram 2

Diagram 5

Diagram 3

STRAIGHT
GRAIN

Diagram 4

GOWNS

Gowns were always ample garments and often lined with fur so they need to be cut at least one size larger than the wearer's measurements. For gowns such as those worn by Henry VIII in the Holbein portrait, follow the basic pattern and pattern for hanging sleeves. Very full gowns need a yoke.

Basic pattern

Peasant doublet pattern (see p. 58) without button stand or front length addition (this will give a generous turn back on the centre fronts; if a narrow turn back is required, use the doublet pattern without button stand).

> *Sheet of paper:*
> Width of doublet pattern at waist + 5cm (2")
> x
> Required length of gown + 5cm (2")
> Extra paper as required in the instructions

Diagrams 1 & 1a

1 Mark the back pattern A, B, C, D, E, F as diagram.

2 Mark the front pattern G, H, I, J, K, L as diagram.

Diagram 2

3 Place A–B along the left-hand side of the paper with A 5cm (2") from the top.

4 Place the front pattern so that D–C meets J–I.

5 Mark the bottom corners of the paper M and N as diagram.

6 From L square out to meet the right-hand edge of the paper at O.

7 From H square out to meet O–N at P.

8 From D/J (the underarm point) square down to meet M–N at Q/R as diagram.

9 Mark S midway along F–E (the back shoulder line).

10 T is midway between M–Q; join S–T.

11 Mark U midway along K–L (the front shoulder line).

12 Mark V midway between I–P.

13 Join U–V and square down to W.

14 Cut along S–T and U–V–W.

15 Join E–D with a straight line – this will be the back armhole.

16 Cut off surplus paper as Diagram 3.

Diagram 4

17 Spread the back pattern pieces to the required width as diagram.

18 Place paper under the gap and weight down the pattern.

19 Rejoin the shoulder line keeping it the original length which will mean leaving a small gap as diagram.

20 Secure the extra paper and cut off surplus.

Diagram 4a

21 Repeat the process with the front pattern checking that the shoulders match.

Note. When spreading the front pattern mark L, the neck end of the shoulder line, as this will establish the crease line for the collar.

GOWNS

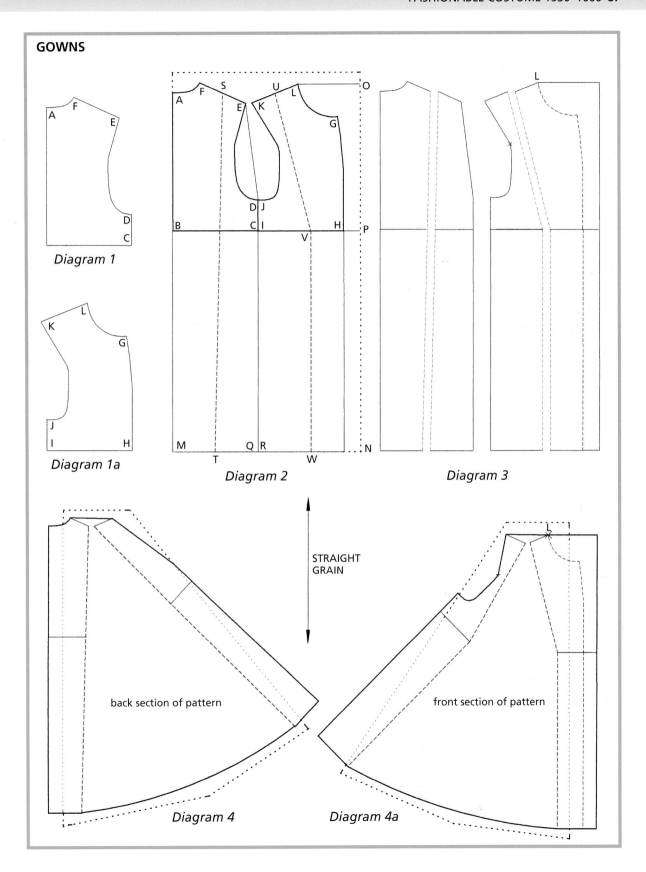

Diagram 1

Diagram 1a

Diagram 2

Diagram 3

STRAIGHT
GRAIN

back section of pattern

front section of pattern

Diagram 4

Diagram 4a

COLLAR FOR BASIC GOWN

Diagram 5

1 From L on the front pattern draw L–U parallel to the centre front.

Diagram 6

2 Place the pattern so that the shoulder lines meet as diagram. With the pattern in this position the armhole may be modified as shown in red (see instructions for sleeves).

3 Fold the front of the pattern along the crease line L–U

4 Match the front and back shoulders and weight down the pattern.

Diagram 7

5 Place a piece of paper under the pattern as diagram and weight it down.

6 V is the required depth of collar; V–W is half the required width of the finished collar.

Note. In the diagram the collar overlaps the end of the shoulder but could be made narrower if worn with sleeves as in the Holbein portrait of Henry VIII.

7 Join W to the edge of the front pattern X (about 30–40cm (12"–16") from the shoulder depending on the height of the wearer).

8 Trace through the red pattern lines onto the new piece of paper and cut off surplus paper.

Diagram 8

9 Unfold the pattern front and attach the collar as diagram.

Diagram 9

The complete collar placed on the gown with the centre fronts and back neck joined to the gown.

Collar variation

A collar cut as the above instructions will stand very square across the shoulders as when worn by Henry VIII in the Holbein portrait. To give sloping shoulders, as worn in Southern Europe, overlap the armhole ends of the shoulders about 6cm (2½") then continue as in the above instructions.

Note. The collar will require a facing, which should be cut in one piece without a centre back seam. This would have been made of fur to match the lining of Northern European gowns.

COLLAR FOR BASIC GOWN

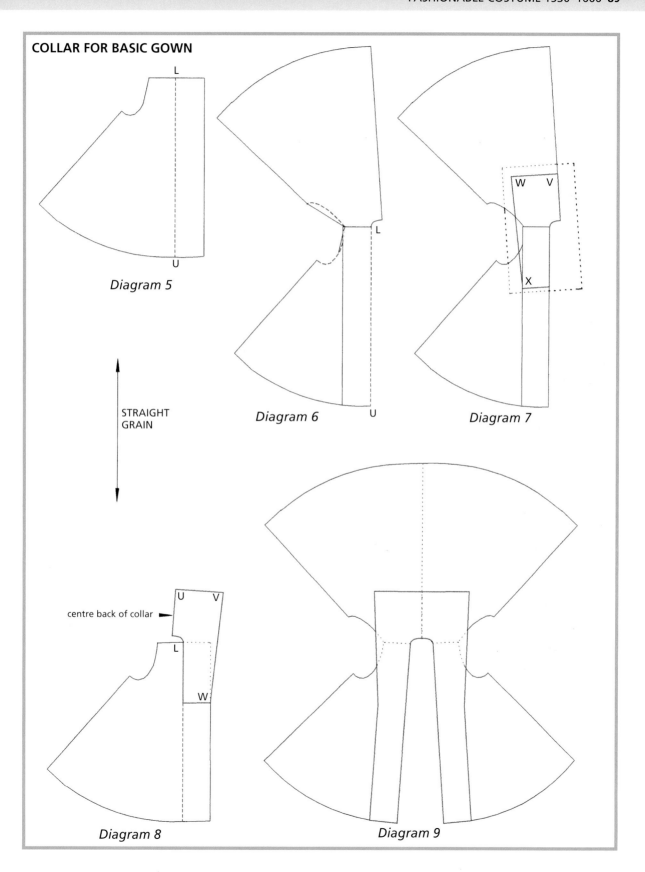

Diagram 5

Diagram 6

Diagram 7

STRAIGHT
GRAIN

centre back of collar ◄

Diagram 8

Diagram 9

FLARED GOWN WITH YOKE

Peasant doublet pattern as for the basic gown (see p. 58).

Sheet of paper:
Total width of doublet pattern
Required length of gown + 5cm (2") (nape to hem measurement)
Extra paper as instructions

Diagrams 1 & 1a
1 Mark the pattern as diagrams.

Diagram 2
2 Place the back section of pattern on the left-hand side of the paper so that A is 5cm (2") from the top corner.
3 Place the front section so that D–C meets J–I.
4 Extend G to meet the right-hand side of the paper so that the centre front is straight.
5 A–M = required depth of the yoke.
6 From M square right across the paper cutting the back armhole at N, the front armhole at O and the centre front at P.
7 Q is midway between M–N. Square down to R.
8 S is midway between I–H. Square up to T and down to U.
9 From D/J (the underarm point) square down to the bottom of the paper. Cut along this line and cut off surplus paper.
10 Make sure that D is clearly marked.

Diagrams 3 & 3a
11 On the back pattern cut along M–N and Q–R.
12 On the front pattern cut along O–P and T–U.

Diagram 4
13 Spread the two skirt sections of the back pattern as for the basic gown pattern.
14 Redraw M–N in a gentle curve as diagram.
15 Check that the measurement M–N on the skirt the same as M–N on the yoke; correct if necessary.
16 Redraw the hem line as diagram.

Diagram 4a
17 Keeping the centre front skirt section straight, spread the side section so that the gap at U–U is ½ the gap at R–R on the back section.
18 Extend the centre front at P and square out to meet O. Re-mark P.
19 Check that O–P on the skirt is the same measurement as O–P on the yoke; correct if necessary.

Diagram 5
The complete yoke which is cut without seams.

FLARED GOWN WITH YOKE

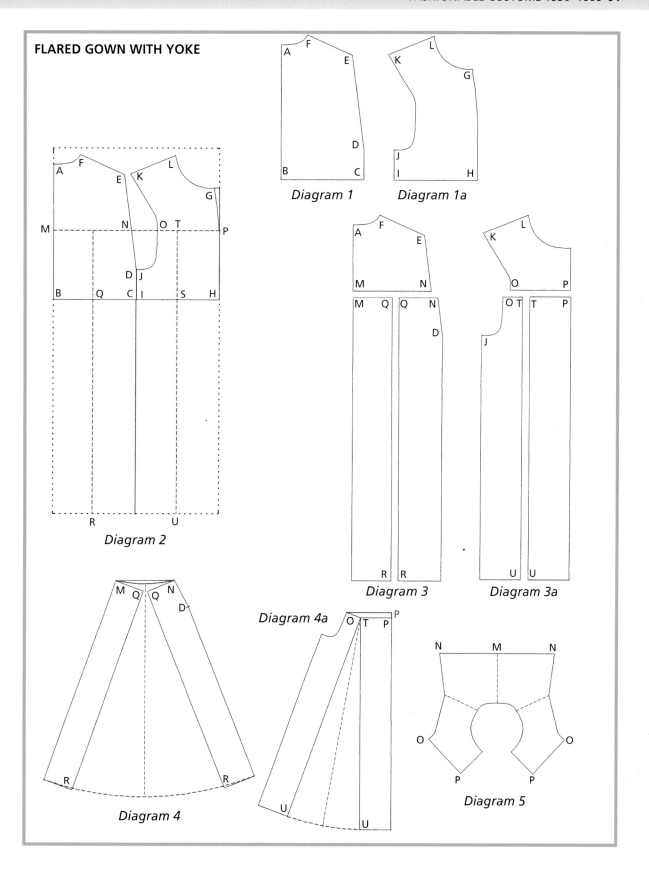

Diagram 1

Diagram 1a

Diagram 2

Diagram 3

Diagram 3a

Diagram 4

Diagram 4a

Diagram 5

PLEATED GOWN WITH YOKE

Note. The skirts of the gown may be flat pleated or cartridge pleated onto the yoke. The top of the skirt should measure at least twice the measurement at the bottom of the yoke. Some gowns do not have a yoke at the front in which case the front section of the Basic Gown pattern should be used. Sometimes the front yoke is shorter than the back.

To cut a pleated gown follow the instructions for Flared Gown with Yoke as far as Diagrams 3 & 3a.

The back pattern

Diagram 4

1 Spread M, Q, R and Q, N, D, R evenly so that M–N measures at least twice M–N on the yoke.

2 Join the pattern with straight lines as diagram.

The front pattern

Diagram 4a

3 Spread J, O, T, U and T, P, U evenly so that O–P measures at least twice O–P on the yoke.

4 Join the pattern with straight lines as diagram.

Diagram 5

5 The complete yoke which can be cut without seams.

Collars for gowns with yokes

1 Cut the yoke pattern along the shoulder line.

2 Join the back section of the yoke to the back skirt pattern so that M on the yoke meets M on the skirt and the centre back is in a straight line.

3 Join front section of the yoke to the front skirt pattern so that P on the yoke meets P on the skirt and the centre front is in a straight line.

4 Follow the instructions for the basic gown collar.

Note. The collar will lie close to the shoulders in the style popular in Southern Europe.

PLEATED GOWN WITH YOKE

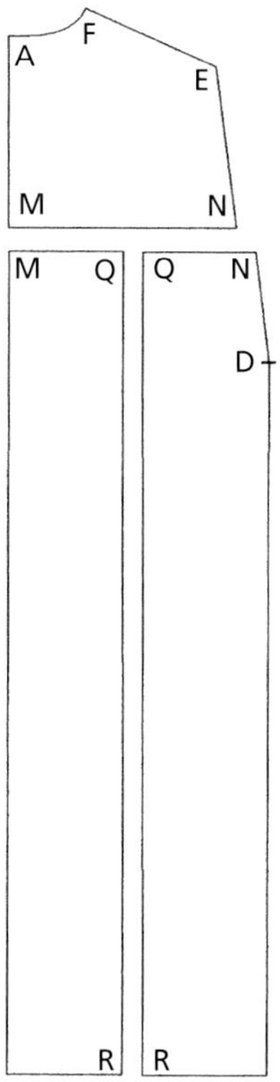

Diagram 3

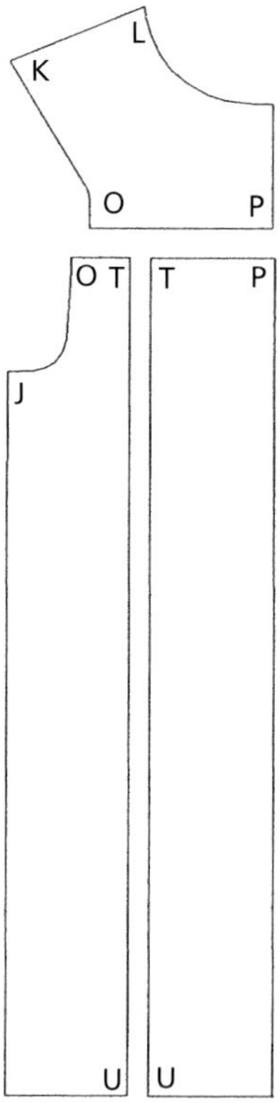

Diagram 3a

Diagram 4

Diagram 4a

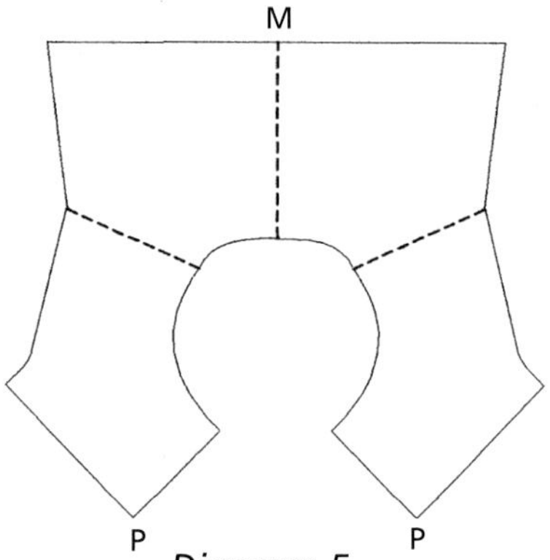

Diagram 5

SLEEVES FOR GOWNS

The measurements used for these instructions are based on Alçega's diagrams; these should be adapted as appropriate.

Basic hanging sleeve

Sheet of paper:
Measurement round armhole
x
Required sleeve length

Diagram 1

1 Mark A 15cm (6") down left-hand side of paper.

2 Square out A–B right across the paper.

3 C is midway between A–B.

4 From C square up to D on the top edge of the paper.

5 Join A–D and D–B. The top of the sleeve head can be curved as drawn in red if the top armhole of the gown is curved.

6 From C square down to E on the bottom edge of the paper.

7 E–F = half required measurement for bottom of the sleeve (15cm (6") is an average measurement).

8 E–G = half required measurement for bottom of the sleeve (15cm (6") is an average measurement).

9 Join A–F and B–G; these are the underarm seams.

10 Cut off surplus paper.

11 From D measure D–H = the position of the slash line; this should not be more than the inner elbow level (i.e. the measurement from the front pitch to the elbow level on the basic sleeve pattern).

12 Mark the slash I–J = half the width of the sleeve at this level.

Diagram 2

The sleeve head should be about the same measurement as the armhole but, as the underarm is not joined this is not critical. The pattern can be widened if necessary (lines drawn in red show an enlarged sleeve), but it is not necessary to increase the depth of sleeve head. The slash might need to be lengthened if the doublet sleeve is very bulky.

Note. When making up the hanging sleeve between ⅔ and ½ is attached to the gown and the underarm left open. The head of the sleeve is usually sewn to the gown but sometimes attached with ties.

Hanging sleeve variation

To cut a hanging sleeve like the one worn by Edward VI cut the pattern along D–E and join A–F to B–G for 30cm (12") from F/G.

The young king Edward VI wears a simpler form of hanging sleeve than the one worn by his father Henry VIII in the Holbein portrait. It is cut with a T-shaped opening; the arm comes through the horizontal part and the vertical slit is closed with gold tags. (*Edward VI*, attributed to William Scrots.)

Hanging sleeve as worn by Henry VIII

Pattern for basic hanging sleeve

Sheet of paper:

For the over-sleeve, an average measurement being140cm (55") x 30cm (12")

The over-sleeve

Diagram 3

13 Mark the paper M, N, O, P as diagram.

14 M–Q = 15cm (6"), N–R = 15cm (6").

15 O–S = 30cm (12"), P–T = 30cm (12").

Diagram 4

When making up the over-sleeve:

16 Pleat Q–R to measure three-quarters of the circumference of armhole of the gown. This is sewn round the armhole of the gown. M–Q and N–R will fold under the arm.

17 Pleat S–T to measure I–J (the length of the slash). This is sewn along the top of the slash. O–S and P–T will hang in triangles under the arm as in the portrait of Henry VIII.

This detail from the portrait of Henry VIII shows a hanging sleeve with a pleated over-sleeve, the ends of which can be seen under the arm. (From *Henry VIII* by Hans Eworth, after Holbein.)

HANGING SLEEVES

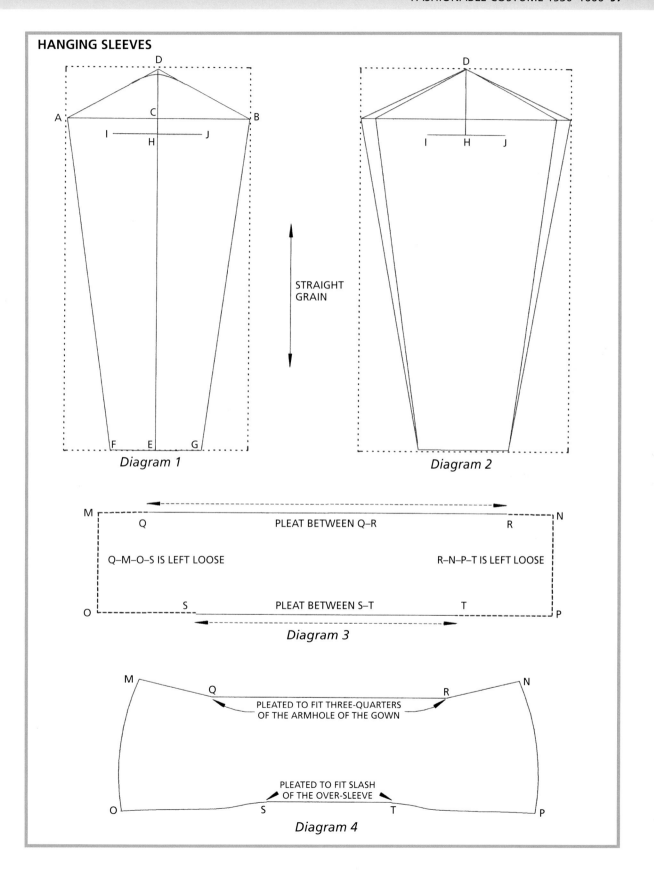

Diagram 1

Diagram 2

STRAIGHT
GRAIN

PLEAT BETWEEN Q–R

Q–M–O–S IS LEFT LOOSE

R–N–P–T IS LEFT LOOSE

PLEAT BETWEEN S–T

Diagram 3

PLEATED TO FIT THREE-QUARTERS
OF THE ARMHOLE OF THE GOWN

PLEATED TO FIT SLASH
OF THE OVER-SLEEVE

Diagram 4

COTES

Basic doublet pattern (see p. 82) with front length addition

Extra paper for the skirts as instructions

Upper body pattern

Diagram 1

1 Upper body pattern with front length addition.

Diagram 2

2 Join the pattern at the shoulders as diagram.

3 Draw the new neckline.

Note. This is an occasion when a stand is very useful as it is easy to make the neckline too wide when the pattern is flat. If a stand is not available, leave good turnings when cutting the fabric.

Diagram 3

4 Cut off surplus paper to complete the upper body pattern.

Note. Very wide necklines are apt to gape, particularly at the point marked with the red line on Diagram 4. To correct this, cut a calico toile and fit it on a tailor's stand or, preferably on the wearer. If the neckline gapes, take in a small dart as diagram and transfer the alteration onto the pattern. Reshape as the neckline will have become slightly distorted.

The skirts

Diagrams 5 & 6

Cut a piece of paper = back waist measurement of the pattern x the required length of the skirt and follow the instructions for increasing patterns in Chapter 2.

Diagram 7

Two evenly flared panels will be required for the back skirts and two without the half flare (drawn in red on Diagram 6) for the front skirt.

Note. The skirts are usually knife pleated or cartridge pleated onto the upper body so one panel can be used as many times as required. More modest cotes had very little fullness which was eased or pleated at the centre back.

The Holbein portrait of Henry VIII is misleading as the proportions have been deliberately altered by shortening the length between waist and knee which gives the illusion of even greater power and strength. Attempts at reproducing the image are always unsatisfactory for this reason. The portrait of Jean de Dinteville in Holbein's *The Ambassadors* gives a more realistic proportion. The cote usually reached just above knee level.

COTES

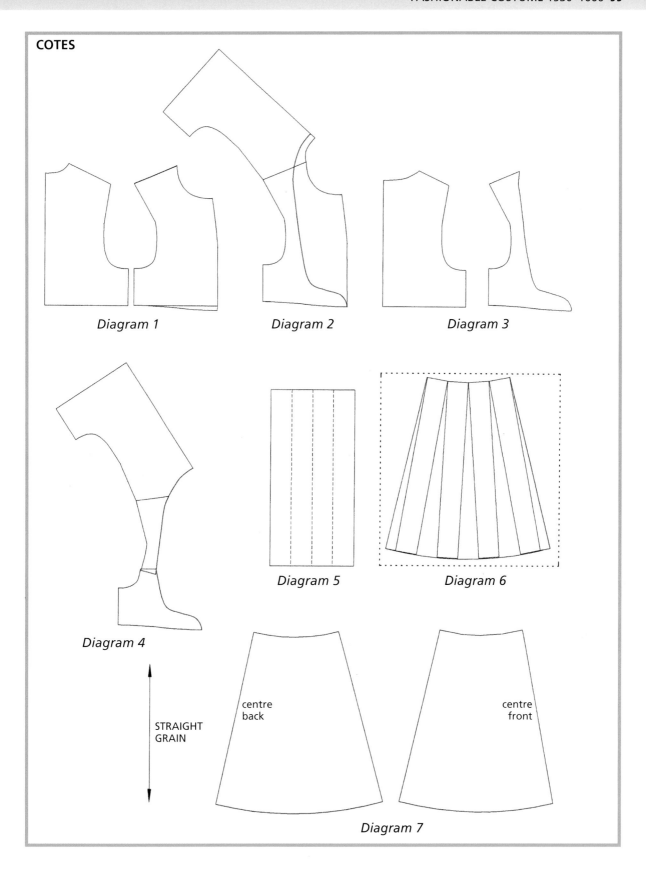

Diagram 1

Diagram 2

Diagram 3

Diagram 4

Diagram 5

Diagram 6

STRAIGHT
GRAIN

centre
back

centre
front

Diagram 7

DOUBLETS AND JERKINS

Note. The back of the doublet is unchanged in both of the following patterns and can be used whether the side seam is under the arm or moved towards the back.

Basic doublet pattern with waist suppression but no front length extension for both patterns
Extra paper for the alterations

Doublet with pointed waist line

Diagram 1

1 Secure a piece of paper under the front waist line as diagram.
2 Mark A where the side seam meets the waist.
3 Mark B on the waist line at centre front.
4 B–C = 10cm (4").
5 Join A–C with a straight line and redraw curving approximately 3cm (1¼") from the centre as diagram.
6 Curve the centre front to avoid a sharp point (which is difficult to sew).
7 Cut off surplus paper to complete the pattern.

Diagram 2

The completed pattern drawn with button stand.

Doublet with peascod belly

Diagram 3

8 Secure a piece of paper under the front pattern as diagram.
9 Mark A where the side seam meets the waist line as diagram.
10 Mark B on the waist line at centre front.
11 B–C = 10cm (4").
12 Join A–C in a straight line and redraw curving approximately 3cm (1¼") from the centre as diagram.
13 D is midway between B–C.
14 Square out D–E = 5cm (2").
15 Mark F at the base of the neck.
16 Join F–E in a straight line.
17 Join E–C in a curve as diagram.
18 Cut off surplus paper to complete the pattern as Diagram 4 (drawn with button stand).

Note. The peascod bellied doublet will require padding to keep its shape. A lining can be cut using the pattern for doublet with pointed waist line.

The measurements given for the above patterns are for average sizes and should be adapted as appropriate.

As jerkins were worn over the doublet they should be cut one size larger and the skirts lengthened slightly.

DOUBLETS AND JERKINS

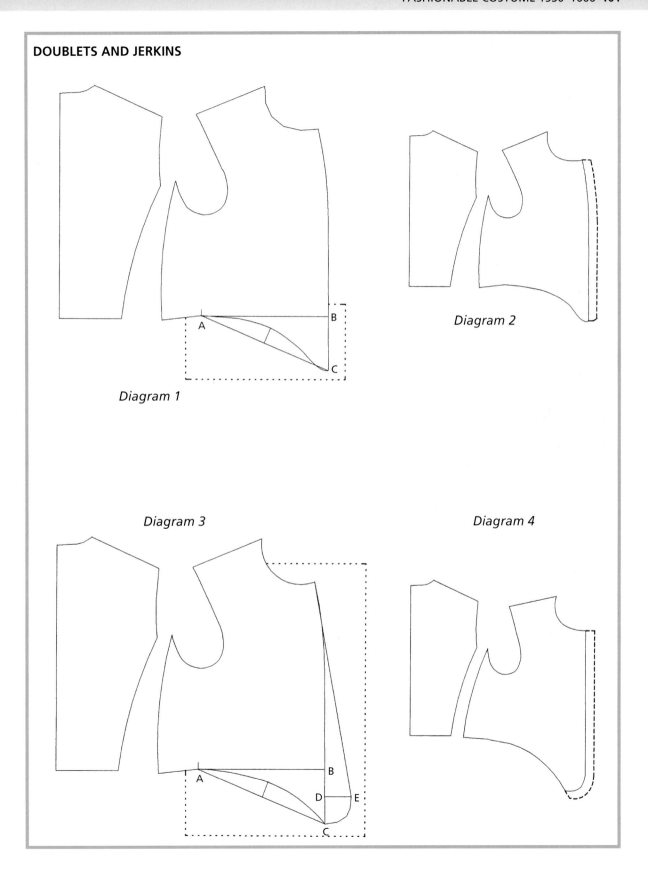

Diagram 1

Diagram 2

Diagram 3

Diagram 4

SKIRTS FOR DOUBLETS AND JERKINS

Skirts for fashionable doublets are cut on the same principle as for the basic doublet pattern (see p. 82). They may be cut in one piece or divided into varying number of tabs. If the doublet is to be worn over full trunk-hose, the skirts need more flare and are usually short – an average depth being 10cm (4") and the flare being about one third more than the waist measurement.

Continuous skirts

Diagram 1
1 Measure the waist of the doublet and cut a strip of paper that length by the required depth of skirt.

2 Mark the strip A, B, C, D as diagram.

3 Fold the strip into eight.

4 Slash the divisions from C–D almost to A–B.

Diagram 2
5 Place the strip on another piece of paper and open the slashes evenly so that the total measurement is approximately one-third larger than the waist.

6 Add half the slash width at the centre back as diagram.

7 Weight down the pattern and draw around it.

8 Cut off surplus paper leaving about 10cm (4") at the centre front.

9 Place the skirt on the doublet pattern so that the waist lines meet as Diagram 3.

10 Continue the centre front line of the doublet and continue the curve of the skirt to meet it.

11 Cut off surplus paper to complete the pattern as Diagram 4.

Skirts divided into tabs

The method for cutting tabs is the same as for continuous skirts except tabs usually overlap about 1–2cm (⅜"–¾") from front to back so this amount must be added to each tab. The tabs are generally all the same size but if the measurement does not divide easily into the required number of tabs the discrepancy should be at the centre front.

Diagram 5
12 Measure the waist line of the doublet and cut a strip of paper to the same length plus 1–2cm (⅜"–¾") for each tab except the one in the centre front.

13 Follow the instructions 2–8 for continuous skirts.

Diagram 6
14 Divide the pattern evenly into the required number of tabs making any necessary adjustment on the centre front tab.

Diagram 7
15 Place the centre front tab as drawn in red on the diagram.

16 Continue the centre front line of the doublet and continue the curve of the tab to meet it.

17 Cut off surplus paper to complete the tabs pattern as Diagram 8.

Note. If the doublet is to be worn with early trunk-hose, Venetians or other less bulky breeches, the waist of the front tabs should be curved upwards, as shown in red in Diagram 8, so that they lie flat.

SKIRTS FOR DOUBLETS AND JERKINS

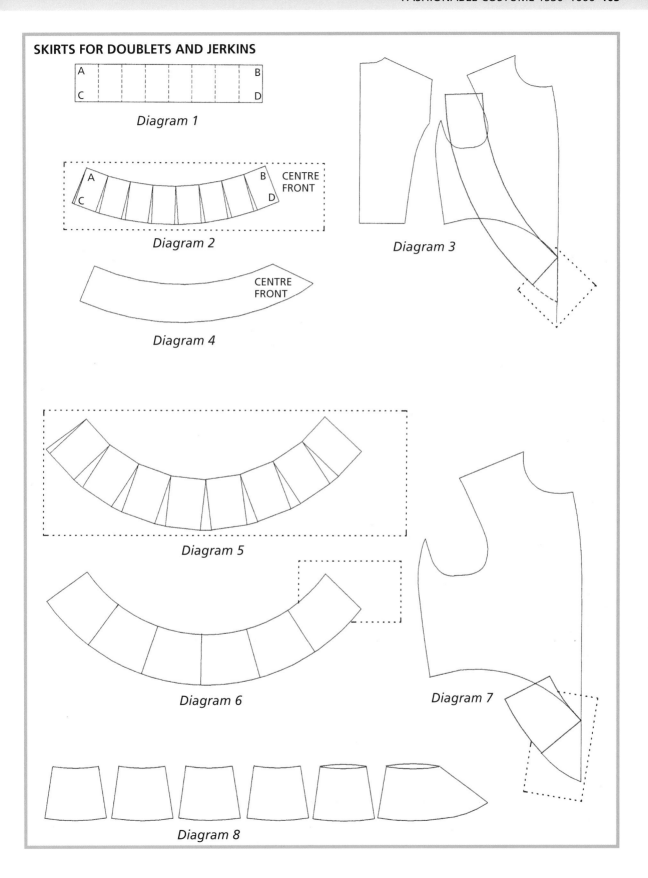

Diagram 1

Diagram 2

Diagram 3

Diagram 4

Diagram 5

Diagram 6

Diagram 7

Diagram 8

STAND COLLAR

Strip of paper:

½ circumference of doublet neck + 1–1.5cm (⅜"–⅝") for button stand if required

X

Required height of collar: 5–6cm (2"–2⅜") is an average, comfortable height

Diagram 1

1 Mark the corners of the strip A, B, C, D as diagram, A–C is the centre back, B–D is the centre front.

2 Divide the paper into three and mark the divisions E–F and G–H as diagram.

Diagram 2

3 From A measure .5cm (¼") and join to C.

4 Mark points .5cm (¼") each side of E and taper to nothing at F.

5 Mark points .5cm (¼") each side of G and taper to nothing at H.

Diagram 3

6 Cut out the darts and rejoin the pattern with adhesive tape.

7 D–I = 1cm (⅜"), join I–H with a smooth curve.

8 Cut along D–I to complete the pattern as Diagram 4.

Note. There will be very small points where the collar has been shaped which can be corrected on the pattern or when the garment is marked out on the fabric.

This collar will require stiffening to keep its shape.

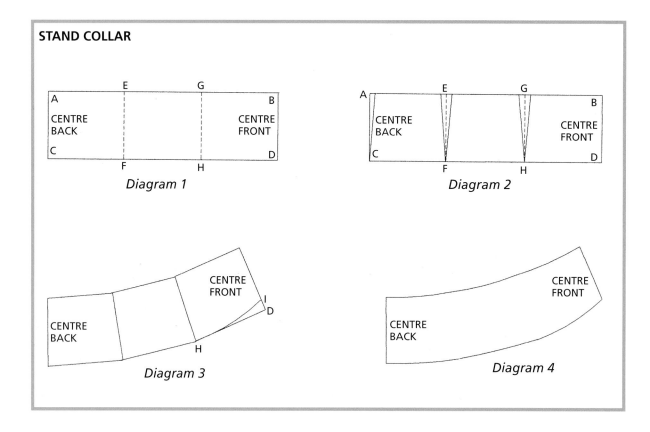

STAND COLLAR

Diagram 1

Diagram 2

Diagram 3

Diagram 4

TRUNK-HOSE AND BREECHES

Trunk-hose were elaborate forms of leg wear worn from c.1530–c.1620. They usually reached from the waist to any level above the knee. In some extreme, Northern European versions, they hung below the knee. At first they were attached to the waist of the doublet with laces, but c.1570 these were replaced by hooks and eyelets. Joined hose were cut with one seam up the back of the leg; trunk-hose had side seams and sometimes inside leg seams. Unlike some later styles of breeches the curved crutch seam was retained which was a logical development from joined hose.

Alçega in his book *Libro de Geometrica, practica y traça* of 1589, does not include patterns for breeches. This is presumably because the trunk-hose of 1589 were almost rectangular and would be cut to fit the width of the fabric so needed no pattern. There are breeches patterns in Francisco de la Rocha Burguen's *Geometrica y traça* of 1618, but these are for the breeches called Venetians, and have more shape. Early pattern books were not intended to teach the art of cutting but to show how to get the garments out of given widths/lengths of fabric.

In the north, the passion for slashing resulted in extreme examples, where garments were cut to ribbons in diagonal, vertical and curved lines. They must have been made of very durable fabric, possibly leather, and even so were liable to be damaged in wear.

The most common form of trunk-hose consisted of three layers. The outer layer was slashed into panes; the middle layer was cut longer and wider. The inner layer was the foundation, cut to fit the body and shorter than the others; it held the garment together and caused the middle layer to bulge out between the panes. When there were three layers the middle layer was usually made of fine silk. The outer layer was stiffened with interfacing and often embroidered, which kept the panes in shape. At first trunk-hose were worn with an erect codpiece but it became superfluous when the girth of the garment increased.

As the skirts of the doublet shortened, trunk-hose became more elaborate and increased in width. They reached their maximum girth and rigidity by c.1570. Padding, known as bombast, was necessary to keep a full rounded shape; this might be horsehair, flax, cotton, flock, rags or bran. Sometimes large pocket bags were inserted between the

This is an example of extreme slashing worn by soldiers in the style popular in Northern Europe. (Detail from *The Sermon of John the Baptist* by Pieter Bruegel the Younger.)

The archduke is wearing a short gown without a fur lining. The shoulders are wide but sloping; its dark colour and the vertical lines of decoration give an overall impression of slimness and height. The trunk-hose are cut with wide panes and an ample middle layer which would be held in shape by the linings but are still fairly close to the body. (*Archduke Ferdinand of Tyrol* by Jakob Seisenegger.)

lining and middle layers which were stuffed with a variety of household textiles as well as bombast. From c.1570–1620 short trunk-hose were often worn with canions which were close-fitting extensions reaching to the knee or just below. Canions were often of a contrasting fabric.

Towards the end of the 16th century, a style developed that did not have the panes layer; the middle layer became the outer layer and was cut very full, often of magnificent brocade as in the portrait of Prince Charles Stuart. Venetians were another version; this style was bulky round the hips but the legs tapered to just below the knee where they might be gathered into a band or left loose. In the portrait of Sir Walter Raleigh and his son, the boy is wearing a version with the fullness at both the waist and knee.

In the early years of the 17th century, the fullness increased as shown in the portrait of Charles I when he was Prince of Wales on p. 120. This style was soon succeeded by narrower breeches that tapered towards the knee. For a short period during the 1660s, a knee-length style became fashionable that was cut straight and so wide they were known as petticoat breeches.

In its last phase, the body and sleeves of the doublet shrank revealing quantities of shirt; it was worn with petticoat breeches. (*Portrait of a Young Man* by Gerard ter Borch.)

TRUNK-HOSE WITH PANES

Sheet of paper:
½ seat measurement + 3cm (1¼") ease + front crutch width x 3

x

Rise + 3cm (1¼") ease + 5cm (2") + required leg length (10cm (4") leg length used on following pattern)

Basic pattern

Diagram 1

1 Mark the corners of the paper A, B, C, D as diagram.

2 A–E = 5cm, square right across the paper to F.

3 From E measure down E–G = rise measurement.

4 From G square across to H.

Diagram 2

5 A–I = front crutch width x 2, square down to meet G–H at J. Draw back crutch seam as diagram.

6 B–K = front crutch width, square down to meet E–F at L and G–H at M. Draw back crutch seam as diagram.

7 Join I–L with a straight line and redraw with a curve as diagram.

Diagram 3

8 N is midway between I–L, square down to O.

9 Cut off surplus paper to complete the basic pattern.

Linings

Diagram 4

10 Make a copy of the basic pattern.

11 C–P = 5cm (2"), join P–G.

12 D–Q = 5cm (2"), join Q–H.

13 Cut off C–G–P and D–H–Q.

14 Cut along N–O.

15 Rejoin the pattern matching H–Q to G–P.

Diagram 5

16 Redraw the crutch line in a smooth curve.

17 Secure a small piece of paper at the bottom of the inside leg and redraw the line as diagram.

18 Cut off surplus paper to complete the pattern as Diagram 6.

Note. The linings are not cut to the waist or finished leg size. When the garment is made up the outer layers are put together then the lining is made up, turned inside out and eased on enclosing the raw edges. The excess fabric adds to the padding.

If the doublet that is to be worn with the hose has a lowered waist line, reshape the centre front of the pattern and cut the waistband as instructions for slops. When the hose are sewn to the waistband, the centre front should be left fairly flat so that the stiffened point of the doublet will lie flat.

TRUNK-HOSE WITH PANES

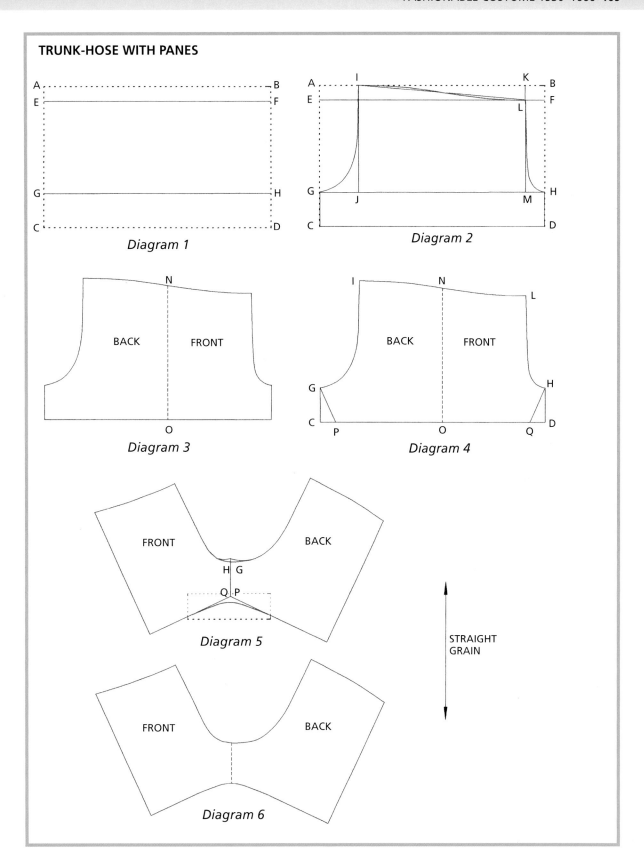

Diagram 1

Diagram 2

Diagram 3

Diagram 4

Diagram 5

STRAIGHT
GRAIN

Diagram 6

The middle layer

Sheet of paper:
As wide and as deep as required for the style, see Note 3

Diagram 7
19 Make a copy of the basic pattern (as diagrams 1–3) and cut it down N–O.

Diagram 8
20 Join H–D to G–C.

Diagram 9
Mark the middle of the paper R–S as diagram.

21 Place the basic pattern so that I meets the top of the paper and H/G–D/C lies along R–S.

22 Widen and lower the crutch by moving L, H/G and I, 1cm (⅜") and redrawing the line as marked in red on the diagram.

23 Mark the new H/G.

Diagram 10
24 Cut off surplus paper to complete the middle layer pattern.

The panes layer

Diagram 11
25 Make a copy of the middle layer pattern and divide it into the required number of strips. Note that the divisions do not meet the crutch line.

26 Widen and lower the crutch line a further 1cm (⅜").

27 Mark the new H/G.

28 Cut off surplus paper to complete the panes layer pattern.

Note 1. The strips should be of equal width but if this is not practical make the difference on the inside leg.

Note 2. If using felt or other non-fraying fabric for interfacing the panes, it is easier and more accurate to draw around the complete pattern and then mark the divisions on the fabric.

Note 3. The size of paper required for the middle and panes layers is entirely dependent on the style of trunk-hose but as a general rule a reasonable width is 1½ to twice the seat measurement and the depth 10–15cm (4"–6") longer than the back of the basic pattern.

Note 4. The waistband can either be a straight strip or cut with a point at the centre front as instructions for sops, linings, canions and waistband. It should be cut 3–4cm (1¼"–1½") longer than the waist measurement.

Note 5. When making up the trunk-hose, the middle layer should be cartridge pleated onto the waistband and leg bands or canions and the panes either eased on or cartridge pleated. If padding is to be added, it should be attached before the lining. The lining should be eased or gathered onto the waist and leg bands or canions wrong sides facing so that all the raw edges are enclosed.

Note 6. The diagram shows the middle layer and panes layers the same size; often the middle layer is cut wider and deeper than the panes.

TRUNK-HOSE WITH PANES

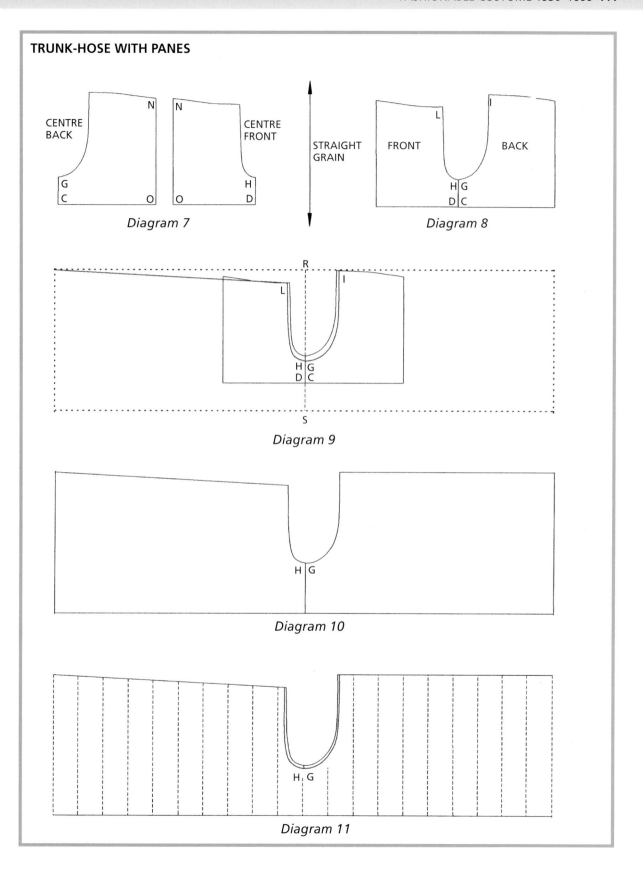

Diagram 7

Diagram 8

Diagram 9

Diagram 10

Diagram 11

SPANISH CODPIECE

Sheet of paper:

20cm (8") x required length of codpiece

Piece of paper for the gusset:

5cm (2") x 10cm (4")

If the codpiece is made without a gusset, it should be attached so that the top, G–H on Diagram 1, is approximately 5cm (2") below the normal waist line. The bottom should be sewn 1 or 2cm (⅜"–¾") below the fly opening. If the codpiece is made with a gusset (Diagram 4), W meets H/G on the trunk-hose.

Diagram 1

Mark the corners of the paper A, B, C, D as diagram.

1 A–E = 7.5cm (3").

2 Square down E–F to bottom of paper.

3 From A measure down A–G = 3cm (1¼").

4 Square out G–H = 6.25cm (2½").

5 E–I = 7cm (2¾").

6 Join H–I.

7 From I square out I–J.

8 From I curve top of codpiece almost to J as diagram.

9 From F measure out K 1.25cm (½") towards C and L 1.75cm (¾") towards D.

10 Join G–K with a straight line and redraw curving .75cm (¼") either side of the mid-point as diagram.

11 Join end of curve near J to L and redraw in a smooth curve as diagram.

12 I–M = 2.5cm (1").

13 F–N = 1cm (⅜").

14 Join M–N with as curved line as diagram.

15 Fold the pattern along E–F and trace through the line from M to N. Mark the new line O–P as diagram.

16 Cut off surplus paper as Diagram 2.

The gusset

Diagram 3

17 Mark the paper Q, R, S, T as diagram.

18 V is midway between Q–R.

19 W is midway between S–T.

20 Join Q–W and R–W.

21 Cut of surplus paper to complete the pattern.

Constructing the codpiece

22 Mark around the pattern on double fabric; cut out and trace the lines through in the usual way.

23 Tack along the lines drawn in red on Diagram 2, to mark them on the right side, on both pieces.

24 Join the pieces together by sewing round the curve I–L.

25 Join the pieces together along H–I.

26 Turn the pouch right side out.

27 Sew halfway down I–F through both layers.

28 Pad out the top of the pouch firmly carefully keeping the shape.

29 Sew the remaining part of I–F.

30 Match the tacked lines M–N and O–P and stitch the pouch to the backing.

31 Attach the gusset joining Q–R to the bottom of the codpiece.

32 Cut a lining as Diagram 4 with I–F on the fold, and sew in place.

33 Make eyelets to lace the codpiece to the trunk-hose as indicated.

SPANISH CODPIECE

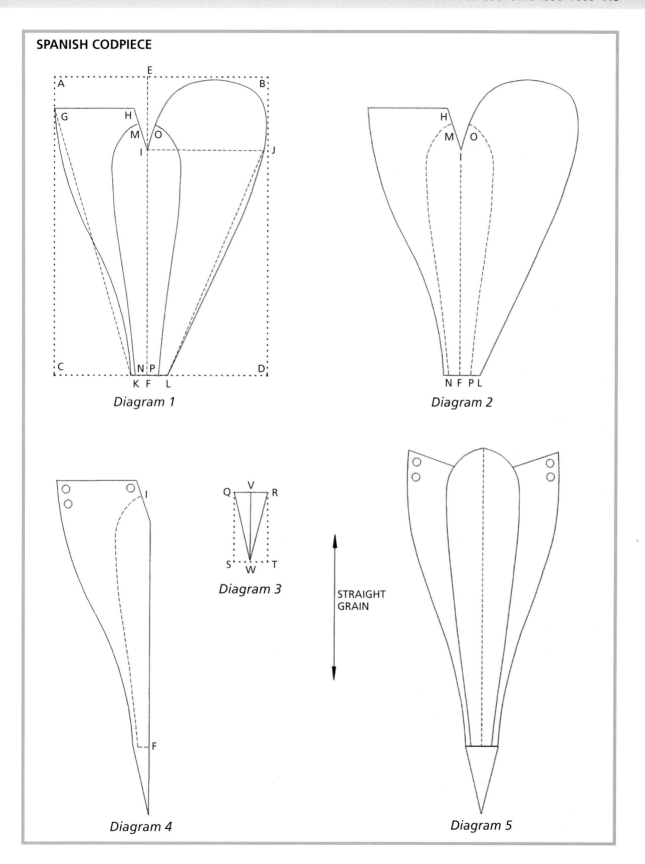

Diagram 1

Diagram 2

Diagram 3

STRAIGHT
GRAIN

Diagram 4

Diagram 5

Diagram 5

The completed codpiece.

Note. If the codpiece is to have elaborate decoration, it is easier to make a cotton foundation and a separate cover.

SIMPLE CODPIECE

Diagram 6

34 Divide the pattern for Spanish codpiece down I–F.

35 Cut away and discard I–O–P–F on the pouch section as Diagram 7.

Making up the simple codpiece

36 Cut two pieces of the pouch section in industrial felt.

37 Cut two pieces for the backing as Diagram 8 (using felt or other fabric) and join along H–I–F.

38 If a gusset is required use the pattern for Spanish codpiece.

39 Use the lining for Spanish codpiece.

40 Pad out the pouch and attach to the backing along the lines drawn in red.

The archduke is wearing the costume of an aristocratic young man (he was 16 when this portrait was painted). The black velvet jerkin emphasises his slimness despite being cut with a small peascod belly. His face is framed by a crisply pleated lace-edged ruff, which matches his cuffs. The trunk-hose are padded to give a melon shape and the codpiece is still worn. (*Archduke Rudolph* by Alonso Sánchez Coello.)

SIMPLE CODPIECE

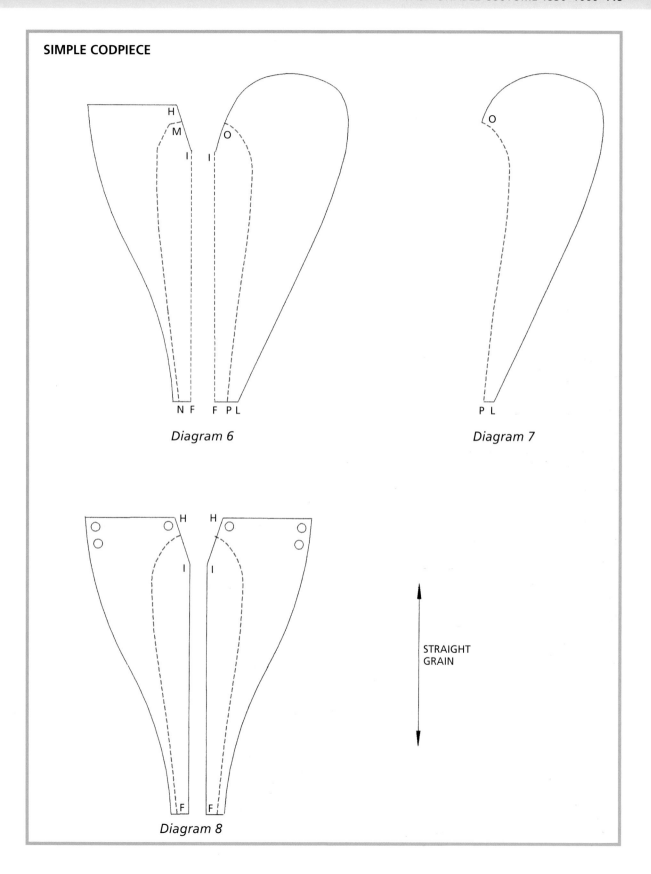

Diagram 6

Diagram 7

Diagram 8

STRAIGHT
GRAIN

SLOPS

Slops with cartridge pleated legs

Sheet of paper:

Seat measurement x 4

x

Approximately 1½ times the required length depending on the amount of padding to be used

Diagram 1

1 Mark the corners of the paper A, B, C, D as diagram.

2 E is midway between A–B.

3 From E square down to F.

4 E–G = 18cm (7").

5 From G square down 50cm (20") to H.

6 E–I = 18cm (7").

7 From I square down 50cm (20") to J.

8 Join H–J.

9 I–K = 5cm (2").

10 Draw G–K in a curve as diagram.

11 F–L = 23cm (9").

12 From L square up 12cm (4¾") to M.

13 F–N = 23cm (9").

14 From N square up 12cm (4¾") to O.

15 Join M–O.

16 A–P = 2.5cm (1").

17 Join P–G in a gentle curve as diagram.

18 B–Q = 2.5cm (1").

19 Join K–Q in a gentle curve as diagram.

Diagram 2

20 M–R = L–M. O–S = N–O.

   When the slops are made up, M–L will be sewn to M–R and N–O to O–S.

21 Cut off surplus paper to complete the pattern as Diagram 2.

Note. If the doublet being worn with the breeches has a pointed waist, lower the centre front 8cm (3") and join to a point 15cm (6") from K as red line on diagram. Make the fly opening 24cm (9"). Point T.

Slops with stitched pleats

Diagram 3

Use the same instructions as for slops with cartridge pleated legs for the basic pattern.

An alternative method of joining the legs of the hose to canions or leg bands is to pleat the excess fabric. A good width for the pleats is 3cm (1¼") with 2cm (¾") spaces. The pleats are sewn which holds out the legs in a more formal shape than if they were cartridge pleated. This is a satisfactory method if the breeches are not excessively wide and the thigh measurement not too small. The length between R and S is not pleated; the first pleats should be about 10cm (4") long and the remainder 12cm (4¾") as Diagram 4. If the width cannot be divided evenly, a small discrepancy will be inconspicuous at the side seam.

SLOPS

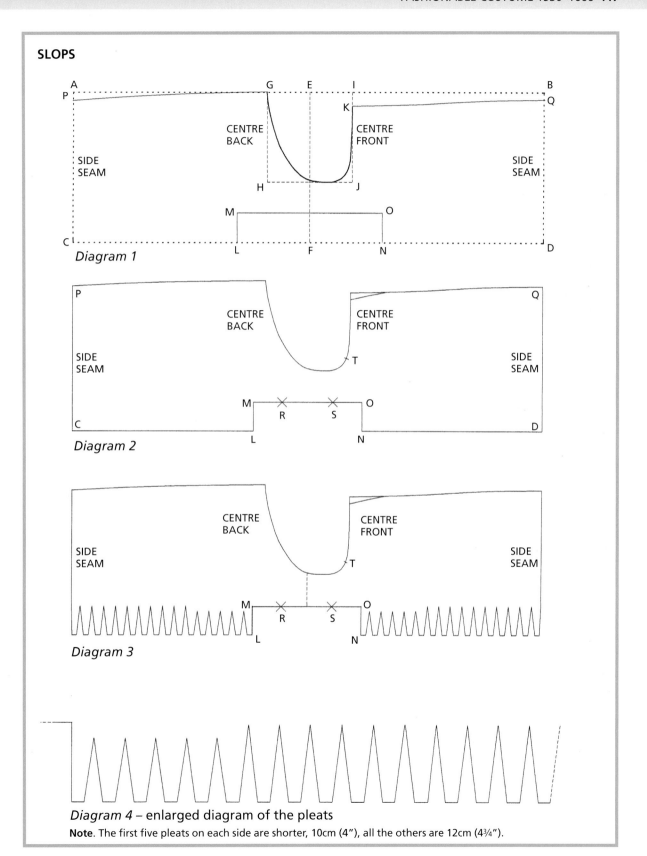

Diagram 1

Diagram 2

Diagram 3

Diagram 4 – enlarged diagram of the pleats

Note. The first five pleats on each side are shorter, 10cm (4"), all the others are 12cm (4¾").

Linings

Sheet of paper:

Depth of pattern for slops from G to M–O (Diagram 1)

x

½ seat measurement + 3cm (1¼") + the front crutch measurement x 3

Diagram 5

22 Mark the corners of the paper A, B, C, D as diagram.

23 A–E = rise measurement + 10cm (4").

24 From E square across to F.

25 A–G = front crutch width measurement x 2.

26 From G square down to meet E–F at H.

27 B–I = front crutch width measurement.

28 From I square down to meet E–F at J.

29 I–K = 5cm (2").

30 Join G–K with a straight line and redraw with a curve as diagram.

31 Draw G–E in a curve as diagram.

32 Draw K–F in a curve as diagram.

33 C–L = 4cm (1½"), join E–L.

34 D–M = 4cm (1½"), join F–M.

35 N is midway between G–K, square down to O.

36 Cut off surplus paper.

Note. If the slops are to be worn with a pointed front doublet, shape the front of the lining as for the outer layer – 8cm (3") down from K and 15cm (6") from K towards N.

Diagram 6

37 Cut along N–O.

38 Rejoin the pattern matching F–M with E–L.

39 Secure a small piece of paper under the pattern and round off the point at M/L as diagram.

Diagram 7

The completed lining pattern; mark the inside leg point, P.

Canions

Sheet of paper:

Measurement round top of thigh + 3cm (1¼")

x

Required length of canions

Diagram 8

40 Mark the corners of the paper Q, R, S, T as diagram.

41 Q–U = half the difference between the top of the canions and required measurement of the bottom.

42 From U square down to V.

43 V–Y = V–U, join U–Y with a curved line.

44 R–W = Q–U, square down to X, X–Z = X–W, join W–Z with a curved line.

45 Cut off surplus paper to complete the pattern.

SLOPS – Linings, canions and waistband

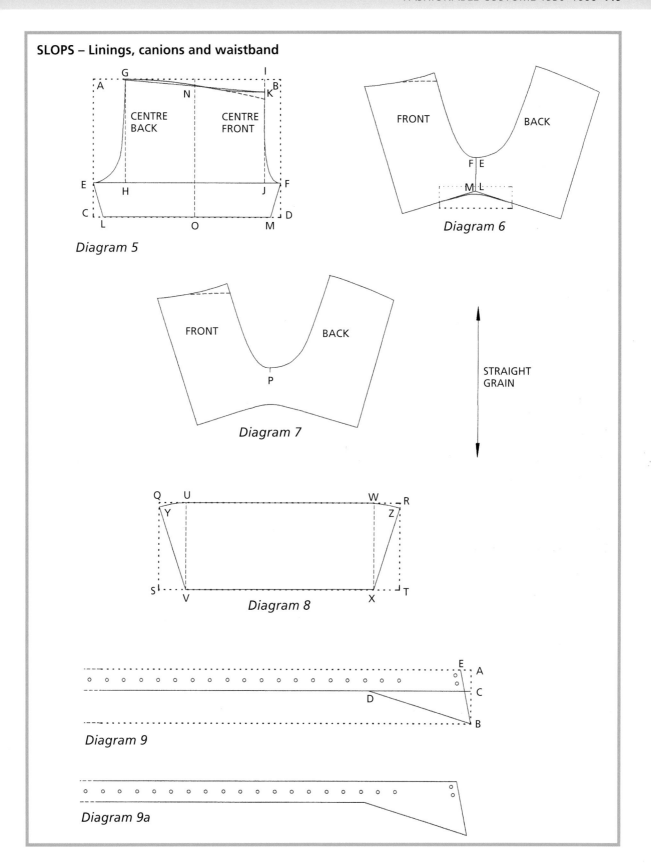

Diagram 5

Diagram 6

Diagram 7

STRAIGHT GRAIN

Diagram 8

Diagram 9

Diagram 9a

Waist bands

Strip of paper:

½ required waist measurement + 1.5cm (⅝")

x

8cm (3")

Diagram 9

46 Mark one end of the paper A–B as diagram.

47 A–C = 2.5cm (1").

48 From C square right across the paper, A–C is the width of the waist band.

49 C–D = 15cm (6").

50 Join B–D.

51 A–E = 1.5cm (⅝").

52 Join E–B.

53 Cut off surplus paper and mark the position of the eyelets as Diagram 9a.

Note. The allowance for a pointed doublet is a depth of 8cm (3") on the above instructions, this should be adjusted as appropriate.

The seam on the lining has been moved to the side to reduce bulk on the inside leg.

The seam Y–V/Z–X on the canions should be at the centre back of the leg when the garment is made up.

Breeches were attached to the doublet with laces and eyelets or hooks. Wide elastic braces are more convenient if authenticity is not important.

The prince is wearing a doublet with narrow sleeves and a slightly raised waist, which gives added importance to his full breeches. He wears a stiff collar edged with needle lace and matching cuffs. His cloak is lined with matching red and silver shag. (*Charles I as Prince of Wales* by Robert Peake the Elder.)

Sir Walter is dressed in the typical costume of an Elizabethan courtier. An elaborate jerkin is worn over matching doublet and trunk-hose, which are worn with canions but no codpiece. He wears a small formal ruff round his neck and tiny frills at his wrists. In contrast, the boy is wearing a simple doublet and matching soft breeches. Instead of a ruff, he has a lace-edged collar. This softer style was to be developed in the 17th century. (*Sir Walter Raleigh* by unknown artist.)

VENETIAN BREECHES

Sheet of paper:

½ seat measurement + 3 times front crutch width measurement + 10cm (4")

x

Required breeches length + 10cm (4")

Diagram 1

1 Mark A 5cm (2") down the left-hand side of the paper.

2 Square out A–B right across the paper.

3 A–C = required breeches length.

4 Square out C–D right across the paper.

5 A–E = trouser rise + 4cm (1½").

6 Square across to F.

7 A–G = 9cm (3½").

8 Join G–E in a smooth curve as diagram.

9 B–H = 5cm (2").

10 Join H–F In a smooth curve as diagram.

11 From G square up G–I = 4cm (1½").

12 J is midway between A–B.

13 Square up J–K = 4cm (1½").

14 Join I–K in a straight line and curve down to H as diagram.

15 From J square down to meet C–D at L.

16 L–M = ½ required knee measurement.

17 L–N = ½ required knee measurement.

18 Draw the knee line M–L–N curving 3cm (1¼") above M–L and 3cm (1¼") below L–N.

19 Cut along E–M and F–N.

20 Join E–M to F–N and check the knee line at M/N.

21 Check the crutch line at E/F.

22 Cut off surplus paper to complete the pattern, Diagram 2.

Note. The Venetians are gathered to fit a waistband with most of the fullness to the back and sides keeping about 14cm (5½") in the centre front flat.

A placket approximately 30cm (12") long x 5–6cm (1½"–2") should be sewn to the right front.

The knees can be left with or without an opening or they can be made wider and gathered onto bands.

VENETIAN BREECHES

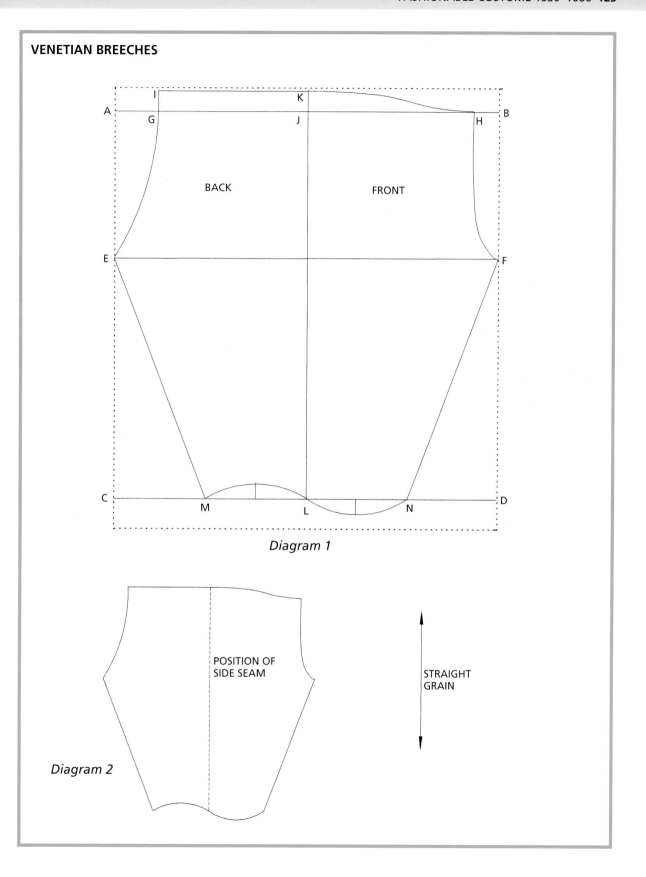

Diagram 1

Diagram 2

HIGH-WAISTED DOUBLET

Basic doublet pattern (see p. 82) with the chest line marked, without waist suppression or front length addition. The centre front straightened if required

Small pieces of paper for the alterations

Diagram 1

1 Join the side seams and mark the underarm point.

2 Mark the pattern A, B, C, D as diagram.

Diagram 2

3 E is midway between A–B.

4 Join D–E with a straight line.

5 D–E cuts the chest line at F.

6 F–G = approximately ¼ F–D.

7 E–H is the waist suppression.

8 Join H–G with a straight line.

9 Redraw the armhole from the underarm point to G as diagram.

10 If the point formed at G is very sharp curve H–G as diagram.

11 Mark G clearly on the back and front sections of the pattern.

12 From A measure up A–I = the amount to be deducted from the length of the doublet.

13 From I square right across the pattern to M, cutting E–D at J, H–G at K, and the original side seam at L.

14 Cut along I–M.

15 Cut along J–D to separate the pattern.

16 Cut along K–G.

Diagram 3

17 Rejoin the pattern matching G on the back section with G on the front section.

18 Secure a piece of paper under the pattern as diagram.

19 Join J–L with a straight line.

20 From M extend the centre front line the required amount for the pointed front, N.

21 Join L–N with a straight line and redraw curving 2cm (¾") from the centre of the line as diagram.

22 Cut off surplus paper.

The king was a small man but the cut of his clothes gives him an air of elegance and dignity. The high-waisted doublet and tapering breeches make his legs look longer and this impression is complemented by the vertical slashes on his doublet. The ruff has been replaced by a lace collar. (*Charles I* by Daniel Mytens.)

17th-CENTURY HIGH-WAISTED DOUBLET

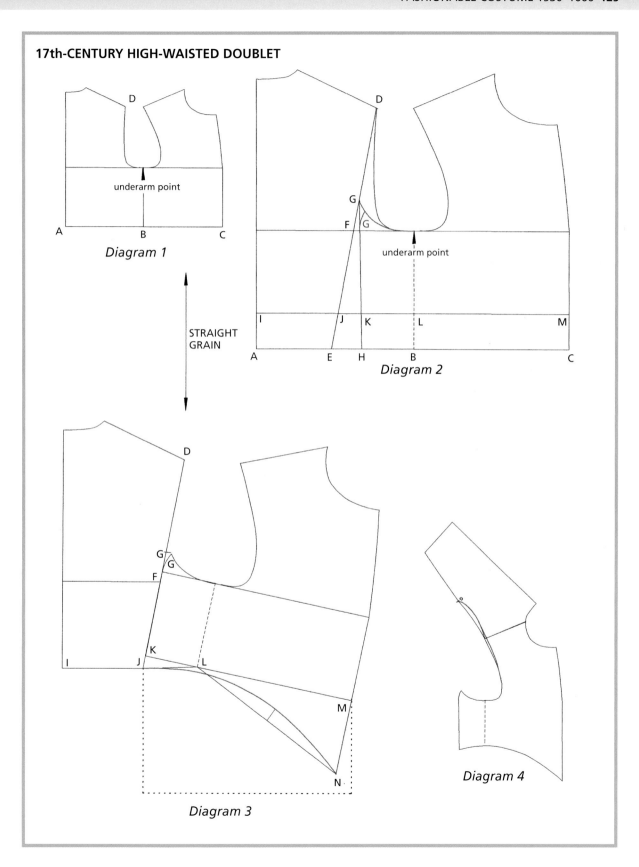

Diagram 1

STRAIGHT
GRAIN

Diagram 2

Diagram 3

Diagram 4

Diagram 4

23 Join the shoulder seams and weight down the pattern.

24 Check the line of the armhole and correct if necessary as diagram.

The skirts

Diagrams 5 & 5a

If the skirt is to hang level all around, measure the new waist line ignoring the point as Diagram 5.

If the skirts are to be cut into tabs, follow the line of the point and measure around the new waist line and the point as Diagram 5a. Add 2cm (¾") to the width of the paper for each tab except the one at the centre front.

Diagram 6

25 Cut a rectangle of paper = waist measurement x the required length of skirt.

26 Mark the paper O, P, Q, R as diagram.

27 Divide the paper into eight as diagram and cut along the divisions from Q–R almost to O–P.

Diagram 7

28 Place the pattern on another piece of paper and spread the slashes evenly the required amount.

29 Add half a slash width to the centre back as diagram.

30 Cut off surplus paper.

31 Mark P is the centre front of the pattern.

32 Mark O is the centre back of the pattern.

Diagram 8

33 P–S on the skirt = M–N on the centre front of the doublet as Diagram 5.

34 O–T = I–L on the waist of the doublet as Diagram 5.

35 Join T–S with a straight line and redraw curving 2cm (¾") above the line as diagram.

If the skirt is to be divided into tabs, measure the waist as drawn in red on Diagram 5a and follow the instructions for the basic doublet pattern.

The sleeves

Follow the basic period sleeve pattern (see p. 84).

The upper part of the sleeve can be cut into strips as Diagram 9. Cut the pattern along the elbow line and divide the top part evenly. The side seams can be straightened as drawn in red.

The front of the sleeve can be left open and fastened at the wrist with buttons and loops as drawn in red on Diagram 10.

High-waisted doublet with or without waist seam

The pattern for simple buff coat in the non-fashionable section is virtually the same shape as a fashionable doublet. The simple shape can look very elegant when made in beautiful fabric with expensive trimmings and lace collar (known as a falling band). The doublet could be given more shape by increasing the amount of waist suppression. A stand collar would be necessary to support the falling band. The sleeves are cut from a basic period sleeve pattern with the front seam left open.

17th-CENTURY HIGH-WAISTED DOUBLET – continued

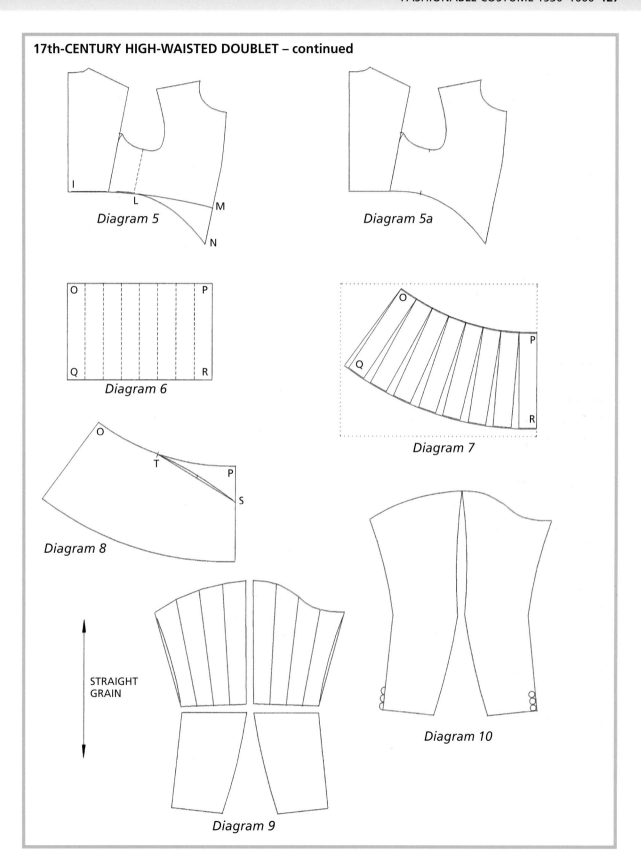

Diagram 5

Diagram 5a

Diagram 6

Diagram 7

Diagram 8

STRAIGHT GRAIN

Diagram 9

Diagram 10

THE LAST PHASE OF THE DOUBLET

In the middle years of the 17th century the doublet shrank to its smallest size, well above waist level. If there were skirts they were tiny tabs. The sleeves were also short, often open down the front seam or made entirely of narrow strips. The doublet was worn with petticoat breeches, often low on the hips and consequently there was a great deal of shirt on display. The entire outfit was generally decorated with quantities of ribbons and lace.

Basic doublet pattern (see p. 82) with the chest line marked, straightened centre front (see basic coat blocks, p. 142) and no front length addition as Diagram 1.

Diagram 2

1 Join the side seams.

2 Raise the underarm point 1cm (⅜").

3 A is midway up the back armhole: A–B = 1cm (⅜").

4 Redraw the armhole through the new underarm point and B as diagram.

5 From the back chest line square up approximately ⅓ of the armhole to meet the new armhole at C.

6 C–D = 3cm (1¼").

7 E is midway along the back waist line.

8 Join E–D with a straight line.

9 E–F = ½ the usual waist suppression.

10 Join F–D with a straight line.

11 From the centre back waist line measure up 5cm (2") to G, and square right across to the centre front H.

12 G–H cuts D–E at I and D–F at J.

13 Cut along C–D–E and D–F.

14 Rejoin the pattern so that D on the back section meets D on the front as Diagram 3.

15 Smooth out any corner at I/J if necessary.

16 Cut along G–I–J–H to complete the pattern as Diagram 4.

Tabs

Diagram 5

Measure the waist of the doublet and divide by four (or the required number of tabs). Cut a piece of paper this length x 4cm (1½") + 2cm (¾").

17 Mark the corners of the paper K, L, M, N as diagram.

18 K–O = 1cm (⅜"). L–P = 1cm (⅜").

19 Join O–M and P–N.

20 Cut off surplus paper.

Collar

If a collar is required, follow the instructions in doublets and jerkins (see p. 104).

Sleeves

Follow the instructions for basic period sleeve (see p. 84).

THE LAST PHASE OF THE DOUBLET

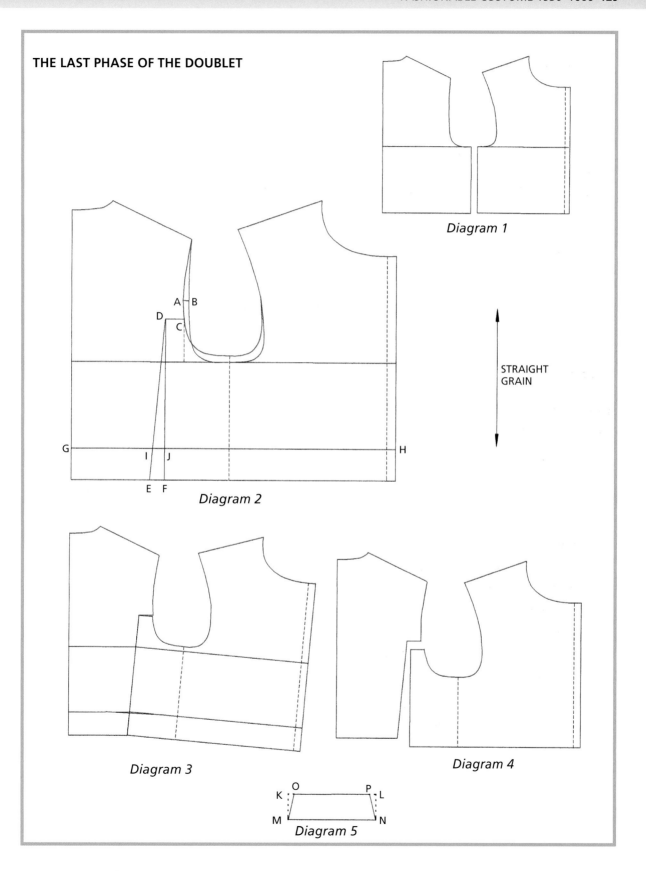

Diagram 1

Diagram 2

STRAIGHT
GRAIN

Diagram 3

Diagram 4

Diagram 5

MID-17TH-CENTURY BREECHES

The cut of these breeches is very simple; the pattern can be adapted to be longer, shorter, wider or narrower. The instructions are based on a seat measurement of 100cm (44"). For the diagrams, the seat measurement has been increased by half and for the bottoms of the legs, the measurement is approximately the calf measurement increased by half. The fly opening should have the buttons on the right front and the buttonholes on the left. Sometimes the placket is on the outside of the breeches, sometimes inside. Non-fashionable breeches often do not have fly buttons or other fastenings and the shirt is visible in the opening.

The outside and inside leg measurements should be shortened as required.

When making up the breeches there is often a 5cm (2") inverted pleat at the centre front and the rest of the fullness gathered to fit the waistband, otherwise they can be gathered evenly all round. The waistband should have a seam in the centre back in case alterations are needed.

Sheet of paper:
Seat measurement + required extra width + front crutch measurement x 3
x
Required length + 10cm (4")

Diagram 1
1 Mark the paper A, B, C, D as diagram.
2 C–E = new inside leg measurement.
3 Square E–F right across the paper.
4 F–G = front crutch width.
5 Square up G–H = trouser rise measurement. Curve the front crutch line as diagram.

6 E–I = front crutch width x 2.
7 From I square up to meet A–B at J.
8 K is midway between E–I.
9 Join K–J with a straight line and redraw as diagram.
10 Join J–H with a straight line.
11 Join K–J with a curved line as diagram.
12 L is midway between I–G.
13 From L square up to meet J–H at M and down to meet C–D at N.
14 O–P = ½ required bottom of leg width deduct this measurement from N–D.
15 D–O = P–N. N–Q = N–P.
16 Q–R = O–P. Join R–E.

Diagram 2
17 Curve the leg seams in (approximately 2cm (¾")) as diagram.
18 Measure the front inside leg seam and adjust the back inside leg seam to match.
19 Redraw the back crutch seam as drawn in red.
20 Cut off surplus paper and divide the pattern along L–M rounding off any points at L.

Diagram 3
The completed back section.

Diagrams 3a & 3b
21 Draw the fly placket as diagram (reverse the pattern) making it about 4cm (1½") wide and 7cm (2¾") from F.

Diagram 4
22 Cut a waist band 5cm (2") deep x ½ waist measurement + 3cm (1¼"). The waist band will have a join at the centre back.

MID-17TH-CENTURY BREECHES

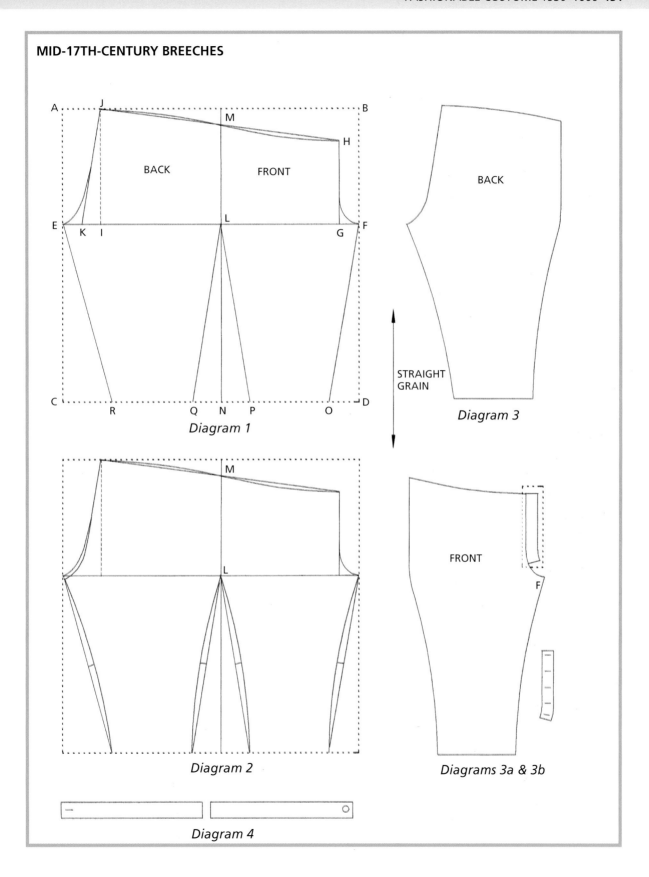

Diagram 1

Diagram 2

Diagram 3

STRAIGHT GRAIN

Diagrams 3a & 3b

Diagram 4

OPEN BREECHES

Open breeches varied from the simple short baggy trousers seen being worn by people in modest circumstances in Dutch paintings to breeches so wide they look like skirts and were known as petticoat breeches. Either style could be decorated with ribbons, braid, lace and flounces. Sometimes the use of ribbons was quite modest, small bunches being attached at the centre front waist and bottom of the legs. Petticoat breeches were profusely decorated with huge quantities of ribbon round the waist and on the outside leg. This style was originally worn with very short doublets; it proved impractical when the long narrow coat came into fashion. At first the coat hem was pinned up to accommodate the breeches but they were soon replaced by simple, closed knee breeches.

Basic pattern

Simple trousers pattern (see p. 214) with the legs reduced to the required length; this is generally knee level, a little longer for plain breeches and a little shorter for breeches with flounces

Extra paper as instructions

Diagram 1

1 Mark the pattern A, B, C, D, E, F as diagram.

2 E–G = 10cm (4").

3 F–H = 10cm (4").

4 Join G–C and H–D.

5 Cut off C–G–E and D–H–F.

Diagram 2

6 J is midway between G–H.

7 From J square up to meet A–B at K.

8 Cut along J–K.

Diagram 3

9 Spread the pattern to the required width.

10 Secure extra paper under the pattern as diagram.

11 Rejoin A–B and J–J.

12 Mark the fly opening, L, 5cm (4") from D.

13 Cut off surplus paper to complete the basic pattern.

The waist band

Strip of paper:
½ required waist measurement + 2cm (¾") ease + 2cm (¾") for button stand

Diagram 4

14 Mark the paper M, N, O, P as diagram.

15 M–Q = 4cm (2½").

16 R is midway between M–N.

17 From R square down 4cm (2½") to S.

18 Join Q–S–P.

19 N–T = 2cm (¾").

20 M–Q is the centre back. Mark two eyelets.

21 Mark the position of two buttons/buttonholes parallel to T–P.

22 Cut off the surplus paper to complete the pattern as Diagram 4a.

OPEN BREECHES

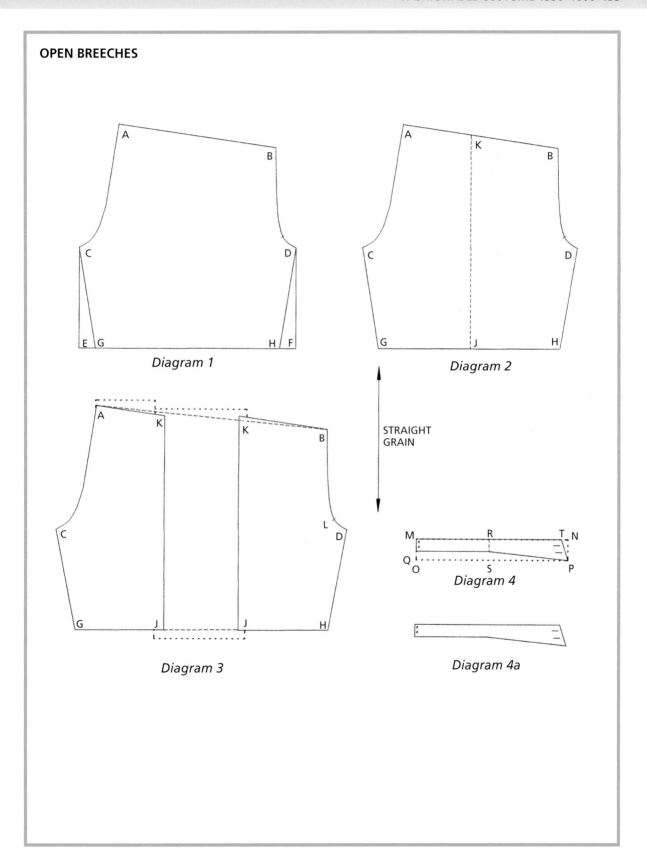

Diagram 1

Diagram 2

STRAIGHT GRAIN

Diagram 3

Diagram 4

Diagram 4a

PETTICOAT BREECHES WITH FLOUNCES

Basic open breeches pattern (see p. 132) widened by half the leg width

The diagrams are drawn with the bottom of the leg = 60cm (24") and the flounce width = 14cm (5½") which would make moderate breeches

---

Marking the position of the flounces

Diagram 1

1 Mark the pattern A, B, C, D, E, F as diagram.

2 Divide A–F into 6.

Diagram 2

3 Mark the divisions G, H, I, J, K as diagram – if the measurement does not divide easily make the discrepancies at E–G and K–F.

4 From E square up 10cm (4") to E*.

5 From G square up 12cm (4¾") to G*.

6 From H square up 14cm (5½") to H*.

7 From I square up 16cm (6¼") to I*.

8 From J square up 14cm (5½") to J*.

9 From K square up 12cm (4¾") to K*.

10 From F square up 10cm (4") to F*.

The flounces

See Calculating Circles (p. 22).

Diagram 3

11 E–F = the measurement at the bottom of the leg, this will be the circumference of the inner circle of the flounce. The radius can be calculated from this (see Calculating Circles (p. 22), it will be approximately one-sixth of the circumference). Draw a circle of this radius.

12 From the same centre point draw a circle adding the required flounce width measurement.

13 Divide the outer circle into six – the radius of a circle goes into the circumference approximately six times.

Diagram 4

14 Mark the divisions L, M, N, O, P, Q as diagram.

15 Join L–O, M–P, and N–Q.

16 Join L–M, M–N, N–O, O–P, P–Q, Q–L as diagram.

17 Mark the divisions on the inner circle R, S, T, U, V, W as diagram.

Diagram 5

18 Q–L–M–S–R–W–Q is the pattern for the middle section of the flounce, drawn in red.

19 O–X = 10cm (4").

20 Join X–U.

21 M–N–O–X–U–T–S–M is the pattern for the two outer sections drawn in blue.

22 Discard the remainder of the pattern as Diagram 6.

When the flounce is cut out, the pattern drawn in blue should be reversed for one section. The pieces are joined as indicated in Diagram 7. The outer edge will be rather more than a circle and have seven points which should be matched to the starred letters on the breeches.

PETTICOAT BREECHES WITH FLOUNCES

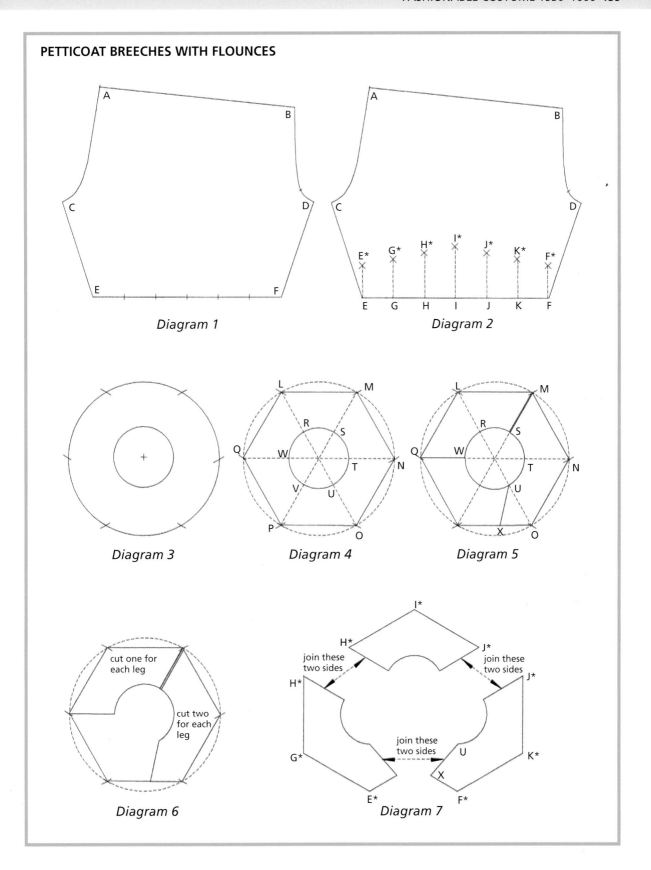

Diagram 1

Diagram 2

Diagram 3

Diagram 4

Diagram 5

Diagram 6

Diagram 7

7

The coat

The doublet and petticoat breeches reached ultimate fussiness and elaboration by the middle years of the 17th century and, as ever when a fashion reaches its limits, were replaced by something very different. There were moves to establish simpler clothes and the coat was the first step. It began as a simple, slightly flared, knee-length garment cut with two back pieces, two front pieces and straight sleeves reaching just below the elbow. The skirt seams were left open sufficiently to accommodate a sword. At first the narrow coat was worn over bulky petticoat breeches so the skirts had to be pinned up at the sides. The problem was soon solved by narrower breeches which hardly showed and so were virtually undecorated.

In its early form, the coat could be worn over the shirt without a doublet. The doublet soon became unfashionable and was replaced by the vest, which was also known as the waistcoat. The vest was cut on the same lines as the coat and originally had sleeves the ends of which were pulled over the coat sleeves but by the middle of the 18th century this was unusual.

Early vests were the same length as the coat but became slightly shorter by the second quarter of the 18th century. The parts of the vest that did not show, the back and upper sleeves, were usually made of inferior fabric but the rest could be very decorative. To this day very decorative waistcoats with plain backs are sometimes worn with conservative suits. The costume consisting of coat, waistcoat and breeches which developed in the 17th century was the origin of the three-piece suit which is still the accepted formal male attire.

In the early years, the fashionable coat, waistcoat and breeches were made of silk. The French aristocracy spent most of their time at court and dressed accordingly. The English, on the other hand, spent a great deal of time on their country estates engaged in country pursuits such as hunting and shooting for which silk clothes were inappropriate. Wool was a much more suitable fabric. Gradually wool became the

This small, finely detailed statue (84cm/33") shows the costume as it would have looked when being worn. (*Joseph Collet* by Amoy Chinqua.)

accepted fabric for all but gala occasions such as celebrations of royal birthdays and other court functions. Eventually woollen coats were acceptable wear even at court, although these were elaborately embroidered. The techniques for working with wool are very different from those needed for silk. The high quality of British wool and the expertise of British tailors who worked in this field have continued to this day. Gradually wool became popular for most occasions throughout the fashionable world.

The long lines of the early coat were rather elegant and had the advantage of making the wearer look taller, but by the end of the 17th century the skirts had widened so much that they had to be controlled in pleats. They reached their greatest width in the 1740s and then started to decrease. The front edges began to curve from the chest towards the back so that the coat could no longer be buttoned at the waist and this resulted in the side pleats being eliminated, once more giving a slender silhouette. The waistcoat became shorter until it was cut straight across a little below the waist. As a general rule, coats remained knee-length throughout all these changes. Now that more of the breeches was revealed, they were cut closer to the thigh and usually had four buttons to close them at the knee.

Early coats had the shoulder seam on top of the shoulder and the side seams only slightly towards the back. Gradually the shoulder seam moved further back and by the middle of the 18th century sloped down at the armhole end. The side seams also moved back, curving sharply and causing the back panels to become very narrow at the waist. The resulting shape gave the appearance of a very straight back and full chest.

The sleeves of the earliest coats were short and wide and turned back to form cuffs. By the 1680s sleeves were cut closer to the arm and had developed long, narrow cuffs known as hound's ears. Towards the end of the century the coat sleeves were still quite short, reaching just below the elbow, and had developed huge cuffs which balanced the wide skirts. As the skirts narrowed the sleeves lengthened, were close fitting and had small cuffs. Many coats were collarless although some had small stand collars. An informal version called the 'frock' was cut on simple lines with less fullness in the skirts and always had a turned-down collar which could be buttoned against inclement weather. Pockets varied in position and shape during the 17th century, but by the middle of the 18th century they were always horizontal, level with the top of the side pleats and had scalloped pocket flaps.

All the coats required some support to maintain the correct shape; some only needed it at the centre fronts and back vents but those with very full skirts needed considerably more. The areas needing support are shown on the individual patterns. Most coats were lined with linen or silk. One example in the Williamsburg Collection is unlined but this is unusual. Broadcloth was very heavily fulled so that it did not fray, consequently the edges could be cut without seam allowance and the lining topstitched about .25cm (⅛") from the edge. As this is not possible with most modern materials, the edges need to be turned in and the linings topstitched or felled in place.

BASIC COAT BLOCKS

The coat blocks are based on the basic upper body pattern without waist suppression (see p. 24). The pattern is widened and the shoulders raised according to the type of fabric being used and the garments being worn underneath. Early coats were usually made of thin silk or velvet which will not require as much enlargement as thick wool coats or coats worn over substantial waistcoats. The line of the centre front was perfectly straight in early coats.

Note. For exceptional measurements such as a beer belly or extra long back alter the basic upper body pattern before proceeding with the following instructions.

Basic coat block with centre front line shaped in the usual way

Small pieces of paper
Basic upper body pattern without front length extension

Diagram 1

1 Add 1.5 – 2.5cm (¾"–1¼") on each side seam.

2 Add 1.5cm (¾") button stand parallel to the centre front line.

3 Raise the shoulders .5–1cm (¼"–½") at the neck end and 1–1.5cm (½"–¾") at the armhole end.

4 Check that the neckline and armhole are smooth curves. Correct if necessary.

Basic coat block with straight centre front line

Small pieces of paper
Basic upper body pattern

Diagram 2

5 Draw a line from the bottom of the front dart to the point where the cross chest line meets the armhole as dashed line on diagram.

6 Cut along this line.

Diagram 3

7 Open the slash so that the front dart width is reduced by half.

8 Add 1.5cm (¾") at the waist and draw a button stand in a straight line to the neck level and join to the neck line.

9 Redraw the armhole as diagram.

10 Check neckline and armhole curves in the usual way.

Note. Straightening the centre front line in this way increases the armhole measurement and pushes the shoulder seam towards the back. In small sizes this is not a problem but the increase may be too much in large sizes. This can be adjusted by joining the back and front shoulders and moving the armhole end towards the front as Diagram 4 and raising the armhole as in Diagram 5.

BASIC COAT BLOCKS

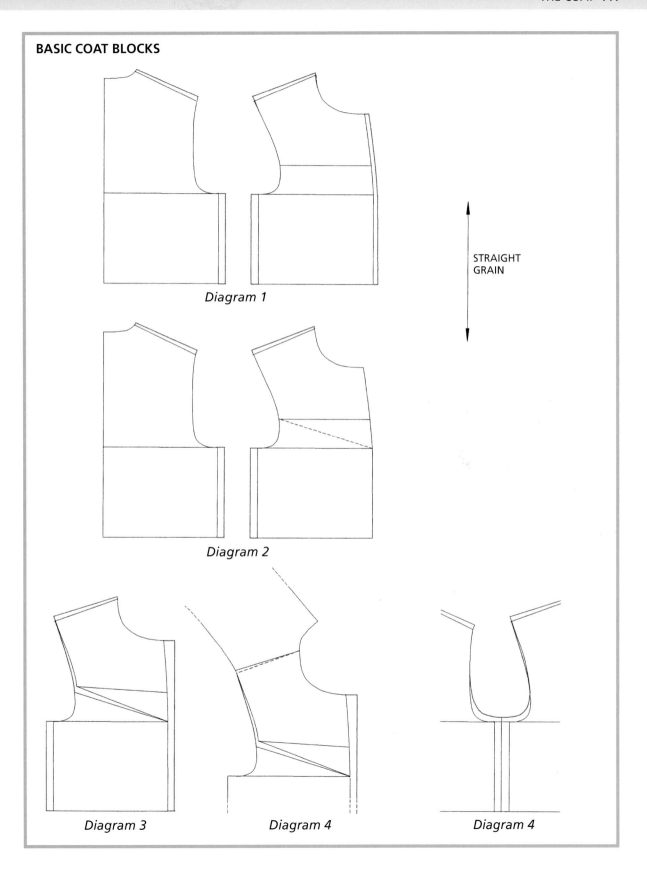

STRAIGHT
GRAIN

Diagram 1

Diagram 2

Diagram 3

Diagram 4

Diagram 4

Moving the side seam

The side seams on men's coats are usually moved towards the back as with doublets. The position and shape of these seams varies with the prevailing fashion but they always run from the armhole towards the centre back as described in Cutting curved seams (see p. 20).

Diagram 6

11 Join the side seams with adhesive tape.

12 Mark A where the seam is to meet the armhole.

13 Mark B where the seam is to meet the waist line.

14 Join A–B with a straight line and redraw in a gentle curve.

15 B–C = the amount of suppression required.

16 Join C–A with a straight line and redraw in a gentle curve.

17 Measure A–B and lengthen A–C at the waist to correspond.

18 Join C to the waist line at the side seam position.

To make a neater fit across the back of the jacket

Diagram 7

19 A–D 1–2cm (⅜"–¾").

20 Join D–C with a straight line and redraw in a gentle curve.

21 Join the seam together matching B/C.

22 Adjust the armhole as Diagram 8.

Moving the shoulder seam

Note. Shoulder seams are usually moved towards the back on fashionable coats from the second quarter of the 18th century and gradually became general on working men's coats.

Diagram 9

23 Join the shoulders with adhesive tape as diagram.

24 E–F = 1.5cm to 2cm (½"–¾").

25 G–H = 6cm (2½").

26 Join F–H and cut along this line.

Diagram 10

The completed pattern with adjusted shoulder line.

BASIC COAT BLOCKS – continued

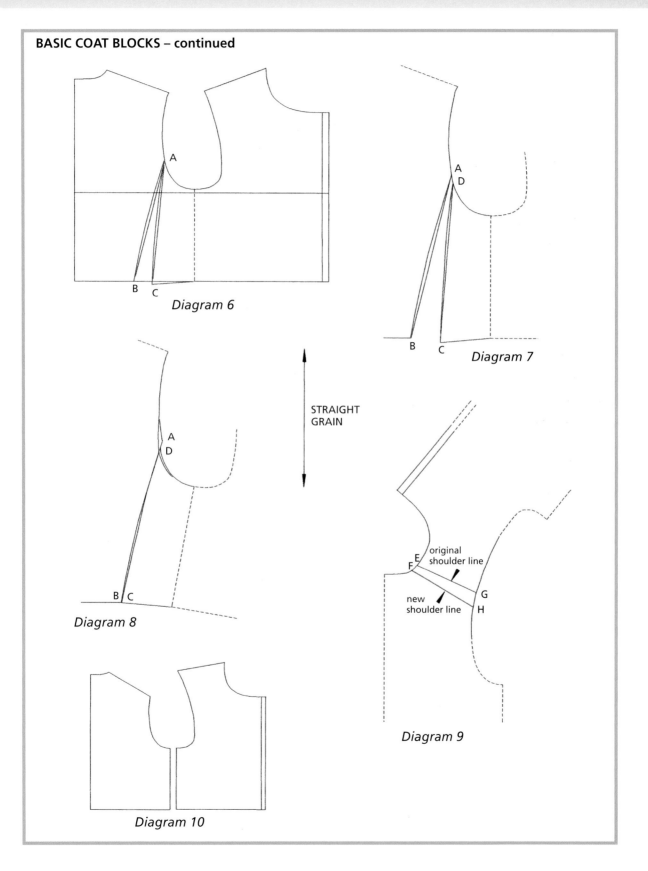

Diagram 6

Diagram 7

STRAIGHT
GRAIN

Diagram 8

original
shoulder line

new
shoulder line

Diagram 9

Diagram 10

EARLY COAT

Basic coat block (see p. 140) with centre front straightened and button stand

Two sheets of paper:

Required length of coat skirt (usually knee length) minus 5cm (2")

x

Total waist measurement of the basic coat block

Diagram 1

1 Lengthen the pattern by 5cm (2") as diagram.

2 Mark the pattern A, B, C, D as diagram.

3 From C measure approximately one-sixth of the back waist line measurement of the pattern and draw a line parallel to the side seam as diagram. Cut along this line.

Diagram 2

4 Join the piece from the back to the front as diagram.

5 Mark the new side seams E–F and G–H as diagram.

On the back section

Diagram 3

6 Attach one of the sheets of paper so that B is 5cm (2") from the top left-hand corner as diagram.

7 F–I = 2.5cm (1").

8 Join I–E.

9 B–J = 1.5cm (⅝").

10 Redraw the back seam in a gentle curve as diagram.

11 Join J to the bottom left-hand corner of the paper.

12 J–K = required skirt length.

On the front section

Diagram 4

13 H–L = 2.5cm (1").

14 Join L–G.

15 Attach the remaining sheet of paper along the waist line as diagram.

16 Join L to the bottom left-hand corner of the paper.

17 L–M = J–K.

18 Draw the flared part of the hemline in a gentle curve.

19 Curve the side seam as marked in red.

20 Cut off surplus paper to complete the front pattern.

Note. The front length addition measurement should be added to the hem of the front skirt, as drawn in red on Diagram 4 for larger sizes but is not essential for smaller sizes.

EARLY COAT

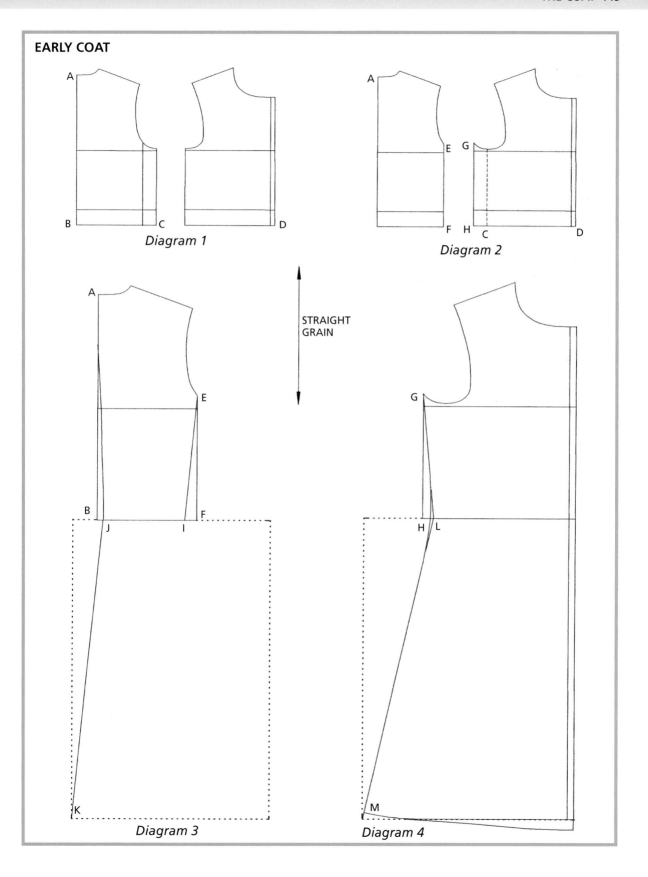

Diagram 1

Diagram 2

STRAIGHT
GRAIN

Diagram 3

Diagram 4

On the back section

Diagram 5

21 Reverse the front pattern and place on top of the back as diagram as drawn in red on Diagram 6.

22 Trace along the front side seam and hem line.

23 Cut off surplus paper to complete the back pattern.

Diagrams 7 & 8

24 Mark the centre back and side openings approximately one-third of the centre back length.

25 The buttons and buttonholes down the centre front and skirt openings are 2.5cm (1") long and set the same distance apart. The pocket flaps are 20cm x 2.5cm (8" x 1") set approximately 10cm (4") lower than the side openings and 6cm (2½") from the centre front.

The early coat was designed to counter the elaborations of mid-century costume. The line is long and narrow, accentuated by the vertical pocket slits and simple row of buttons and buttonholes, most of which were left undone. (Detail showing Charles I from the engraved frontispiece of *Morgan's Map of London*.)

EARLY COAT – continued

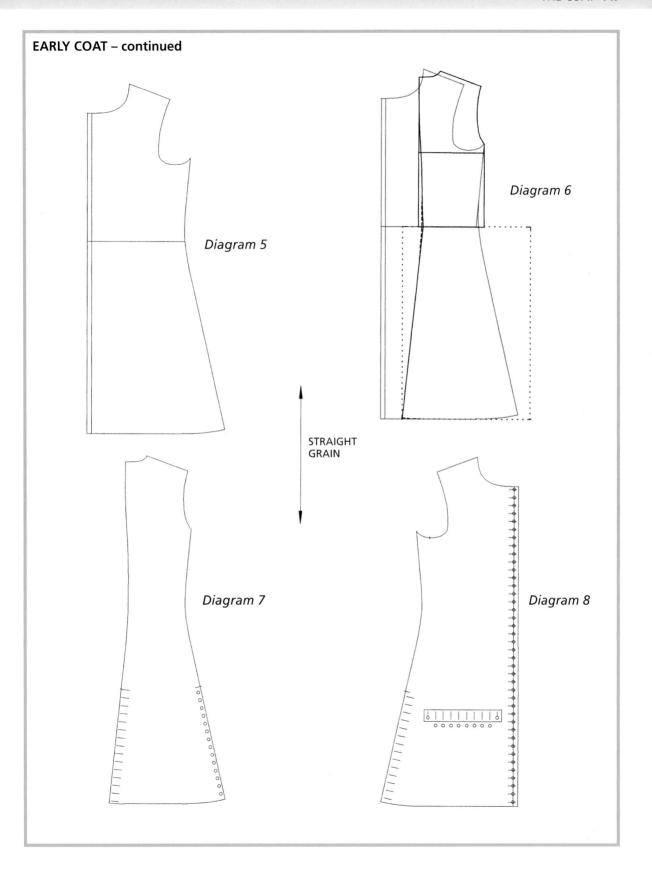

Diagram 5

Diagram 6

STRAIGHT
GRAIN

Diagram 7

Diagram 8

The sleeves

Note. If the coat is to be made of thin fabric, the armhole of the coat can be reduced by raising the side seam which will make the sleeve narrower and more elegant.

The measurements for the cuffs are a guide and should be adapted as required.
Only the upper section of the sleeve pattern is drafted, the under section being exactly the same except for the sleeve head.

   Pattern for basic period sleeve (p. 84) cut to fit the armhole of the coat pattern
   Small pieces of paper for the alterations

Diagrams 9 & 9a

26 Mark the basic period sleeve pattern A, B, C, D as diagram.

27 Cut along A–B and open the slash 2cm (¾") at A and secure a piece of paper underneath.

28 Mark E as diagram.

29 D–F = ⅓ D–B.

30 C–G = ¼ C–E.

31 Join F–G and cut along the line, discard the bottom piece of the sleeve pattern.

Diagram 10

32 Secure a piece of paper along G–F as diagram and fold it under the pattern as diagram.

33 F–H = 1.25cm (⅝").

34 From B continue the upper arm curve to H as drawn in a dashed red line on diagram.

35 From H measure up H–I = 10cm (4"). I is .75cm (⅜") from B–H.

36 G–J = 5cm (2").

37 From J square up J–K = 12.5cm (5").

38 Join I–K with a straight line and redraw in a gentle curve.

39 Complete the cuff joining K–J curving approximately 2.5cm (1") from the line.

40 Mark the lines of the cuff with a tracing wheel and unfold the paper.

Diagram 11

41 J–L = 5.5cm (2⅜").

42 From L square up L–M = 5cm (2").

43 Draw the back seam A–M–J as diagram.

44 Cut off surplus paper to complete the pattern as Diagram 12.

Note. When the sleeve is made up, the back seam and cuff are left open from M.

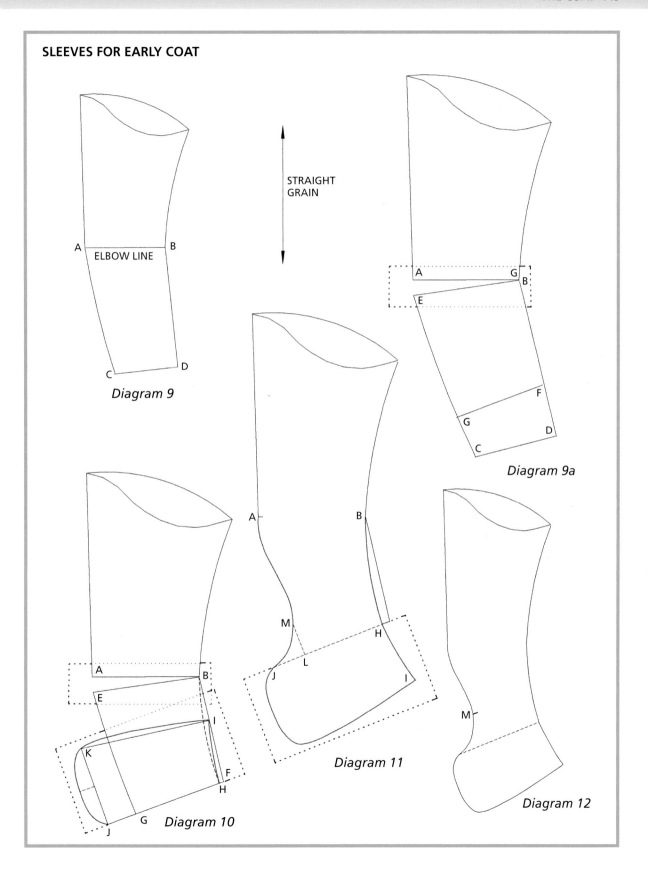

SLEEVES FOR EARLY COAT

STRAIGHT GRAIN

Diagram 9

ELBOW LINE

Diagram 9a

Diagram 10

Diagram 11

Diagram 12

DEVELOPMENTS IN THE CUT OF 18TH-CENTURY COATS

The patterns that follow are for four typical coats which illustrate the major changes in style during the first three-quarters of the century. There are very many variations on these styles and the examples should not be taken as definitive. Coats could be worn for many years and only the most fashionable would discard a good coat when it was a little out of date. Examination of examples in museum collections is always worth while but care must be taken as garments have sometimes been altered for the original owner, to fit someone else, or in more in more recent times, for fancy dress and theatricals. Some silk coats were made from recycled fabric, possibly a dress, and may have puzzling features such as evidence of unpicked stitching or odd joins. Unusual joins are also found in inconspicuous places when the fabric had to be cut economically or adjustments were made at the fitting. These unusual features are generally easy to recognise and will not be confused with interesting design elements. Pockets sometimes had buttons on the flaps, sometimes under the flaps; the buttons may have been removed; if there is no evidence of stitching there may never have been any buttons. Some collars were made in two pieces with a join and small point at the centre back, it may seem strange but that was how it was supposed to be.

Some features were constant throughout the period:

- The coats were approximately knee length and had vents at the centre back and side seams.
- The vents were approximately half the nape to hem measurement.
- The fullness in the skirts was controlled in graduated pleats.
- The side vents were joined at the bottom with a button or a few stitches.
- After c. 1725 the tops of the pocket flaps and the top of the vents were on the same level.

The centre fronts of early coats were straight from neck to hem. Waistcoats were almost as long as the coat; they sometimes had sleeves and were worn buttoned. The breeches, which hardly showed, were very plain. As the century progressed, the coat fronts began to slope towards the back, the waistcoat became shorter and the breeches more elegant.

Interfacing was used where necessary, down the fronts, the vents and in the cuffs, pocket flaps and collars, and to support the pockets, whether the fabric was silk or wool. Two layers were used where extra strengthening was needed, particularly where there were buttons and buttonholes and at the tops of the vents. Some silk was so stiff it did not require interfacing although the very wide skirted coats of the first half of the century usually had the entire front skirts, the vents and centre fronts interfaced. Silk coats had the raw edges turned in and the edge of the lining, usually also of silk, turned in and top-stitched close to the edge.

Wool was so heavily fulled it did not fray, so the coat edges were simply cut and the linings top-stitched close to the edge.

EARLY 18TH-CENTURY FASHIONABLE COAT

- **Side seams**: a little towards the back (approximately one-sixth of the back waist measurement before waist suppression is deducted).
- **Shoulder seam**: in the natural position along the top of the shoulder.
- **The fronts**: straight, meeting, able to be buttoned from top to bottom.
- **Skirt width**: wide, approximately a full circle which in the earliest coats hung in soft folds and was not pleated. The flare on the skirts varied with quality of the garment, if it was to be an everyday coat there would be less width in the skirts.

  The proportion of the coat in the diagrams is:

  The hem line of the back skirt is approximately 4 times the back waist measurement.

  The hem line of the front skirt is approximately 3 times the front waist measurement.
- **Sleeves**: short, ending between the wrist and elbow, could be wide.
- **Cuffs**: very large.
- **Waistcoat**: almost as long as the coat with buttons from neck to hem, with or without sleeves.

The pattern

Basic coat block (see p. 140) with straightened centre front, no waist suppression or front length addition

The skirt length will be the measurement from waist to knee

2 sheets of paper:

Skirt length

x

Skirt length + 10–15cm (4"–6") according to size

Note. The measurements given in the following instructions are for average sizes.

Diagram 1

1   Join the front and back patterns at the side seam.

2   Move the side seam towards the back by approximately one-sixth of the back pattern measurement at the waist line and cut along this line.

3   Mark the new back section A, B, C, D as diagram.

4   Mark the new front section E, F, G, H as diagram.

The back pattern

Diagram 2

5   Join the back pattern to the top edge of one of the pieces of paper so that C is 5cm (2") from the left-hand corner.

6   From C square down 15cm (6") to I.

7   From D square down 15cm (6") to J.

8   Join I–J.

9   C–K = 5cm (2") square across to meet D–J at L, K–L is the new waist line.

10   L–M = 2cm (¾").

11   Draw B–M–J in a smooth curve as diagram.

12   K–N = 1 – 1.5cm (½"–¾").

13   Draw A–N–I in a smooth curve as diagram.

14   Join I to the bottom left-hand corner of the paper with a straight line; mark this O.

15   From J square down to meet the bottom edge of the paper, P.

16   From J repeat the length J–P as diagram to draw the skirt flare.

17   Mark the end of the hemline Q.

18   Round off the angle at J and re-mark J on the curve.

19   Cut off surplus paper to complete the back pattern.

The front pattern

Diagram 3

20   Join the second sheet of paper to the waist line of the front pattern so that H meets the right-hand side of the paper (on the diagram this sheet of paper is overlapped by Diagram 2).

21   From H measure down 5cm (2") to R.

22   From G measure down 5cm (2") to S.

23   Join R–S.

24   S–T = 2cm (¾").

25   Reverse the back pattern and place over the front so that B meets F and M meets T.

26   Trace round the back pattern from B through M and round the skirt to Q; mark this V on the front pattern.

27   Mark the position of J onto the front pattern; this will be U.

28   Remove the back pattern.

29   From H measure down the edge of the paper H–W = total skirt length + the front length addition.

30   Join W to the traced hem line measurement as diagram.

EARLY 18th-CENTURY FASHIONABLE COAT

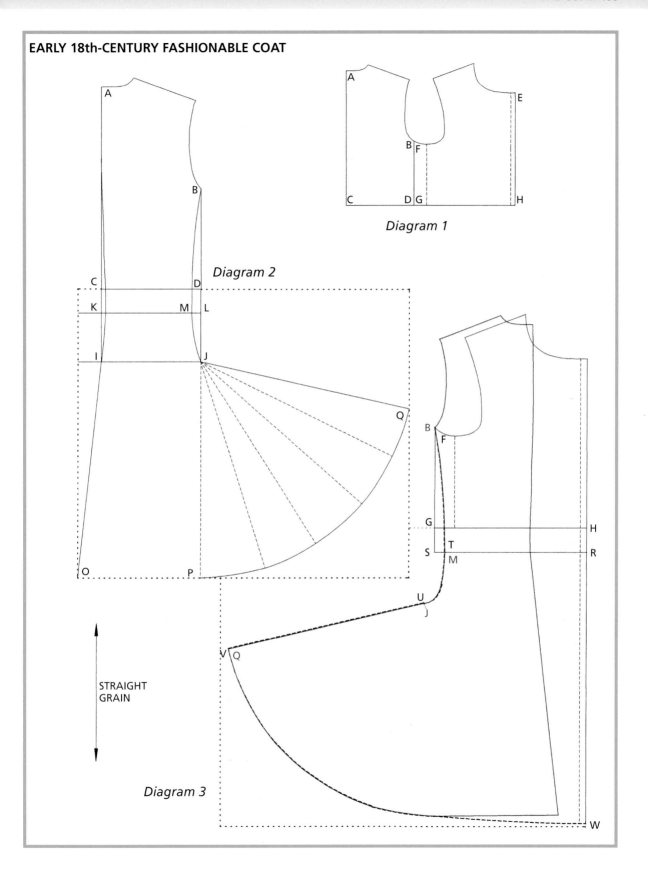

Diagram 1

Diagram 2

Diagram 3

STRAIGHT
GRAIN

Diagram 4

31 From V square out V–X = 5cm (2").

32 From U square out U–Y = 3cm (1¼").

33 Join X–Y and continue for 1cm (⅜") Z, redraw X–Z in a gentle curve.

34 Join Y–Z.

35 Cut off surplus paper to complete the front pattern.

Diagram 5

36 Place the back pattern so that J meets U and Q meets V as diagram and check that the hem line makes a smooth curve.

37 Trim V–X.

38 Cut off surplus paper.

Although the prince was only seven when this portrait was painted, he is dressed like an adult. His coat is cut close to the upper body and flares out from the hips. It is worn over matching breeches, which are barely visible, and a long-sleeved waistcoat. (Detail from the portrait of *Prince James Francis Edward Stuart* with his sister by Nicolas de Largillière.)

EARLY 18TH-CENTURY FASHIONABLE COAT – continued

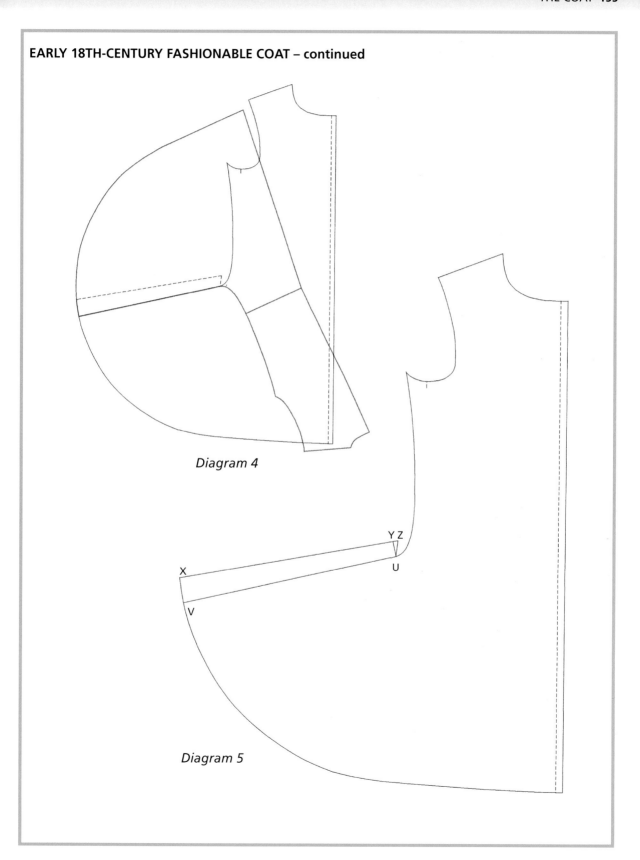

Diagram 4

Diagram 5

The sleeves

Basic period sleeve pattern (see p. 84) with the elbow line marked, to fit the armhole of the coat

Piece of paper for the cuff

Diagram 6

39 Mark the pattern A, B, C, D, E, F as diagram.

Diagram 7

40 Cut along the elbow line from D almost to C.

41 Open the slash 2cm (¾") and secure a piece of paper underneath, rejoin D–D.

42 E–G = approximately ¼ A–E.

43 F–H = approximately ⅛ B–F.

44 Join G–H and cut along this line; discard the bottom of the sleeve.

Diagram 8

45 Place a piece of paper under the pattern so that the top edge is approximately 8cm (6¼") below D and 4cm (2⅝") below C.

46 G–I = 30cm (12").

47 Join I to the D–H in a curved line as diagram.

Diagram 9

48 Cut along D–I and from I to the end of the crease as diagram.

49 Fold the extra paper under the pattern as diagram.

50 G–J = 16cm (6½"); move J out 1cm (⅜").

51 Join G–J with a straight line and redraw in a gentle curve as diagram.

52 From I square up 22cm (8¾") to K.

53 Join J–K with a straight line and redraw with a gentle curve.

54 Join K–I with a straight line and redraw with a gentle curve.

55 Mark J–K with a tracing wheel.

56 Unfold the paper and cut off the surplus to complete the pattern as Diagram 10.

Note. The cuff pattern is the same for the upper and lower sections of the sleeve.

EARLY 18TH-CENTURY FASHIONABLE COAT – sleeves

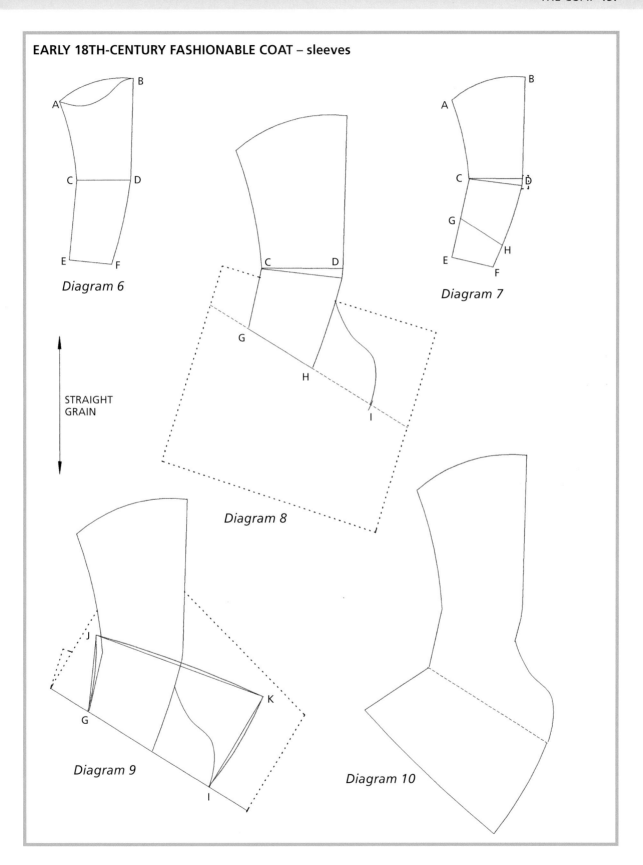

Diagram 6

Diagram 7

STRAIGHT
GRAIN

Diagram 8

Diagram 9

Diagram 10

The buttons and buttonholes

Diagrams 11 & 12

The buttons and buttonholes down the centre fronts, the side seams and centre back are 3.5cm (1⅜") apart and the buttonholes 6cm (2⅜") long. The buttonholes on the pocket flaps are 7cm (2¾") long and 3.5cm (1⅜") apart.

Note. The buttons and buttonholes on the centre front and centre back are drawn on top of each other. Although there are examples of coats with buttons and buttonholes on both sides, the general rule is that men's coats button left over right. Sometimes there are two rows of buttonholes down the centre back and no buttons.

Diagram 13

The buttons and buttonholes on the cuffs are the same length and distance apart as those on the body of the coat.

The pockets

Diagram 14

The pocket flap on the diagram is cut with the top edge 24cm (9½"), the bottom edge 25cm (10") and it is 8cm (3¼") deep.

The top of the pocket flaps are set 25cm (10") above and parallel to the hem, 10cm (4") from the centre front.

The buttonholes on the pocket flaps are almost the full depth of the flap.

Note. The measurements and numbers of buttons and buttonholes in the above instructions are intended as a guide and are by no means definitive. Frequently many of the buttonholes, particularly those at the centre back, were uncut and purely decorative.

EARLY 18TH-CENTURY FASHIONABLE COAT – buttons and buttonholes

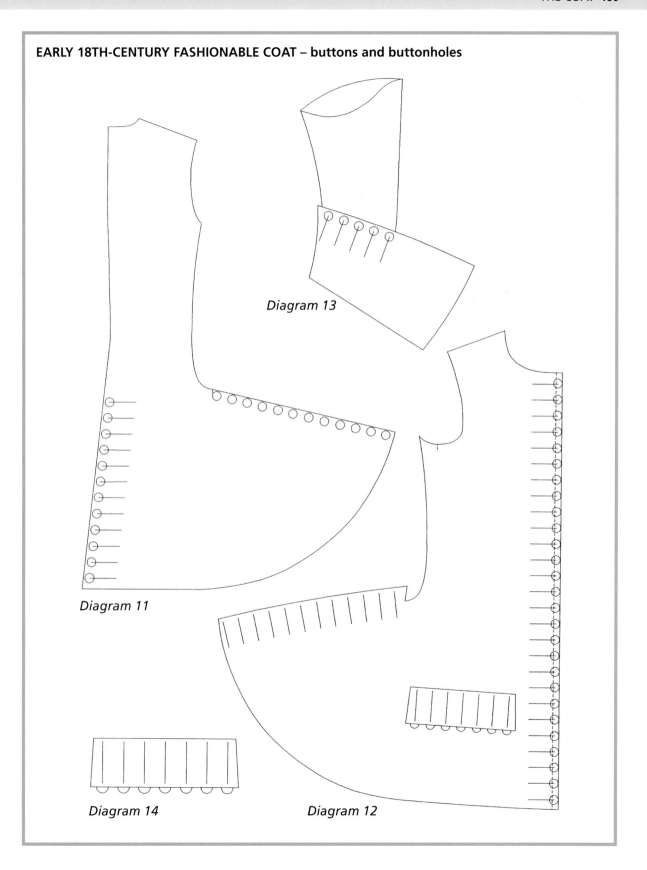

Diagram 13

Diagram 11

Diagram 14

Diagram 12

1720s COAT

- **Side seams**: a little towards the back (approximately ⅙ of the back waist measurement before waist suppression is deducted).
- **Shoulder seam**: set slightly further back.
- **The fronts**: straight, able to be buttoned from top to bottom but usually only buttoned at the waist.
- **Skirt width**: very wide, total circumference approximately 6m (6½ yards), controlled in graduated pleats as the sides and back.
- **Sleeves**: short and wide.
- **Cuffs**: very deep cuffs reaching above the elbow, called boot cuffs.
- **Waistcoat**: almost as long as the coat with buttons from neck to hem; cut on the same lines as the coat.

Diagram 1

The early coat pattern (see p. 144)

Extra paper for the pleats

The extra fabric at the side vent is controlled in pleats, the number varies but three at the back is usual. They are all approximately the same width at the top, 2cm (¾"), but vary at the hem with the exception of pleats 2 and 3 which are the same width.

The back pattern

1 Mark the pattern A, B, C, D as diagram.

2 From A square out A–E = 8cm (3").

3 From E square down to meet the hem at F.

4 Place a piece of paper under the pattern.

5 F–G = 12cm (4¾").

6 From B square out 2cm (¾") to G.

7 From D square out D–H = width of first pleat.

8 G–H = B–D.

Note. The tops of the pleats are all the same length i.e. 2cm (¾").

Pleat 2 is wider at the hem than pleat 1.
Pleat 3 is the same width as pleat 2.
Pleat 4 is wider than pleat 3.
Pleat 5 is a single layer and is narrower than pleat 4.

9 Mark the lines of the pleats with a tracing wheel.

Diagram 2

10 Cut out A–E–F–C.

11 Redraw A–C in a gentle curve as diagram.

12 E–I = 10cm (4").

13 From I square across to J.

14 Join I–J.

Diagram 3

15 Secure a piece of paper along E–F on the back pattern as diagram.

16 Place the section A–E–F–C so that E meets E on the main pattern.

17 Pivot section A–E–F–C so that a gap of 12cm (4¾") opens at the bottom as diagram and draw along E–F.

18 Cut along I–J and join the lower part to the back pattern as diagram. Join F–F with a curved line.

19 Do not discard the pattern piece A–E–I–J.

20 Fold the pleats and continue the hem line as diagram.

21 Cut off excess paper.

Note. Sometimes the pleats are cut in a straight line rather than following the line of the coat hem.

1720s COAT

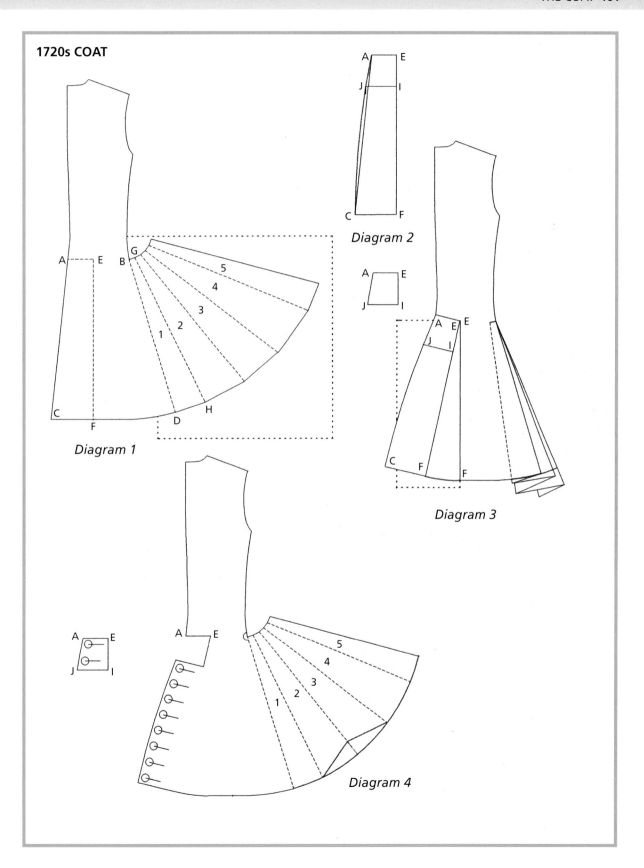

Diagram 1

Diagram 2

Diagram 3

Diagram 4

Diagrams 4 & 4a

22 The join between pleats 2 and 3 is usually shortened (approximately 5cm (2")).

23 When the coat is made up the pattern piece A–E–I–J is inserted in the gap at the centre back.

24 The top of the side vent is finished with a button; the ends of the hem are joined either with a button or a few stitches.

25 Mark the position of buttons, buttonholes or any other trimming down the back vent.

The front pattern

Diagram 5

26 Lower the neck line 5cm (4") at the centre front.

27 Draw the pleats as for the back pattern making no. 2 wider than no. 1, no. 3 wider than no. 2, no. 4 is narrower than no. 3.

Diagram 6

28 Fold the pleats and trim the excess as for the back pattern.

Note. The pleats are sometimes arranged so that the hem line continues in a straight line from X on the diagram.

29 Mark the position of the buttons and buttonholes.

30 Mark the position of the pocket flaps which are usually in line with the tops of the vents after c. 1725.

31 The dashed lines under the pocket flap indicate the shape and position of the pocket opening and pocket bag.

The sleeves

Diagram 7

32 Measure round the armhole and cut a basic period sleeve pattern (see p. 84).

33 Increase the slash at the elbow by approximately 3cm (1¼").

34 N–O = 3cm (1¼"). P–Q = 5cm (2").

35 Join O–Q and cut along this line.

Diagram 8

36 Place a piece of paper under the pattern as diagram.

37 Q–R = approximately 21cm (8¼").

38 The depth of the cuff is variable but should come well above elbow level.

39 Draw the cuff as diagram and complete as for early 18th-century coat (see p. 156).

40 Unfold the paper and cut 3cm (1¼") above O–Q as drawn in red on Diagram 9.

41 Mark the position of the buttons and buttonholes as required.

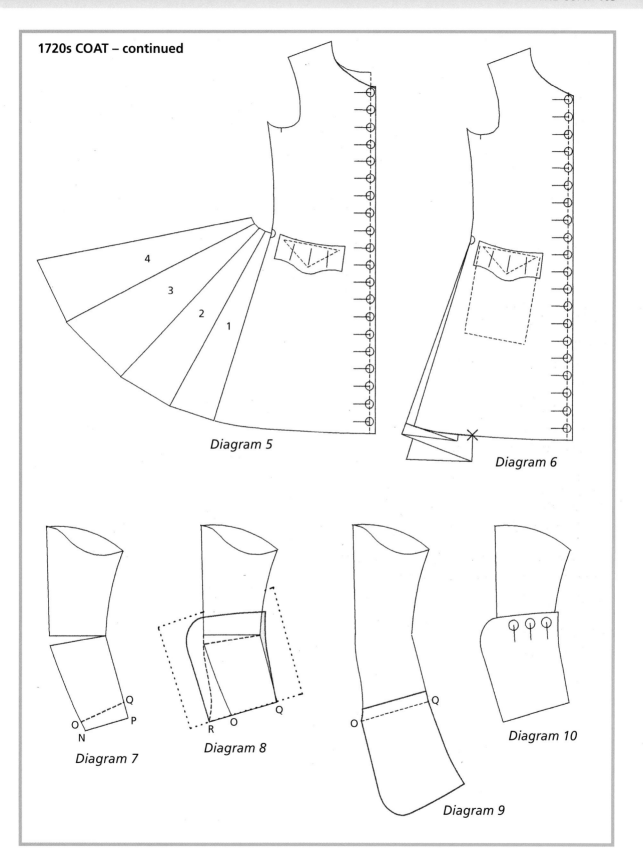

1720s COAT – continued

Diagram 5

Diagram 6

Diagram 7

Diagram 8

Diagram 9

Diagram 10

COATS IN THE SECOND HALF OF THE 18TH CENTURY

Middle of the century

- **Side seams**: start to move slightly further back.
- **Shoulder seam**: set slightly down the back.
- **The fronts**: curving out over the chest, padded from shoulder over fullest part of the chest, straight from waist down. Buttons and buttonholes from neck to hem but usually only those at the neck and waist are functional.
- **Skirt width**: reached maximum width about 1740, could be as much as 7m (7½ yards), thereafter decreased rapidly.
- **Neck**: usually finished with a narrow band graduated to nothing about 4cm (1½") from the centre fronts when the lining and outer fabric are top stitched edge to edge.
- **Sleeves**: fairly wide, narrowing above the elbow.
- **Cuffs**: wide, deep cuff.
- **Pockets and vents**: always on the same level.
- **Waistcoat**: reached top or mid-thigh; sometimes had buttons to the hem, sometimes only to the waist.

The coat fronts now slope towards the back, revealing the shorter waistcoat and breeches. (*James Grant, John Mytton, the Hon. Thomas Robinson and Thomas Wynn* by Nathaniel Holland Dance.)

The young man in the middle of the picture is wearing a fashionable, short double-breasted waistcoat which reveals the breeches. The two older men are more con-servatively dressed. (*The Connoisseurs: John Caw (died 1784), John Bonar (1747–1807) and James Bruce 1783* by David Allan.)

1775–80

Gradually the movement of the centre front towards the back becomes more pronounced giving a more slender and elegant line.

- **Side seams**: moved well towards the back.
- **Shoulder seam**: moved towards the back and sloped at the armhole end.
- **The fronts**: sloping towards the back from waist or mid-chest in more fashionable coats.
- **Skirt width**: much less fullness; about 1.3m (1½ yards) for fashionable coats and 1.75m (2 yards) for ordinary coats. The pleats were much shallower, the centre back skirts sometimes met edge to edge or had a simple overlap.
- **Neck**: small stand collar usual for fashionable coats; ordinary coats often had small turn-down collars.
- **Sleeves**: narrow, reaching the wrist.
- **Cuffs**: small and close to the arm.
- **Pockets and vents**: always on the same level.
- **Waistcoat**: about 25cm (10″) below the waist with buttons from neck to the level of the vents.

Patterns can be cut for these coats using the basic coat block (see p. 140) with shaped front and button stand; otherwise the method is similar to that for 1720s coat. The measurements given are purely as a guide and should be adapted as required. The general procedure is as follows.

Diagram 1

1 Join the side seams.

2 Secure a strip of paper to lengthen the pattern 20cm (8").

3 Mark the bottom edge of the paper A, B as diagram.

4 From the waist draw the position of the new side seam with a straight line.

5 Take out 1.5cm (⅝") of the waist suppression at the centre back, C.

6 Join C–A with a very gentle curve as diagram.

7 Mark the new seam line D/E and F as diagram.

8 F–G = 5cm (2"). Join G–E.

9 From F square down to meet A–B at H.

10 H–I = 1.5cm (⅝"). Join I–F and join I–G.

11 Redraw the new seam in a gentle curve taking a little from the back section and smoothing out the point at F as diagram. Re-mark F on the new line.

12 Redraw E–G with a curved the line as diagram.

13 Redraw G–I with a curved line as diagram.

14 Cut along D–F–I and E–G–I and separate the front and back sections of the pattern as Diagram 2.

Diagram 3

15 Join the shoulder seams with adhesive tape and move the line towards the back of the neck and armhole.

16 Cut along the new shoulder line as Diagram 4.

Diagram 5

Match the side seams of the front and back patterns as closely as possible and redraw the armhole.

COATS IN THE SECOND HALF OF THE 18TH CENTURY

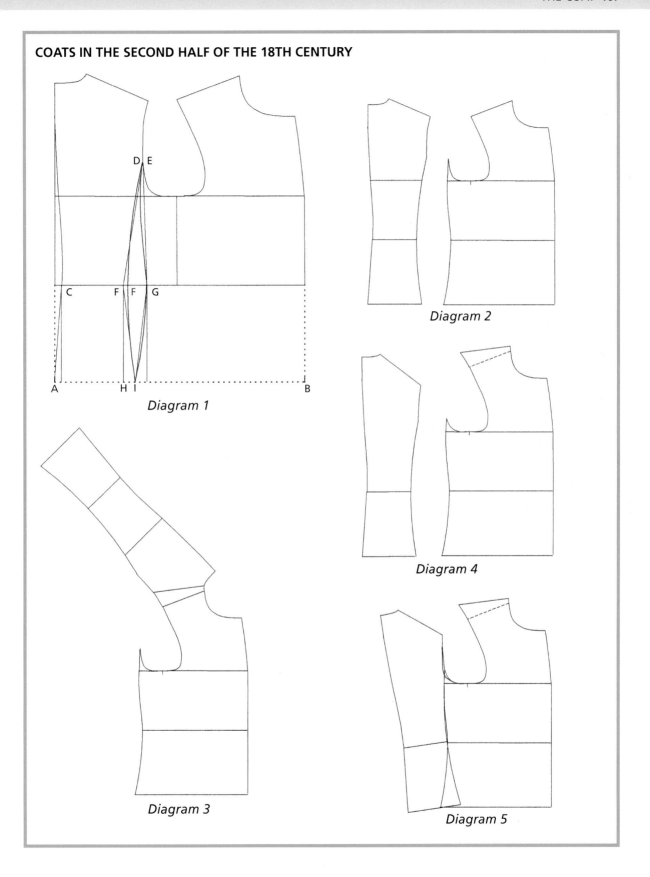

Diagram 1

Diagram 2

Diagram 3

Diagram 4

Diagram 5

On the back section

Diagram 6

17 Secure a sheet of paper (required length of skirt from A–I to hem + 5cm (2") x the required width of back skirt and side pleats) under the back pattern so that the top edge is 5cm (2") above A–I and A is 8cm (3") from the left-hand edge of the paper as diagram.

18 From A square down to the bottom of the paper, K.

19 K–L = twice the back waist measurement (C–F).

20 Join I–L.

21 From A square out 4cm (1⅝") to M.

22 Join M to the bottom left-hand corner of the paper, N – this line can be straight or slightly curved.

23 Draw the pleats as required taking the lines to the bottom of the paper as diagram.

24 Repeat the measurement I–L along edge of each pleat and join with a smooth curve.

25 Shorten the inside folds of the pleats (approximately 2cm (⅝")) and redraw the hem as diagram.

26 Cut along the edge of the last pleat leaving some surplus paper at the top.

27 Cut surplus paper from the centre back.

On the front section

Diagram 7

28 Secure a sheet of paper (required length of skirt x the required width of the front skirt and pleats) under the front pattern so that the top edge is 5cm (2") above I–B and B meets the right-hand edge.

29 Reverse the back section of the pattern, fold the pleats back, and place on top of the front section so that A–I lies along I–B and I on the back section meets I on the front.

30 Trace along I–L as drawn with a solid red line on the diagram. Remove the back pattern.

Diagram 8

31 Draw the front pleats as required.

32 Cut along the edge of the last pleat leaving some paper at the top.

33 Trim the bottom of the pleats as for the back pattern and shorten the inside folds.

The centre front line

34 Mark the top of the shoulder O.

35 O–P = 8cm (3").

36 Join P to the end of the chest line Q and redraw curving approximately 2cm (⅝") from the centre.

37 B–R = 2.5cm (1"). Join Q–R with a gentle curve.

38 Mark the bottom right-hand corner of the paper S.

39 S–T = 13cm (5").

40 Join R–T.
    O–P–Q–R–T is the new centre front line.

41 Cut off surplus paper.

Diagrams 9 and 9a show the skirts with the pleats folded in position.

COATS IN THE SECOND HALF OF THE 18th CENTURY – continued

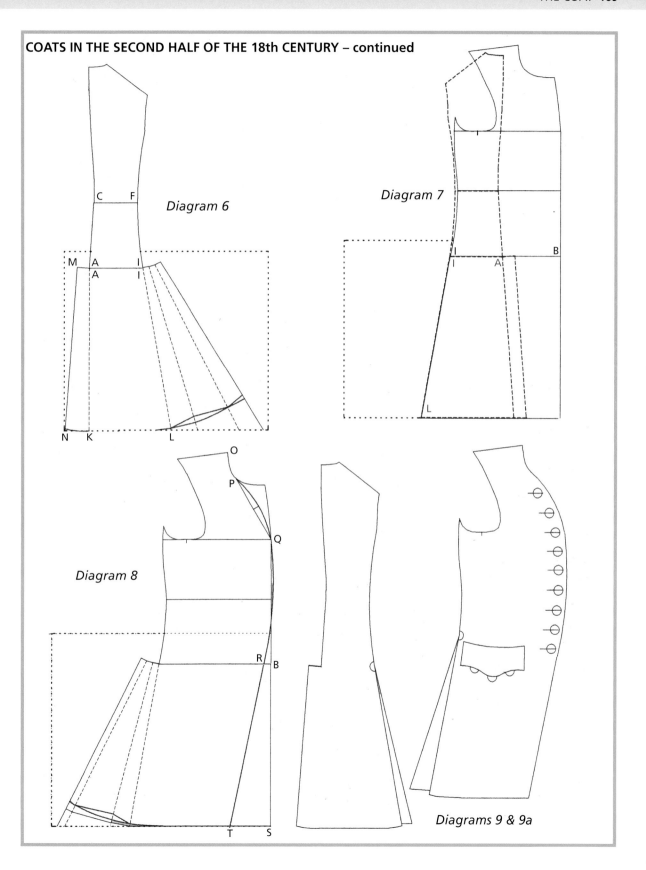

Diagram 6

Diagram 7

Diagram 8

Diagrams 9 & 9a

The sleeves

Diagram 10

42 Measure the armhole of the coat and draft a basic period sleeve.

43 Narrow the wrist and redraw the front seam in a gentle curve.

Simple cuff

Diagrams 11, 11a & 11b

44 A simple cuff can be drafted on the same principle as the cuffs for the 1720s coat as diagrams.

Cuff with an opening

Diagram 12

45 A–B = the required depth of cuff.

46 From B square across to C.

47 On the upper section of the sleeve, mark A–D = position of the opening (about 4cm (1½") from the front seam.

48 From D square up to meet B–C at E.

49 Cut along D–E.

50 A–F = 1.5cm (¾") square up approximately 16cm (6¼"). A–F is the position of the scalloped flap.

Diagram 13

51 Cut a strip of paper:

B–C x 2 + 1.5cm (⅝")

x

A–B + 6cm (2⅜")

52 Mark the paper H, I, J, K as diagram.

53 From H measure down 2cm (¾"), L and square across to meet G–I at M.

54 From J measure up 4cm (1½"), N and square across to meet G–I at O.

Diagram 14

55 Draft a pattern for the scalloped flap making it about 16cm (6¼") x a maximum of 9cm (3½").

Diagram 15

When making up the cuff, the flap is made with three button holes but only the two lower ones are functional. The flap is sewn along F–G and held in place by the top button. The cuff is sewn from the opening E–D, eased round the sleeve, and sewn over the edge of the flap. The top edge of the cuff is turned in and the bottom edge eased round the inside of the sleeve. Two buttons are stitched onto the cuff to correspond with the buttonholes.

There are many variations of this cuff and the simple one described in Diagrams 11, 11a & 11b. Some were unadorned, others were decorated with buttons, braid, contrasting fabrics or embroidery. It is emphasised that the measurements are only a guide.

Collars

Collars are usual on later coats, stand collars for formal wear and simple turned-down ones for ordinary coats. The pattern for stand collars in the Fashionable Doublet section (p. 104) can be used on formal coats and a straight strip (neck of coat measurement x required depth) for turned-down collars.

SLEEVES FOR COATS IN THE SECOND HALF OF THE 18th CENTURY

Diagram 10

Diagram 11

Diagram 11a

Diagram 11b

Diagram 12

Diagram 13

Diagram 14

Diagram 15

WAISTCOATS IN THE SECOND HALF OF THE 18TH CENTURY

The patterns for waistcoats are simplified versions of the coat patterns. Although sometimes exquisitely embroidered the basic shape is not complicated. As coat fronts sloped towards the back, waistcoats grew shorter, often the back was of inferior fabric as it would not normally be worn without the coat. The front of the waistcoat was worn buttoned and although the skirts also sloped they were wide enough to wrap well to the back and covered the top of the breeches.

If the coat is to be worn over a waistcoat it should be at least 3cm (1¼") larger round the chest on the half pattern. The pattern given for coats in the second half of the 18th century can be adapted for most waistcoats. The armhole should be enlarged as drawn in red on the diagram and adjustments for size made at the side seams. Some waistcoats had small stand collars or they might have a simple binding round the neck. Mid-century waistcoats usually had a narrow binding to 4 or 5cm (1½–2") of the front edges. The last bit having the lining and outer fabric turned in edge to edge and top stitched. Pockets on ordinary coats were usually undecorated and set at the same level as the coat pockets.

MID- TO LATE-18th-CENTURY WAISTCOAT

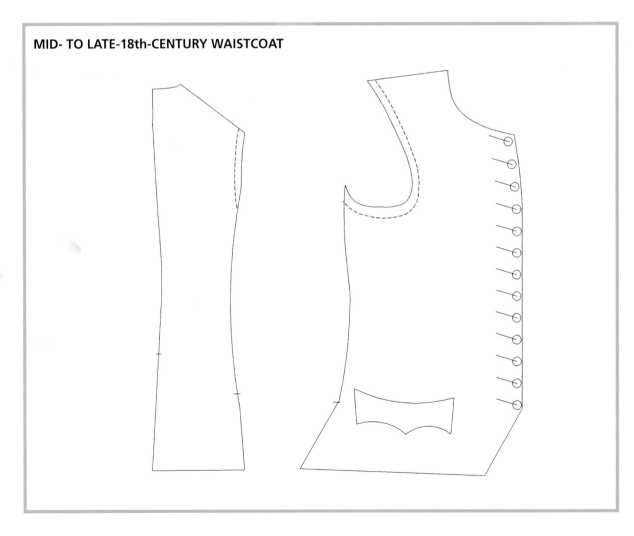

18TH-CENTURY BREECHES

Breeches for early 18th-century coats

The pattern for Venetians (see p. 122) is suitable for breeches to be worn with full-skirted coats. The knees can be left open for early coats. For 1720s, the breeches can have casings around the knees for drawstrings or be pleated into narrow bands and button fastenings up the leg openings.

Breeches for mid- to late-18th-century coats

Sheet of paper:
½ seat measurement + front crutch width x 3 + 10cm (4")

x

Required length + 20cm (8")

Diagram 1

1   Mark the corners of the paper A, B, C, D as diagram.

2   A–E = 10cm (4"), square right across the paper to F.

3   E–G = body rise, square right across the paper to H.

4   G–I = front crutch width, I–J = front crutch width.

5   From J square up to meet E–F at K.

6   Join I–K with a straight line and continue to meet A–B at L.

7   M is approximately ⅓ I–L; join M–G with a curve as diagram.

8   H–N = front crutch width.

9   From N square up to meet E–F at O.

10   P is approximately ⅓ N–O; join P–H with a curve as diagram.

11   Q is midway between J–N.

12   From Q square up to meet E–F at R and,

also from Q, square down to meet C–D at S.

13   Join R–L with a straight line.

14   S–T = ½ knee measurement; S–U = ½ knee measurement.

15   Redraw S–T curving 3cm (1¼") above the line.

16   Redraw S–U curving 3cm (1¼") below the line.

17   Join G–T with a straight line and redraw in a curve as diagram.

18   Join H–U with a straight line and redraw in a curve to match G–T.

19   Check that the inside leg seams match and correct as drawn in red on diagram.

20   From O square up O–V = 3cm (1¼"); from V square across 10cm (4") to W.

21   From W square down 12cm (4¾") to X. W–X is the line for the falls; cut along this line.

22   W–X cuts R–F at Y.

23   From Y measure down 3cm (1¼"), Z.

24   Join R–Z with a straight line and redraw in a gentle curve as drawn in red on diagram.

25   Cut along R–Q–S to separate the back and front sections. Cut off surplus paper.

The waist band

Note. The waist band is made in two pieces joined across the centre back with a strap and buckle. The top of the centre back seam is left open about 5cm (2") as marked on diagrams.

Diagrams 2, 2a & 2b
Strip of paper:
Required waist measurement + 3cm (1¼") for ease + 1.5cm (⅝") button stand

x

10cm (4")

26 Place the paper so that the distance from V to the bottom of the paper = 6cm (2¼") and the button stand extends beyond the centre front as Diagram 2.

27 Trace along R–Z.

28 The centre back of the waist band = 7cm (2¾"); join to R.

29 Cut off surplus paper.

30 Mark the position of buttons and button-holes at the centre front as Diagram 2b.

31 Mark the position of buttons for braces (filled in solid colour on diagram) if required.

32 Cut a strap approximately 17cm x 3cm (6¾" x 1¼"). This will be attached to the right-hand side of the back and correspond to a buckle on the left. Buttons are sometimes used instead of a buckle.

Diagram 3

33 From S measure up 15cm (6").

34 Secure a small piece of paper as diagram and draw a button stand 4cm (1½") wide parallel to the side seam; shape the bottom to match the back section.

35 Mark the position of the buttons and buttonholes.

36 Redraw the side seams to match.

Diagram 4

The diagram is drawn with the falls folded down and the front of the waist band in position to show the shape of the guards.

37 Cut a pattern for the guards as drawn in red. They do not reach the centre front of the waist band and are lower than the bottom of the fall. The guards will be sewn to the waist band.

Diagram 5

The diagram shows the falls in place.

38 The cut edges of the falls are finished with narrow strips ending in points.

39 Mark the position of the buttons and buttonholes at the top of the falls.

Note. The bottoms of the legs can be eased onto narrow bands to fit the small knee measurement or pulled in with drawstrings threaded through casings. Pockets can be inserted along the seams joining R–Z or on the waist band as drawn on Diagram 5. The back and sides of the breeches are pleated onto the waist band with the front left flat under the falls.

MID- TO LATE-18TH-CENTURY BREECHES

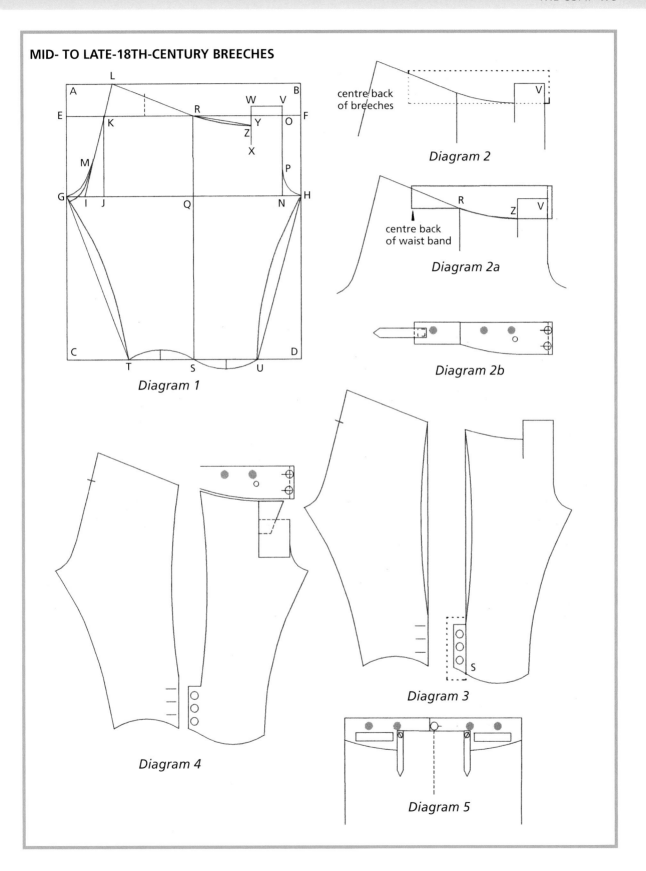

Diagram 1

centre back
of breeches

Diagram 2

centre back
of waist band

Diagram 2a

Diagram 2b

Diagram 3

Diagram 4

Diagram 5

8

Non-fashionable costume 17th–19th centuries

While the difference in cut between fashionable and non-fashionable costume was very marked in the 16th and early 17th centuries, it became much less so thereafter. The simple cut of the doublet and breeches worn by King Charles I and military buff coats could easily be adapted for working people, albeit in very different fabrics. This development was by no means instant; working people wore their clothes until they fell apart, by which time fashions may have changed several times. Pieter Bruegel would have recognised the clothes some of the men are wearing in the work painted by Adriaen Brouwer and Adriaen van Ostade a century later.

As no examples of early working men's clothes survive, the most useful reference is from paintings. The Dutch genre painters are invaluable for 17th-century reference as they painted all classes in engaged in everyday activities. By the 18th century there is much more source material; William Hogarth's work, particularly the etchings, is useful for the mid-18th century, but good reference for this period can also be found in unexpected places such as the paintings of George Stubbs. He is principally known for painting horses, but they are often accompanied by grooms, stable lads and other non-fashionable people. One invaluable source for the end of the 18th and early 19th centuries is W.H. Pyne's *Microcosm*, for which he drew working people in all manner of occupations: agricultural workers, pedlars, fishermen, smugglers, colliers, wheelwrights, butchers,

Compare this painting with the Mytens portrait of Charles I (on p. 124); the cut is similar but the fabric very different. This is an informal picture of a young man, not a king posing for an official portrait. This is how he would have looked in real life with some of his buttons undone, his collar untied and wrinkles in his thick hose. (*Young Man with a Pipe* by Pieter Codde.)

gypsies etc. From this time on, pictorial reference becomes more and more plentiful and a few actual garments still exist.

As early as the late 17th century, foreign visitors to Britain were struck by the quantity of good cloth worn by people of modest means. At first the yarn was spun at home and taken to the local weavers and dyers to be made into fabric, but gradually women found it more profitable to work for wages, initially in their own homes and later in factories. Factory-made fabrics were cheaper than those produced at home and were available to most people from shops, fairs or visiting pedlars. Daniel Defoe, writing in the 1720s, noted that there was little difference between the clothing of country- and townspeople. There was in fact little distinction between the general style of fashionable and non-fashionable costume. All but the very poorest had working clothes and best clothes. Usually working clothes were made of fustian and best clothes of wool. Working clothes might include garments relating to the wearer's occupation, such as the protective smocks worn by agricultural workers, and other protective garments like aprons and the trousers worn by sailors, but otherwise they were very similar in style to best clothes. This was noted by H. de Misson in his *Memoirs and Observations on his Travels in England, 1685*.

As a general rule, the poor living in cities, and particularly in London, bought second-hand, third-hand or even fourth-hand clothes, which were much cheaper than even the cheapest new garments. Some of the poorest people in Hogarth's paintings are wearing the tattered remains of once fashionable knee-length coats while others wear the non-fashionable short jackets which may well have been made for them.

The chief distinction between clothes of the rich and poor is in the quality of the fabric; the woollen fabrics of the relatively poor would have been very inferior to the broadcloth worn by prosperous farmers. Coats and jackets made specifically for people of limited means were cut economically and did not have, for instance, the fashionable huge cuffs of the middle years of the 18th century. The short practical jacket which had its origins in the buff coats of the mid-17th century has remained a basic part of working men's clothing almost to the present day.

The groom is wearing a livery coat made of good fabric but cut without any unnecessary features, not even pockets. (Detail from *Bandy* by George Stubbs.)

SIMPLE BUFF COAT

Basic upper body pattern (see p.24)
Extra paper as instructions

Diagram 1

1 Shorten the pattern by 6cm (2½") as diagram.

2 Add at least 1cm (⅜") on each side seam depending on what will be worn underneath the coat.

3 Measure out 1–1.5cm (⅜"–½") midway down the back armhole and reshape as diagram.

4 Cut a piece of paper = back waist measurement x required depth of skirt.

5 Cut a piece of paper = front waist measurement x required depth of skirt.

6 Divide the pieces of paper into four as Diagram 2.

Diagram 3

7 Flare the slashes so that the hem measures approximately 1½ times the waist measurement (see instructions on cutting flares in basic cutting techniques, p. 16).

8 Add 4cm (1½") parallel to the back side seam as diagram; this will fit underneath the front skirt.

Diagram 4

9 Place the back skirt pattern as diagram.

10 Place the front skirt pattern so that it meets the upper body pattern at the side seam but leaving a 1cm (⅜") gap at the centre front as diagram.

11 Add 1cm (⅜") button stand parallel to the centre front.

12 The coat can be made more elegant by shaping the centre back and side seams as diagram.

Diagram 5

Use the basic period sleeve pattern on p. 84 which can be modified by making the wrist narrower as diagram; wings and a stand collar could also be added.

Diagram 6

The finished basic pattern.

Note. When making up the coat, the side seams are joined as far as the overlap on the back pattern and the centre back skirt is left open.

If using leather, it is more economical to have the waist seam as Diagram 7.

The working man's coat can be drafted from these instructions without shortening the nape to waist measurement of the basic pattern.

SIMPLE BUFF COAT

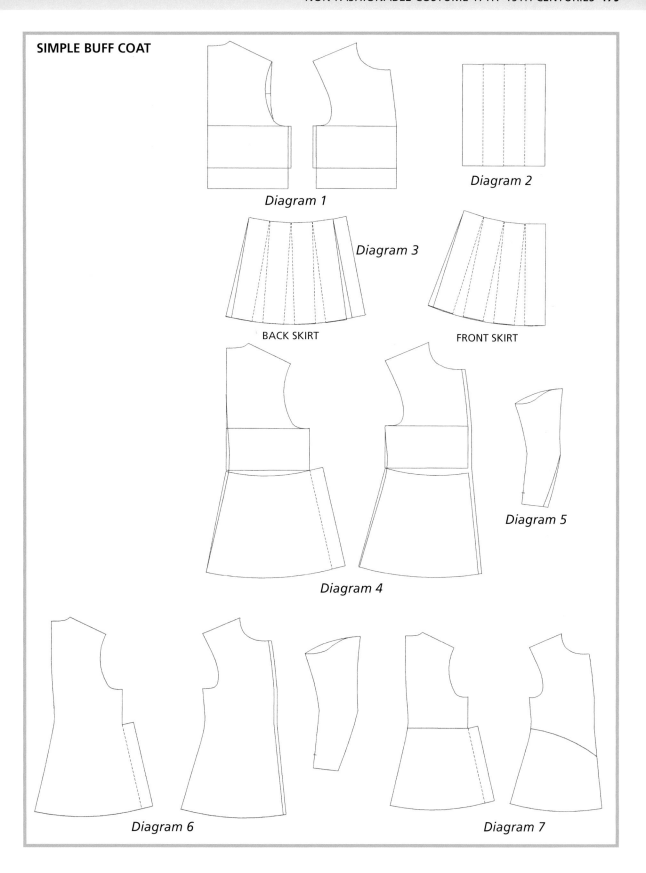

Diagram 1

Diagram 2

Diagram 3

BACK SKIRT

FRONT SKIRT

Diagram 5

Diagram 4

Diagram 6

Diagram 7

NON-FASHIONABLE BREECHES WITH FULL FALLS

Sheet of paper: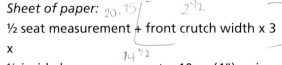
½ seat measurement + front crutch width x 3

x

½ inside leg measurement + 10cm (4") + rise

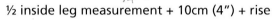

Diagram 1

1 Mark the corners of the paper A, B, C, D as diagram.

2 A–E = 9cm (3½").

3 Square E–F right across the paper.

4 E–G = rise measurement.

5 Square G–H right across the paper.

6 H–I = front crutch width.

7 From I square up to meet E–F at J, and curve as diagram.

8 G–K = front crutch width, K–L = front crutch width.

9 A–M = twice front crutch width.

10 Join M–K and curve as diagram.

11 N is midway between L–I.

12 Square down to meet C–D at O.

13 O–P = 5cm (2").

14 J–Q = ¼ waist measurement.

15 Join Q–M.

16 Join Q–P.

17 O–R = ½ small knee measurement: P–S = ½ small knee measurement.

18 Join R–H and S–G.

19 Measure R–H and check it is the same as S–G; make any necessary alteration at G.

20 From Q square up 4cm (2½") to T.

21 From J square up 4cm (2½") to U.

22 Join T–U.

23 Mark the position of two buttonholes as diagram.

24 Q–V = 15cm (6"): this is the side opening.

25 M–W = 5cm (2"): this is the centre back opening.

26 P–X and O–Y = 10cm (4"): for the leg opening.

27 Add a lap of 4cm (1½") x 12cm (5") to the back leg opening for buttons if required.

The waist band

Diagrams 2 & 2a

Strip of paper for the waist band:
½ waist measurement + 2.5cm (1")

x

6cm (2½")

28 Mark the corners of the paper A*, B*, C*, D* as diagram.

29 A*–E* = 3cm (1¼").

30 D*–F* = ¼ waist measurement + 2.5cm (1").

31 Join E*–F*.

32 Mark the position of buttons and buttonholes as diagrams.

33 Mark the position of eyelet holes as diagram.

34 Cut a rectangle of paper 12cm (5") x 15cm (6") for the falls shields.

Diagram 3

The top of the shield is stitched to the waist band from F*.

The side of the shield is stitched to the back side seam from Q to V.

The falls are buttoned onto the waist band which will be slightly higher than the top of the falls.

WORKING MAN'S BREECHES WITH FULL FALLS

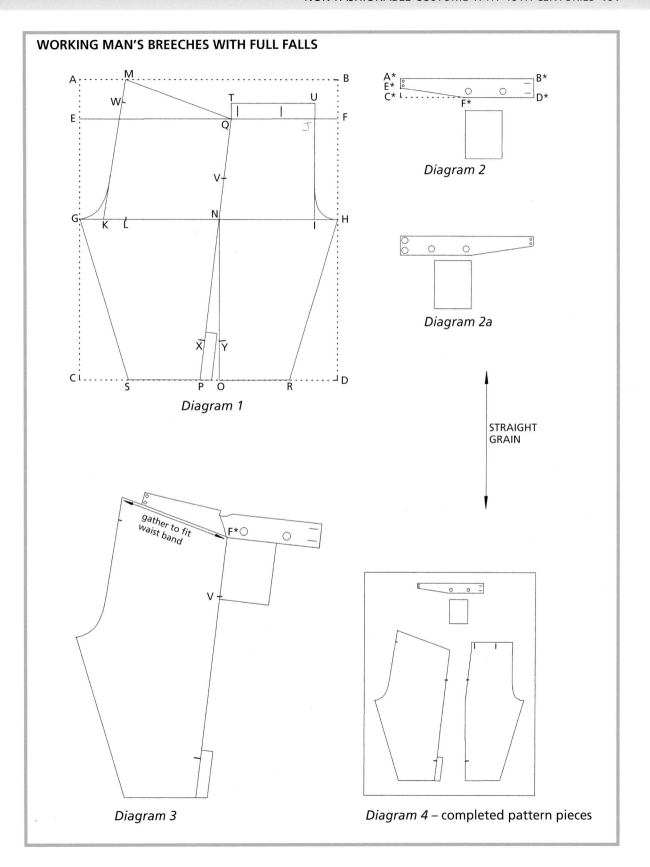

Diagram 1

Diagram 2

Diagram 2a

STRAIGHT
GRAIN

Diagram 3

Diagram 4 – completed pattern pieces

Breeches and trousers with half falls

The pattern uses the front section of the simple trousers pattern (p. 214) but can be applied to all trouser or breeches patterns Small pieces of paper

Diagram 4

35 Mark the waist of the pattern A, B as diagram.

36 C is midway between A–B.

37 Square down C–D = 12–15cm (5"–6") depending on size.

38 Join a strip of paper along C–B to raise it 3cm (1¼").

39 Mark the strip E = F as diagram.

Diagram 5

Half falls require bearers to support them when the falls are unbuttoned. These are cut in the following way.

40 Place a piece of paper under the pattern as diagram.

41 B–G = 2cm (¾").

42 From G square down 5cm (2") to H.

43 Draw H–D in a curve as diagram.

44 Mark the position of two buttonholes.

45 Mark the lines drawn in red on the diagram with a tracing wheel and cut off surplus paper as Diagram 6.

Note. When making up the garment C–D on the bearers will be sewn to C–D on the breeches.

46 Cut a strip of paper the measurement from E–D x 4cm (1½") as Diagram 6a, to bind the cut edges of the falls.

Diagram 7

The breeches will be attached to a straight waist band 5cm (2") deep. The falls button onto the waist band as diagram. Diagram 8 shows the falls in place.

This is presumably an idealised picture of workmen; their clothes are improbably clean and in good repair but the cut of the garments is realistic. (*Labourers* by George Stubbs.)

HALF FALLS

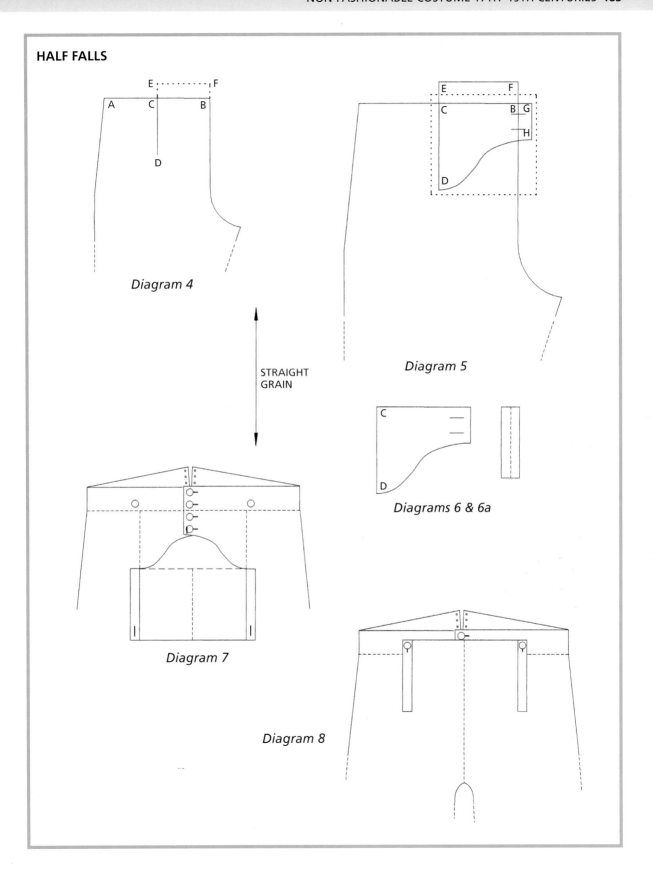

Diagram 4

Diagram 5

STRAIGHT
GRAIN

Diagrams 6 & 6a

Diagram 7

Diagram 8

WORKING MAN'S DOUBLE-BREASTED SHORT COAT

Basic coat block (see p. 140) with straightened centre front and no button stand modified as required

Sheet of paper:

Total width of coat block + 20cm (8")

x

Required length of coat from centre back neck to hem + 8cm (3")

Diagram 1

1 Join the front and back side seams with adhesive tape.

2 Draw the back seam from approximately ⅓ of the way down the back armhole to approximately midway along the back waist line.

3 Take out the required waist suppression, separate the pattern and correct the waist line and armhole as in basic coat blocks.

4 Add 5cm (2") to the bottom of both the pieces of pattern as diagram.

Diagram 2

5 Mark the sheet of paper A, B, C, D as diagram.

6 A–E = 5cm (2") square down to F at the bottom of the paper.

7 A–G = the new nape to waist measurement + 5cm (2") square across to H.

8 B–I = 10cm (4") square down to J.

9 Place the back pattern so that the centre back lies along E–F and the waist along G–H.

10 Place the front pattern so that the centre front lies along I–J and the front waist line along G–H.

11 Mark the back waist line K, L and the front waist line M as diagram.

Note. The front waist addition measurement can be added and H lowered to H* as in diagram.

12 H*–N = 15cm (6"). Square down to O.

13 O–P = 5cm (2"). Join N–P.

14 From M square down to Q.

15 From Q measure out 5cm (2") along C–D.

16 M–R = M–Q.

17 Join R–Q in a gentle curve.

18 From L square down to C–D.

19 L–S = M–Q.

20 From S square out 5cm (2").

21 L–T = L–S. Join S–T in a gentle curve.

22 K–U = 1–1.5cm (⅜"–⅝"). Redraw the centre back line as diagram.

23 Join U–F. U–V = L–S. Join V–S with a straight line.

24 From M square out M–W = 3cm (1¼").

25 From R square out R–X = 3cm (1¼").

26 Join W–X.

27 Repeat this from L and T on the back seam and U and V at the centre back.

28 Cut off surplus paper.

WORKING MAN'S DOUBLE-BREASTED SHORT COAT

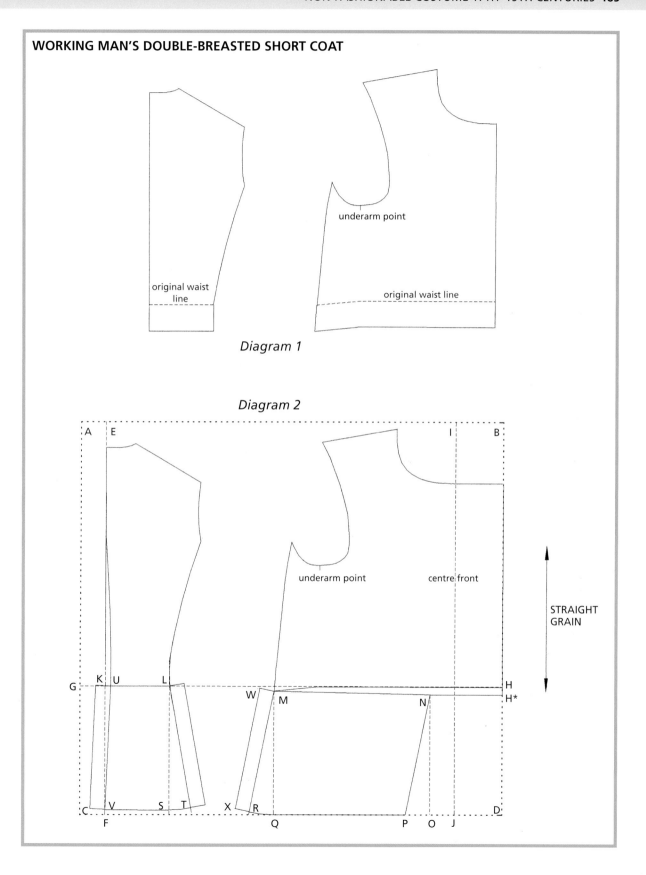

Diagram 1

Diagram 2

The collar

Diagram 3

> *Piece of paper:*
> Measurement round neck from centre back to centre front + 5cm (2")
>
> x
>
> 13.5cm (5¼")

29 Mark the paper A, B, C, D as diagram.

Diagram 4

30 A–E = 9.5cm (3¾").

31 From E square across to F.

32 C–G = measurement round neck from centre back to centre front.

33 C–H = ⅔ C–G.

34 F–I = 5cm (2").

35 Join I–H with a straight line and redraw in a gentle curve as diagram.

36 I–J = 2.5cm (1"). Square up J–K = 2cm (¾").

37 Join K–I with a straight line.

38 B–L = 7cm (2¾"). B–M = 1.5cm (⅝").

39 Join L–M in a gentle curve as diagram.

40 Join M–K with a straight line.

41 Cut off surplus paper to complete the pattern.

Diagram 5

The collar is cut in one piece with A–C on the fold.

The pocket flaps

> *Piece of paper:*
> 18cm (7") x 7cm (2¾")

Diagram 6

42 Mark the paper A, B, C, D as diagram.

43 E is midway between A–B. Square down to F.

44 A–G = 5cm (2"). B–H = 5cm (2").

45 Join G–F with a straight line and redraw in a curve.

46 Join H–F with a straight line and redraw in a curve.

47 Cut off surplus paper to complete the pattern.

To mark the buttons, buttonholes and position of the pockets

Diagram 7

48 The six buttonholes are evenly spaced 1.5cm (¾") from the outer edge.

49 The centres of the buttons are 4cm (3¼") from the centre line.

50 A button is marked at L/M at the top of each back opening.

51 The pocket flaps are placed 2.5cm (1") below the level of H–N and 5cm (4") from N–P.

The sleeves

Use the basic period sleeve pattern (see p. 84) drafted to fit the armhole of the coat.

The gardeners wear neat short, double-breasted coats and knee breeches. (Details from W.H. Pyne's *Microcosm*.)

WORKING MAN'S DOUBLE-BREASTED SHORT COAT – continued

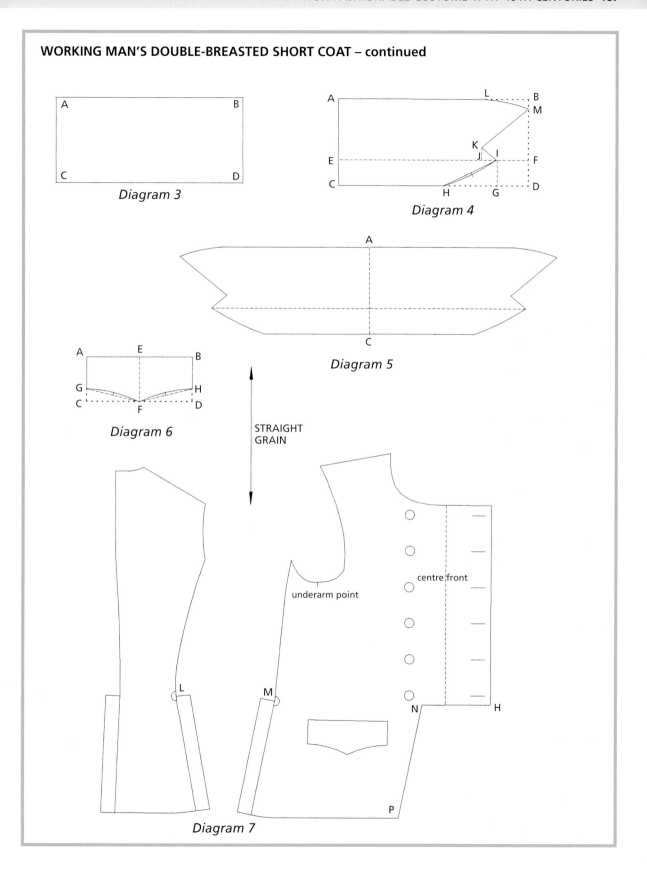

Diagram 3

Diagram 4

Diagram 5

Diagram 6

STRAIGHT
GRAIN

underarm point

centre front

Diagram 7

WORKING MAN'S SINGLE-BREASTED JACKET

Basic coat block (see p. 140) with straightened centre front and button stand

Sheet of paper:

Total width of pattern + 15cm (6")

x

Required length of jacket from centre back neck to hem + 10cm (4")

Diagram 1

1 Join the front and back side seams with adhesive tape.

2 Draw the back seam from approximately halfway down the back armhole to approximately midway along the back waist line.

3 Take out half the usual waist suppression.

Diagram 2

4 Separate the pattern and correct the waist line and armhole as in basic coat blocks.

5 Mark the new seam lines X and Y as diagram.

6 Z is the centre front neck.

Diagram 3

7 Mark the sheet of paper A, B, C, D as diagram.

8 Place the front pattern so that the edge of the button stand lies along B–D and the shoulder line is close to A–B.

9 Mark the centre front waist E. Draw round the pattern and remove it.

10 From E square right across the paper to F.

11 Place the back pattern as diagram.

12 Draw round the pattern and remove it.

13 E–G = required skirt length + front length addition.

14 Y–H = required skirt length.

15 Join G–H.

16 From H square out H–I = 2.5cm (1"). Join I–Y with a straight line.

17 Join X–J = required skirt length.

18 F–C = required skirt length. Join C–J.

19 From L square out J–K = 2.5cm (1"). Join X–K with a straight line.

Note. There is so little flare on the back seams that the hemlines can be drawn with straight lines.

20 Cut off surplus paper.

Note. The back is cut in one piece without a centre back seam and there are no openings at the bottoms of the seams. If preferred the bottoms of the seams can be left open from 5cm (2") below the waist line as with the working man's double-breasted jacket.

The sleeves

Use the basic period sleeve (see p. 84) drafted to fit the armhole of the jacket.

WORKING MAN'S SINGLE-BREASTED JACKET

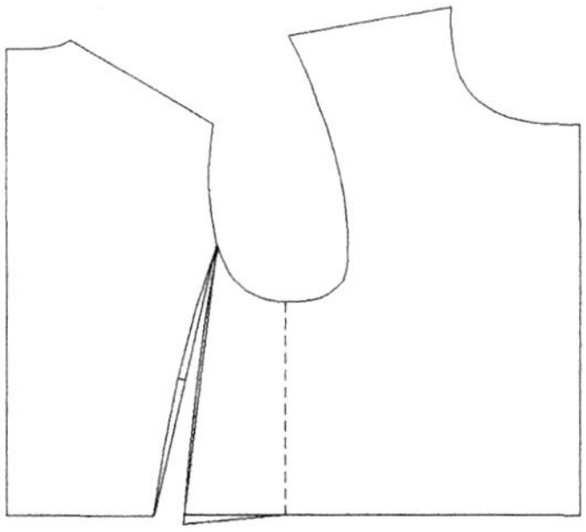

Diagram 1

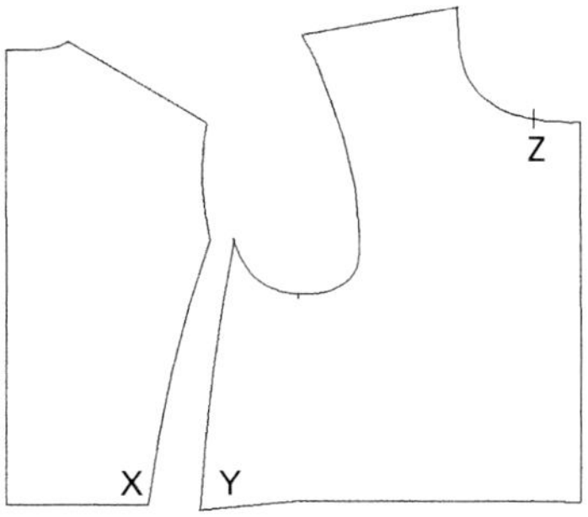

Diagram 2

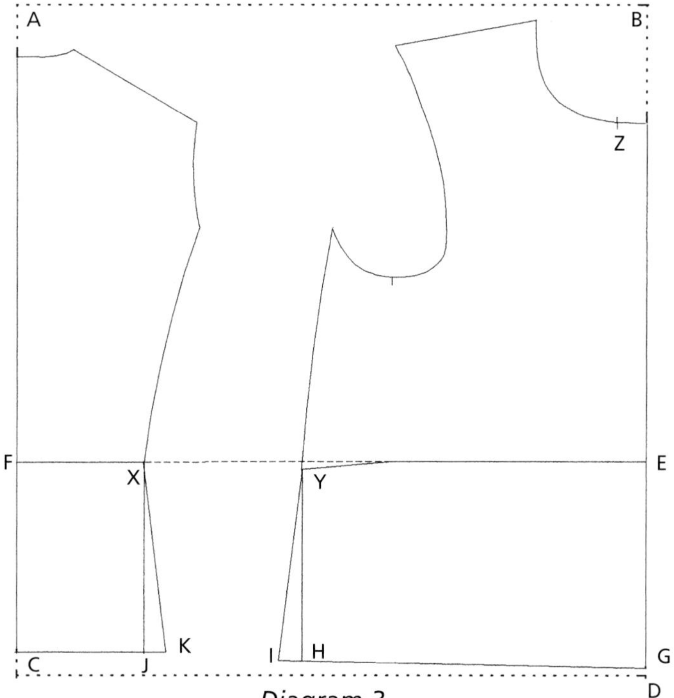

Diagram 3

Diagram 4

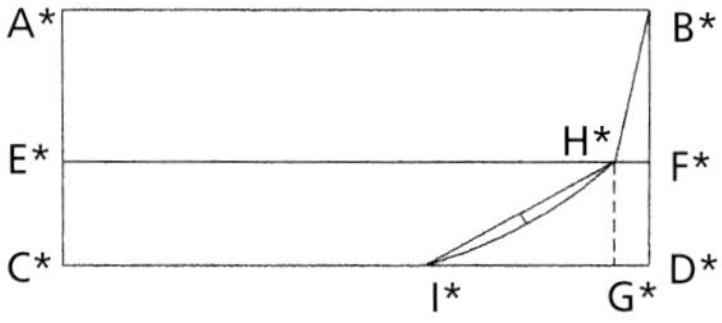

Diagram 5

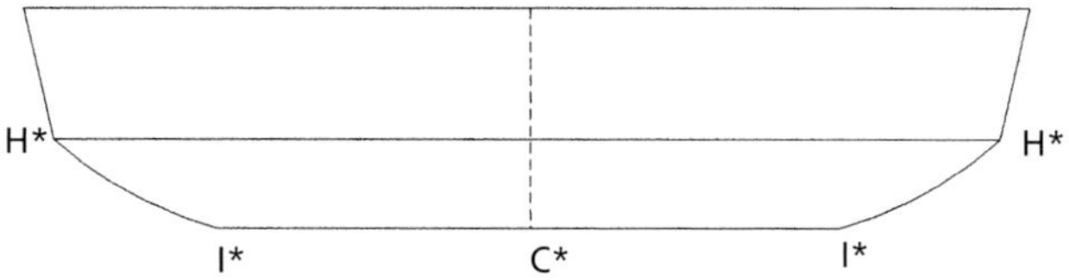

The collar

These simple short jackets were often collarless but sometimes had a simple collar as the following instructions.

Diagram 4

 Piece of paper:

 Measurement round the neck without button stand

 x

 10cm (4")

21 Mark the paper A*, B*, C*, D* as diagram.

22 A*–E* = 6cm (2⅜"). Square across to F*.

23 C*–G* = neck measurement minus 1.5cm (⅝").

24 From G* square up to meet E*–F* at H*.

25 Join H*–B* with a straight line.

26 C*–I* = ⅔ of the neck measurement.

27 Join I*–H* with a straight line and redraw in a gentle curve as diagram.

28 Cut off surplus paper to complete the pattern.

Diagram 5

C* marks the centre back of the collar. When the collar is cut out the edge H*–I*–C*–I*–H* is sewn round the neck starting 3cm (1¼") from the edge of the jacket at both sides (marked Z on Diagram 3).

Diagram 6

The pattern for pocket flaps is the same as for working man's double-breasted short coat (see p. 186).

The buttonholes are evenly spaced as diagram.

Diagram 7

The jacket can be cut without a centre back seam.

These fishermen are wearing single-breasted jackets with trousers. (Detail from W.H. Pyne's *Microcosm*.)

WORKING MAN'S SINGLE-BREASTED JACKET – continued

Diagram 6

Diagram 7

WORKING MAN'S SINGLE-BREASTED WAISTCOAT

Basic coat block (see p. 140) with shaped centre front and button stand modified as required. The waistcoat will not require as much additional width as coats unless it is to be worn over a very bulky shirt; 1–1.5cm (⅜"–⅝") would normally be sufficient.

Sheet of paper:

Total width of prepared block + 5cm (2")

x

Nape to waist measurement + required skirt length + 5cm (2")

Diagrams 1 & 1a

1 Join the front and back side seams with adhesive tape.

2 Draw the back seam from approximately halfway down the back armhole to approximately midway along the back waist line.

3 Take out half the usual waist suppression.

4 Mark the new seam lines X and Y as diagram.

Diagram 2

5 Mark the paper A, B, C, D as diagram.

6 Place the front pattern so that the edge of the button stand lies along B–D and the shoulder line is close to A–B.

7 Mark the centre front waist, E. From E, square right across the paper to F.

8 Draw round the pattern and remove it.

9 Place the back pattern as diagram. Draw around the pattern and remove it.

10 E–G = required skirt length + front length addition.

11 Y–H = required skirt length.

12 Join G–H.

13 From H square out H–I = 2.5cm (1"). Join I–Y.

14 F–J = required skirt length.

15 Square out J–K = F–X. Join K–X.

16 Cut off surplus paper.

Diagram 3

17 Join the shoulders as diagram.

18 L–M = 2cm (¾"). N–O = 6cm (2½"). Join M–O.

19 N–P = 2.5cm (1"). O–Q = 3.5 (1⅜").

20 Cut along M–Q–O.

Diagram 4

21 Join the side seams as diagram.

22 Lower the armhole 2.5cm (1") at the underarm point, R.

23 Redraw the armhole Q–P–R–Q in a smooth continuous curve.

WORKING MAN'S SINGLE-BREASTED WAISTCOAT

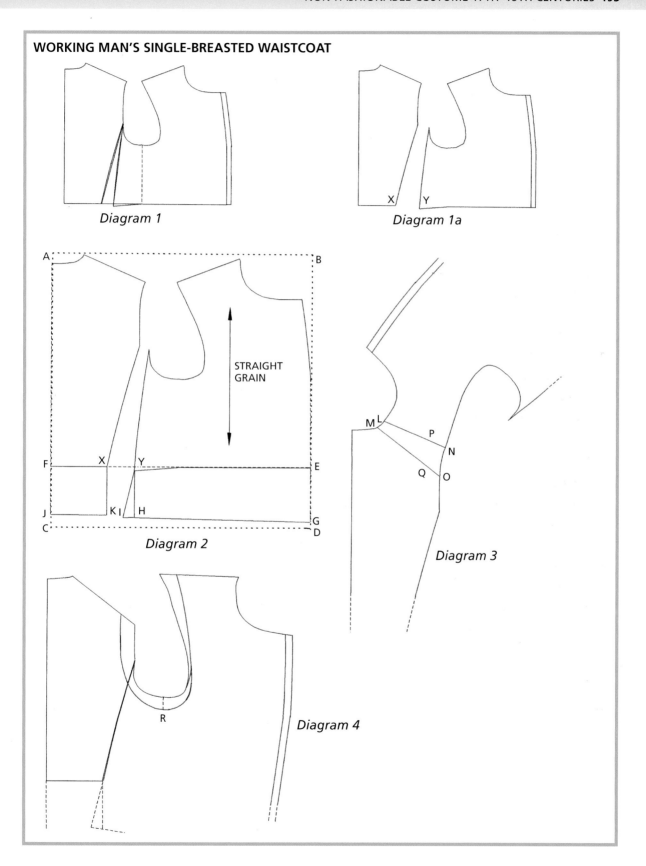

Diagram 1

Diagram 1a

STRAIGHT
GRAIN

Diagram 2

Diagram 3

Diagram 4

The collar

Diagram 5
  Strip of paper:
  Neck measurement of pattern minus
  3cm (1½″)
  x
  3cm (1½″)

  24 Mark the paper A, B, C, D as diagram.

Diagrams 6, 6a & 6b
  25 Divide the paper in three and mark the divisions E–F and G–H as diagram.
  26 A–I = .5cm (¼″) join I–C.
  27 In the same way deduct .5cm (½″) either side of E and join to F and .5cm (½″) either side of G and join to H.
  28 D–J = 1cm (⅜″). Join H–J and redraw in a gentle curve.
  29 Cut and rejoin the pattern as Diagram 6a.
  30 Smooth out the corners as Diagram 6b.

Note. When making up the waistcoat the collar is sewn 3cm (1¼″) from the front edges.

The pocket

Cut a strip 15cm (6″) x 3cm (1¼″) for the pocket welt.

The buttons and buttonholes

Space the buttons and buttonholes evenly starting about 2cm (¾″) from the neck.

Diagram 7
The pieces of the waistcoat, the back section cut without a centre seam and the pockets drawn in position.

This illustration shows overcoats being worn over trousers. (Detail of fishermen from W.H. Pyne's *Microcosm*.)

WORKING MAN'S SINGLE-BREASTED WAISTCOAT – continued

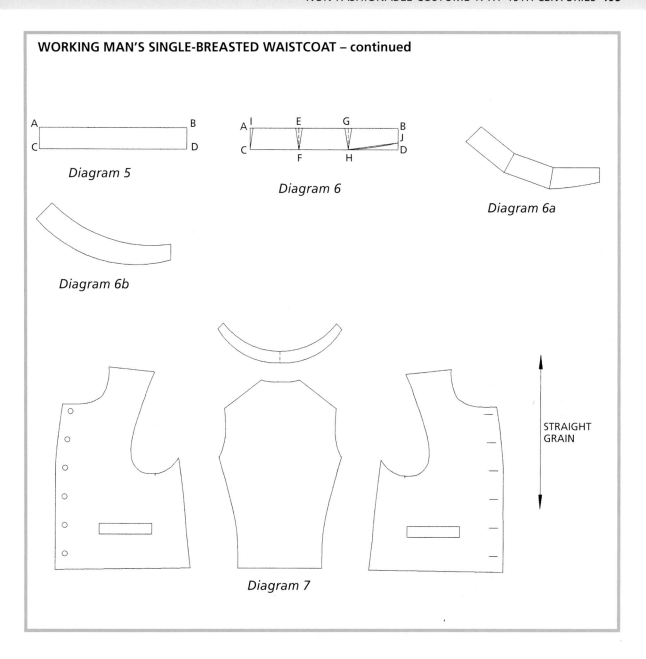

Diagram 5

Diagram 6

Diagram 6a

Diagram 6b

STRAIGHT GRAIN

Diagram 7

NON-FASHIONABLE COAT VARIATIONS

Working men's coats were cut as economically as practicality would allow. The long coat was worn for warmth; cut just wide enough at the hem not to restrict movement and not to require vents in the seams. The collar could be cut from a simple rectangle and sometimes there were one or two capes for added protection.

Long coat

Using either the double- or single-breasted pattern (see pp. 184 and 188) with the chest line marked drafted one size larger if it is to be worn over bulky clothes.

Diagrams 1 & 1a

1 Mark the pattern A, B, C, D, E, F, G, H as diagrams.

2 Increase the pattern to the required length by adding extra paper as diagrams.

3 Mark I at the bottom left-hand corner of the paper on the back pattern.

4 Mark J at the bottom right-hand corner of the front pattern.

5 Continue the side seams to the bottom of the paper, K and L.

6 E–M = approximately ¾ of E–F.

7 From M square up to N, 5cm (2") above the chest line and join to approximately ⅓ of the way up the armhole, O as Diagram 1.

8 From M square down to the bottom of the paper P.

9 Q is midway between L–J. R is midway between C–D.

10 Join Q–R and continue 5cm (2") above the chest line to S and join to approximately ⅓ of the way up the armhole, T as Diagram 1a.

11 Cut along P–M–N–O and Q–R–S–T.

Diagrams 2 & 2a

12 Spread the back section, pivoting it at O, adding 10cm (4") to the hem measurement.

13 Spread the front section, pivoting at T, adding 20cm (8") to the hem measurement.

14 Cut off surplus paper from the side seams.

Note. This will make a long coat wide enough at the hem to not need vents for a man of average height.

15 Secure pieces of paper under the slashes with adhesive tape.

Diagram 3

16 Place the front and back sections so that F and G match.

17 Measure E–I and repeat this measurement from M, F, G and H and draw the hem in a smooth curve.

18 Mark the position of extra buttons, buttonholes and the pockets as Diagram 4.

The sleeves

Use the basic period sleeve pattern (see p. 84) drafted to fit the armhole of the coat.

The collar

19 Measure around the neck of the front and back patterns and cut a strip of paper this measurement minus 3cm (1¼") x 13–18cm (5"–7").

WORKING MEN'S COAT VARIATIONS – LONG COAT

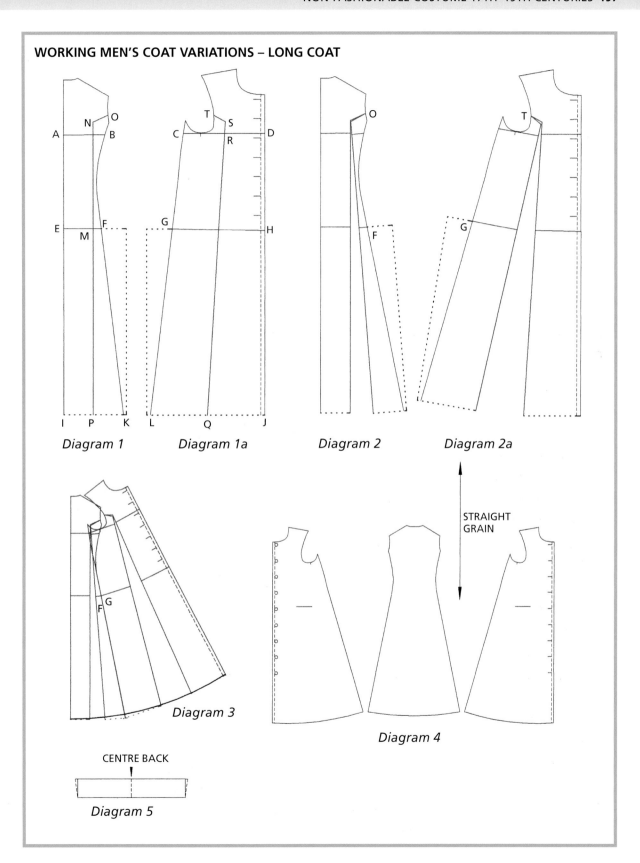

Diagram 1

Diagram 1a

Diagram 2

Diagram 2a

STRAIGHT GRAIN

Diagram 3

Diagram 4

CENTRE BACK

Diagram 5

Note. This will make the simple collar often drawn in W.H. Pyne's *Microcosm*. To make a slightly more sophisticated collar add 2–3cm (¾"–1¼") to the outer edge as dashed lines on Diagram 5.

Tail coat

The pattern for working man's double-breasted short coat (see p. 184) can be adapted to make a simple knee-length tail coat by lengthening the skirts as Diagrams 1 & 1a.

Diagrams 2 & 2a show the finished pattern.

Sleeve variations

The basic period sleeve pattern (see p. 84) can be adapted as follows:

Diagram 3
The back seam can be left open to make a short vent about 10cm (4") which can be buttoned as diagram or left open.

Diagrams 4 & 4a
Cuffs of various depths can be added to the sleeves. If the cuff is small, it can be a continuation of the sleeve.

20 Join a piece of paper to the end of the sleeve pattern.

21 Fold the paper under the pattern as diagram.

22 Draw the cuff making it a little wider than the sleeve as diagram.

23 Mark the line with a tracing wheel.

24 Unfold the paper and cut off the surplus.

Diagram 4b
Button holes can be made in the outer section of the cuff and buttoned to the sleeve. This is generally done on deep cuffs.

Note. If it is necessary to make the cuff separate from the sleeve, it should include part of the sleeve as indicated in red on Diagram 4a so that there is a fold rather than a join at the wrist.

The man's coat comes below the knee and buttons straight down the front; it has a large collar and modest cuffs. It is being worn over a knee-length smock. (Detail of farmer's man with greyhounds from W.H. Pyne's *Microcosm*.)

WORKING MAN'S TAIL COAT AND SLEEVE VARIATIONS

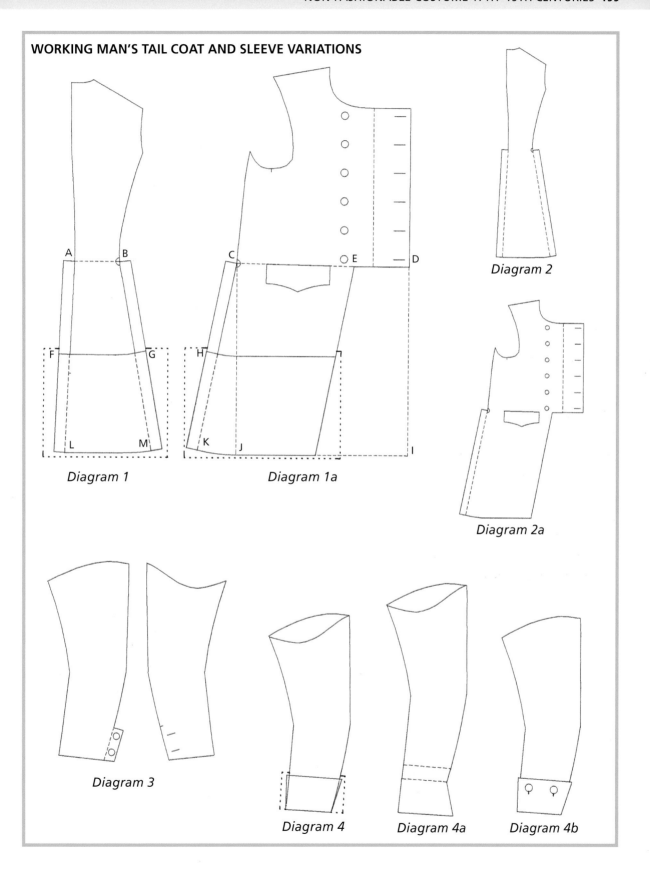

Diagram 1

Diagram 1a

Diagram 2

Diagram 2a

Diagram 3

Diagram 4

Diagram 4a

Diagram 4b

9

Shirts

The mediaeval working man's shirt was cut from a loom-width rectangle of fabric, the back and front in one piece, and two straight pieces for the sleeves. A hole was cut big enough for the head to get through which had to be sufficiently rounded for the edges to be turned in neatly. The shirt usually reached mid-calf and had side vents at the hem. The sleeves were rather wide and had to be rolled up for work but this simple cut made a perfectly practical garment. This is the type of shirt worn by Bruegel's peasants.

By the mid-16th century, fashionable shirts were still composed of rectangular pieces but had acquired collars, cuffs and gussets and developed the shape that was to remain, with few alterations, until the middle of the 19th century. Precise dating is impossible for these innovations as they were not so radical as to make a great deal of difference and old styles continued to be worn, particularly amongst the unfashionable.

As all the parts of the shirt were rectangular they might be expected to fit neatly into a rectangle of fabric. The reason that this is not so is that they were made in batches of six or a dozen. Although they still did not fit into an exact rectangle, it was much more economical to cut them in batches. As there was a great variety of fabric widths, an ideal one could be chosen for each different shirt size. The pattern pieces were marked by drawing threads out of the fabric and cutting along the resulting rows of little holes; the seam allowance was counted as so many threads. As all the pieces were on the grain of the fabric, the shirt did not distort when laundered. The upper body of working men's shirts was reinforced either with a complete layer reaching from half way up the back to below the front opening or wide strips over the shoulders. These reinforcement pieces were called linings.

As a general rule the proportion for cutting shirts until the end of the 19th century was as follows:

This shirt is cut in three pieces – one rectangular piece for the body and two smaller rectangles for the sleeves. The neck hole seems to be finished but the hem and the sleeve ends are raw. (Detail from *Netherlandish Proverbs* by Pieter Bruegel the Younger.)

- **Shirt length**: from the nape of the neck to the back of the knee.
- **Shirt width**: the width of the fabric.
- **Sleeve length**: half the length from shoulder to knee.
- **Collar**: the same length as the sleeves and the cuffs were half this length.

These proportions are only a rough guide and would need to be adjusted for unusual sizes. The present-day average size for a man's collar is between 40–44cm (16"–17") and even allowing for seam allowance and the button stand this is likely to be less than half the shirt length. It would, however, be a good proportion for working men's shirts which should not fit too closely round the neck.

The big change came in the middle of the 19th century when fashion-able shirts were cut much closer to the body and yokes were introduced. The following is quoted from *Cassell's Household Guide* c.1880:

> Shirt making at home has fallen into disesteem, a result chiefly referable to two reasons. First, on the part of the men, because home-made shirts are so ill cut as to be uncomfortable, untidy, and soon soiled; second, because the labour of shirt making is close and unpleasant, and, undoubtedly, trying to woman kind.

> The supremacy shop-made shirts, as they are called, have obtained over home-made, is due to the superiority of their cut. Home-made almost invariably "bag," as the expressive term is, at the front or breast. All the shop shirts are narrow there. The patent shirts are very narrow in the breast, and short on the shoulders, bringing the top of the sleeve, which is roomy, on the shoulder and forward towards the chest. The result of this is a perfectly free play of the arms without moving the shirt front. In the home-made shirt, also, there is too much room given about the collar-bone, and the front is too long; hence a riding up from the waist, and a lopping down from the throat.

The yoke was an important innovation as it did away with the need for neck gussets and gave a much smoother line. Shaped armholes and sleeve heads also improved the fit and did not require underarm gussets. Another innovation which has continued to the present day was to move the wrist opening from the underarm sleeve seam so that it was in line with the little finger. This was brought about because the cuffs were fastened with cufflinks and it was awkward to have them under the wrist when writing.

EARLY WORKING MEN'S SHIRTS

Measurements for early working men's shirts

- **Length**: variable from mid-thigh to mid-calf.
- **Width**: chest measurement + at least 40cm (16").
- **Minimum neck opening**: measurement round head + 5cm (2") average 65cm (26").
- **Sleeve length**: measure from nape of neck to shoulder point to wrist with arm slightly bent. This can be calculated from the charts by adding ½ back neck width + shoulder length + sleeve length

Diagram 1

Layout of simple shirt as worn by Bruegel's peasants in *The Battle between Carnival and Lent* consisting of back and front cut in one piece and two sleeves. The fabric would have been woven or bought the required width.

Diagram 2

The shirt made up. The side seams left open below the marks.

Diagram 3

The same shape as Diagram 1 but with a T-shaped neck opening.

Diagram 4

Sleeves narrowed to the wrist and with a horizontal slit for the neck opening.

Diagram 5

Shirt made from wider fabric; wide neck opening cut and gathered into a narrow band. Side seams left open below the marks.

LATER WORKING MEN'S SHIRTS

The basic shirt pattern which follows was worn by working men with little variation at least until the end of the 18th century when the neck and wrist bands were replaced by cuffs and collars. Sometimes the front and back were cut in separate pieces and the upper body was reinforced with linings. The linings were sometimes small patches reinforcing the shoulders where there was most wear; otherwise the entire body part was double from halfway down the back to under the front opening. When the back and front were cut in one piece, the linings were held in place with stab stitching along the shoulders.

BASIC SHIRT PATTERN

The pieces of the basic shirt

- **A** Body of the shirt, front and back in one piece – sometimes the back is slightly longer than the front. The back and the front can be cut in two pieces.
- **B** Sleeve: cut 2.
- **C** Underarm gusset: cut 2.
- **D** Neckband: cut 1.
- **E** Wristband: cut 2.
- **F** Neck gusset: cut 2 and fold in half or cut 1 and cut in half.
- **G** Side seam gusset: cut 2.

EARLY WORKING MEN'S SHIRTS

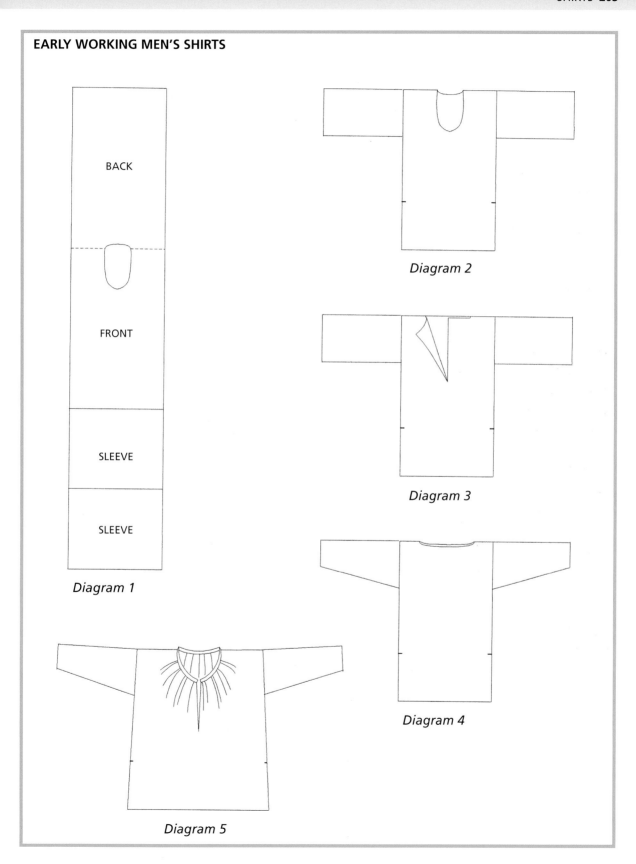

BACK

FRONT

SLEEVE

SLEEVE

Diagram 1

Diagram 2

Diagram 3

Diagram 4

Diagram 5

To calculate the sleeve length, measure from the nape of the neck to the fingertips with arm stretched out, then deduct the measurement C–K (Diagram 1).

Shirt to fit average sizes

Body of the shirt A

1 A–B = width of shirt – (the width of the fabric).

2 A–C = length of the back.

3 Square C–D right across the fabric.

4 C–E = length of the front.

5 Square across E–F and cut along this line.

6 G is midway between C–D.

7 Square down G–H = 30cm (12").

8 C–I and D–J = shoulder length – 23cm (9").

9 I–K and J–L = length of side of the neck gussets – 6cm (2½").

Neck gussets F

10 M, N, O = neck gusset – 7cm (3") square.

Neck band D

11 Cut the neck band, neck size + 2cm (¾") seam allowance + 5cm (2").

When making up the shirt cut along the lines K–L and G–H. The slit G–H is turned in and hemmed all the way around. Fold the gussets in half along M–O and fit in the cuts K–I and J–L. The neckline is gathered to fit the neckband.

The sleeves B

12 P–Q = sleeve width.

13 P–R = sleeve length (measurement as note above minus measurement C–K on the body of the shirt).

14 R–T and S–U = 10cm (4") for the wrist opening.

The wristband E

15 Cut the wrist band 22cm (9") x 5cm (2").

The underarm gussets C

16 Cut 2 underarm gussets 20cm x 20cm (8" x 8").

To make up the sleeves turn in narrow hems between R–T and S–U. Gather R–S to fit the wristband. Attach the wrist-band. Gather P–Q to 26cm (10") leaving seam allowance at either end.

Diagram 2

On the body of the shirt, mark points 13cm (5") either side of C and D; join the tops of the sleeves between these points. Attach the gussets. Sew the side seams leaving approximately 23cm (9") open at the bottom. Attach the side seam gussets in the same way as the neck gussets. Hem round the bottom edges and the slits. Make the fastenings as required.

Diagram 3

The completed shirt.

Note. If linings are required they should be sewn to the inside of the shirt as indicated with dashed blue and red lines. The linings drawn in red should be stab stitched along the shoulder line to keep them in place. Sometimes straps are used along the shoulders as drawn in blue dashed lines on Diagram 2.

BASIC SHIRT

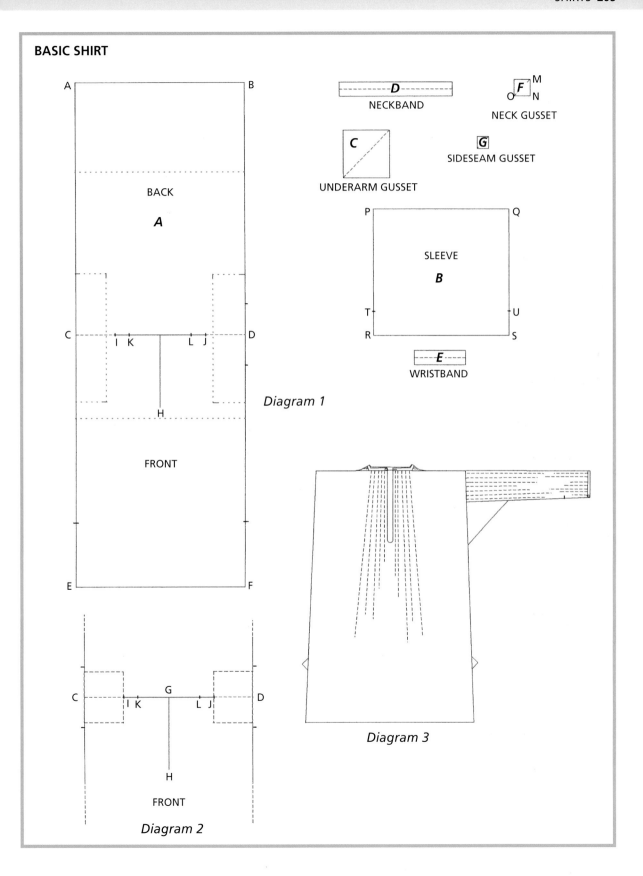

NECKBAND

NECK GUSSET

UNDERARM GUSSET

SIDESEAM GUSSET

BACK

A

SLEEVE

B

FRONT

WRISTBAND

H

Diagram 1

FRONT

Diagram 2

Diagram 3

SIZES FOR LATE 19th-CENTURY SHIRTS						
CHEST SIZE	SHIRT WIDTH	NECK SIZE	COLLAR SIZE	½ BACK YOKE WIDTH	ARMHOLE DEPTH	CUFF LENGTH
90cm	140cm	36.75cm	38cm	20cm	19cm	25cm
105cm	155cm	40.75cm	42cm	22.5cm	21cm	26cm
120cm	160cm	45.75cm	45.75cm	24cm	23cm	27cm
130cm	180cm	46.75cm	47cm	26.5cm	24cm	28cm

CHEST SIZE	SHIRT WIDTH	NECK SIZE	COLLAR SIZE	½ BACK YOKE WIDTH	ARMHOLE DEPTH	CUFF LENGTH
34"–36"	55"	15"	15½"	8"	7½"	9¾"
38"–42"	60"	16"	16½"	9"	8¼"	10¼"
44"–46"	65"	17"	17½"	9½"	9"	10¾"
48"–50"	70"	18"	18½"	10½"	9½"	11¼"

Note. Take the sleeve length from the main measurement chart minus ½ the cuff depth.

CHEST SIZE	MEASUREMENT 1 A–B and M–O	MEASUREMENT 2 A–C	MEASUREMENT 3 M–P	CHEST SIZE	MEASUREMENT 1 A–B and M–O	MEASUREMENT 2 A–C	MEASUREMENT 3 M–P
90cm	8cm	6cm	4cm	34"–36"	3⅛"	2⅜"	1½"
102cm	8.5cm	6.5cm	4.25cm	38"–42"	3⅜"	2½"	1¾"
120cm	9cm	7cm	4.5cm	44"–46"	3½"	2¾"	2¼"
130cm	9.5cm	7.5cm	4.75cm	48"–50"	3¾"	3"	2"

MID-19TH-CENTURY FASHIONABLE SHIRT

2 sheets of paper:
¼ required width + 5cm (2")
x
Required length of shirt (not including the back yoke measurement of 4cm (1⅝") for all sizes)
Piece of paper:
½ sleeve width
x
Sleeve length
Small pieces of paper for the yoke, cuffs etc.

The yoke pattern

Piece of paper:
½ back yoke width + 5cm (2")
x measurement 2 from chart + 4cm (1⅝")

Diagram 1

1 Mark A at the top left-hand corner of the paper.

2 A–B = measurement 1 on the chart.

3 A–C = measurement 2 on the chart.

4 C–D is the centre back.

5 Join B–C with a straight line and redraw curving 1.5cm (⅝") below the mid-point.

6 Mark D at bottom left-hand corner.

7 D–E = ½ back yoke length.

8 From E square up to F – 6.5cm (2½") for all sizes.

9 Draw front yoke line from B through F to G at edge of the paper.

10 E–H = 1.5cm (⅝") for all sizes.

11 Join D–H with a straight line.

12 Cut off surplus paper to complete the yoke pattern as Diagram 2.

MID-19th-CENTURY FASHIONABLE SHIRT

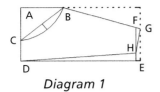

Diagram 1

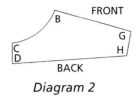

Diagram 2

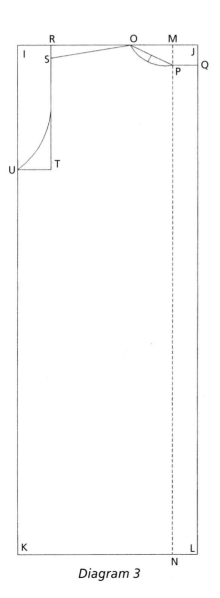

Diagram 3

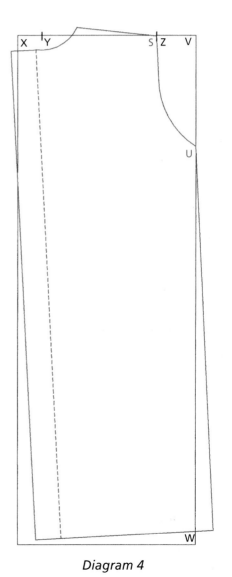

Diagram 4

The front pattern

Diagram 3

13 Mark the corners of one of the large sheets of paper I, J, K, L as diagram.

14 J–M = 5cm (2"); from M square down to meet K–L at N.

15 M–O = measurement 1 on the chart (A–B on the yoke draft).

16 M–P = measurement 3 on the chart, P–N is the centre front of the shirt; from P square out to meet J–L at Q.

17 Join O–P with a straight line and redraw curving 1.5cm (⅝") below the mid-point.

18 O–R = B–G on the yoke pattern.

19 From R square down to S – 2.5cm (1") for all sizes.

20 Join O–S.

21 From R square down R–T = armhole depth + 2.5cm (1").

22 From T square out to meet I–K at U.

23 Draw the front armhole S–U curving the lower part as diagram.

24 Cut off surplus paper to complete the front pattern as Diagram 3.

The back pattern

Diagram 4

On the second large sheet of paper, mark the right-hand edge V–W as diagram.

25 X–Y = 5cm.

26 Y–Z = D–H on the yoke pattern.

27 Reverse the front pattern (drawn in red) and place so that S meets Z and U touches V–W.

28 Trace round the front armhole and remove the front pattern.

29 Cut off surplus paper to complete the back pattern.

Shaping the body

Diagrams 5 & 5a

The sides of the fashionable shirt were shaped in slightly and the tail rounded. This was done by folding the back and front in half, placing one on top of the other and cutting through all four layers. On the diagrams, the sides are curved in 2.5cm (1") at waist level taking the line the same distance below the waist as above. The side seams are sewn to the bottom of the curve where a small triangular gusset, about 4cm (2⅜") including seam allowances, should be inserted. The corners of the shirt are rounded off as much or as little as preferred.

Diagram 5a

The double shirt fronts are approximately half as wide as the cross chest measurement of the shirt and 25–30cm (10"–12") long. Draw the pattern as diagram adding a button stand of 1cm (⅜"). Place a small piece paper under the pattern and trace through. Cut off surplus paper Diagram 6.

The front can be curved as Diagrams 7 & 8 and either shape can be embellished with lace, embroidery, frills or tucks.

The neck band

Diagrams 9 & 9a

Strip of paper: a total measurement of the neck line on the yoke (B–C on Diagram 2) and double shirt front with button stand + 2.5cm (1")

30 Mark the paper A, B, C, D as diagram.

31 E is midway between B–D.

MID-19th-CENTURY FASHIONABLE SHIRT – continued

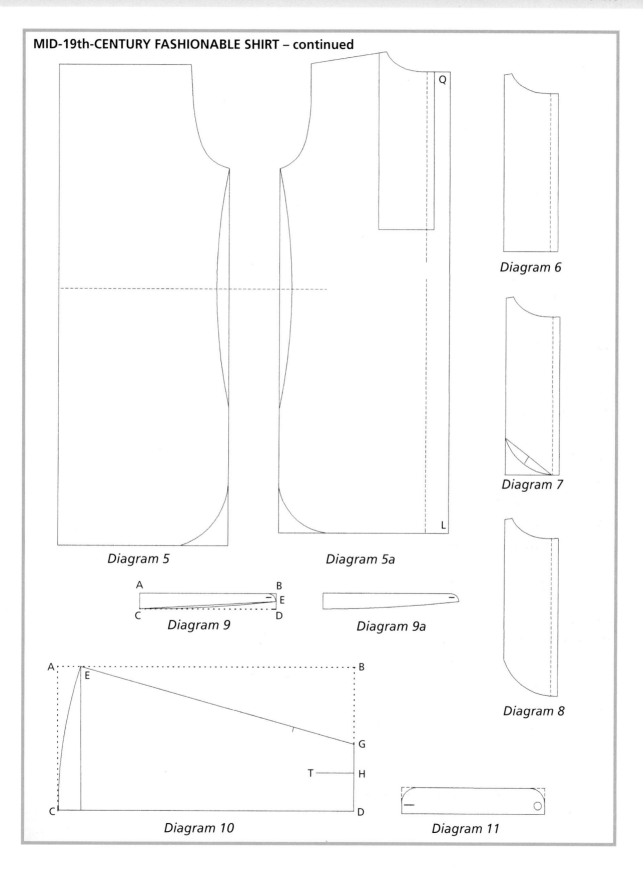

Diagram 5

Diagram 5a

Diagram 6

Diagram 7

Diagram 8

Diagram 9

Diagram 9a

Diagram 10

Diagram 11

32 Join E–C with a straight line and redraw with a gentle curve as diagram.

33 Round off the corner at B and mark a small buttonhole as diagram.

34 Cut off surplus paper to complete the pattern as Diagram 9a.

The sleeves

Only half the pattern need be drafted as the sleeve is symmetrical and can be cut on the fold

Sheet of paper:

Required sleeve length (minus ½ cuff depth)

x

½ armhole measurement

Diagram 10

35 Mark the corners of the paper A, B, C, D as diagram.

36 A–E = sleeve head depth.

37 Join C–E in a gentle curve.

38 D–G = required length of cuff + 5cm (2").

39 Join E–G with a straight line.

40 G–H = 9cm (3½") for all sizes.

41 Square out H–T = 12cm (4¾") for all sizes.

42 Cut off surplus paper to complete the pattern.

The cuff

Strip of paper:

Required cuff length x cuff depth

Diagram 11

43 Round off the top corners as diagram.

44 Mark the position of button and buttonhole or two buttonholes if cuff links are to be worn.

Making up the shirt

When cutting out the shirt, the centre back and Q–L are cut on the fold. Two yokes are cut with C–D on the fold. The neckband is cut with A–C and A–B on the fold. When making up the shirt, the double fronts should be sewn to the shirt front first as follows.

Diagram 12 – drawn with seam allowances added

45 On the wrong side of the shirt place the fronts so that the centre front lines match the centre frontlines on the shirt, marked with dashed lines on the diagram.

46 Stitch .75cm (⅜") from the centre front lines, marked with dotted lines on the diagram.

47 Cut away the area outlined in red and snip into the corners as diagram.

Diagram 13

48 Turn the fronts to the right side and press.

49 Turn in the edges of the sides marked A–A and stitch down.

50 Make 3 small vertical buttonholes down the centre fronts lines (for shirt studs) as diagram.

Diagram 14

51 Bring the right front over the left matching the buttonholes exactly and tack down so that a pleat forms below the shirt fronts.

52 Cut a narrow strip of fabric to cover the raw edges, make narrow turnings and stitch in place as diagram.

53 Cut a second strip and stitch on the inside.

MID-19th-CENTURY FASHIONABLE SHIRT – continued

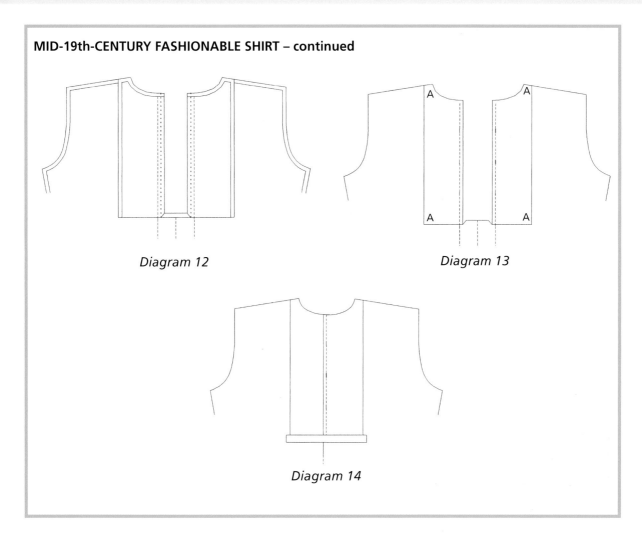

Diagram 12

Diagram 13

Diagram 14

Note. If curved shirt fronts are being made, curved strips will be necessary to cover the raw edges.

54 Once the shirt fronts are in place, the yoke can be attached.

55 Gather or pleat the back to fit the back yoke – the gathers or pleats can be central or distributed over the shoulder blades.

56 Stitch the second yoke on the inside to cover the raw edges.

57 Make up the neckband and stitch in place.

58 Cut along the wrist opening H–T and either turn in a narrow hem all round and reinforce T with a small gusset as at the side seams or a buttonhole stitch bar.

59 Sew the sleeves into the armholes.

60 Sew the sleeve seams and side seams in a continuous line.

61 Make narrow turnings round the shirt tails.

62 Sew the small side gussets in place to reinforce the ends of the side seams.

63 Gather or pleat the ends of the sleeves to fit the cuffs.

64 Make up the cuffs and attach to the sleeves.

10

Two miscellaneous patterns

The patterns for cloaks belong to many periods and simple trousers have been worn by sailors since the Middle Ages as they gave protection from rope burns when climbing the rigging and could be rolled up to wade ashore. Trousers did not become fashionable until the early 19th century but have been worn by the non-fashionable since at least the 17th century.

BASIC CLOAKS

The ubiquitous long, protective cloak which has been worn in Europe since at least the Middle Ages, is cut from a regular circle without making allowance for the shoulders. This means that the hem of the cloak is shorter at the sides than the front and back but this is not conspicuous in a full length garment. Very few fabrics were wide enough for a full-length cloak to be cut in one piece. If the cloak is to be made from wool or similar fabric, it can usually be cut in two pieces needing only one seam. If there is no gathering at the neck, it must be at least ¾ of a circle in order to meet comfortably down the centre front.

It is unnecessary to cut a pattern for a simple cloak; unless a great many are being made the shape can be drawn straight onto the fabric. It will be necessary to leave seam allowance round the neck when the cloak is cut out.

Note. See Calculating Circles on p. 22.

Using wide fabric

Without nap, pile or one-directional pattern

Diagram 1

1 Open out the fabric and press out the central fold if necessary.

2 Measure the width of the fabric.

3 A is the top left-hand corner of the fabric.

4 Measure down A–B = width of the fabric.

5 B is the centre of the semicircle which will form half the cloak.

6 From B measure out to establish the hemline as diagram.

Diagram 2

7 Cut out the section and place it on the fabric as diagram.

8 Using this section as a pattern, cut round the circumference.

9 Calculate the radius of the neckline.

10 From B draw the neckline in the same way as the hemline.

11 Mark the neckline onto the first section with a tracing wheel and carbon paper.

BASIC CLOAKS

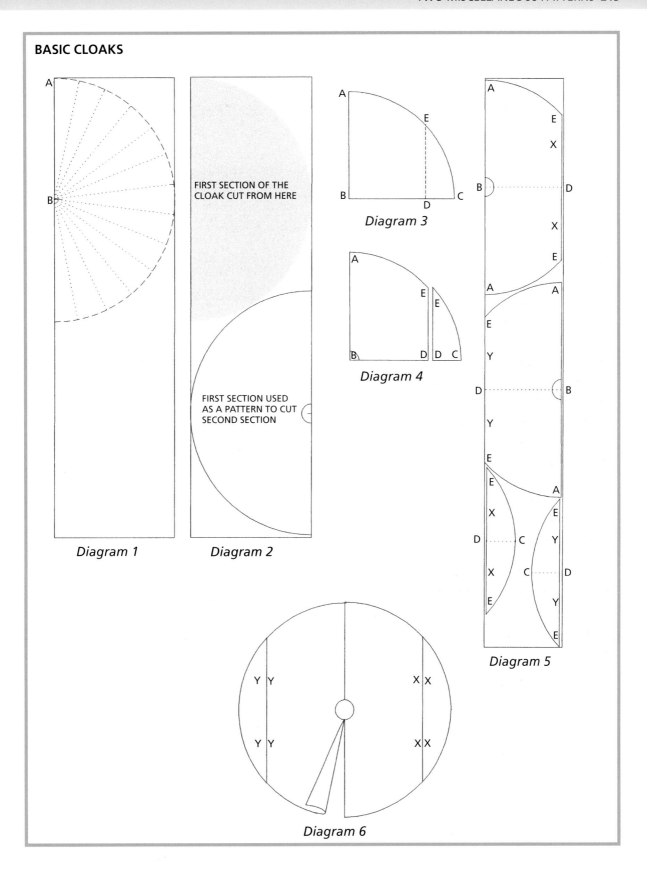

FIRST SECTION OF THE
CLOAK CUT FROM HERE

FIRST SECTION USED
AS A PATTERN TO CUT
SECOND SECTION

Diagram 1

Diagram 2

Diagram 3

Diagram 4

Diagram 5

Diagram 6

12 Cut round the neckline leaving about 2cm (¾") seam allowance. There will be sufficient off-cuts to make a neckband or collar.

Using narrow fabric

Note. Unless it is to be a very rough cloak cut a ¼ circle pattern.

Diagram 3

13 A–B and B–C = length of the cloak plus the radius of the neck.

14 B–D = width of fabric minus 2cm (¾") for seam allowance.

15 Square up D–E.

Diagram 4

16 Cut along D–E.

17 From B measure out the radius of the neckline and draw a ¼ circle as diagram.

Diagram 5

18 Place the main part of the pattern along the selvedge of the fabric as diagram and draw around.

19 Reverse the pattern and place as diagram.

20 Repeat the process along the opposite selvedge.

21 Using the small piece of pattern mark out the rest of the cloak as diagram.

Diagram 6

If the fabric has a pattern or is directional in other ways e.g. velvet or shot silk, it is important to make up the cloak as the diagram matching the edges X–X and Y–Y. The small pieces should be at the sides where they are less conspicuous.

When the piecings are very small, it is possible to cut them across the width of the fabric provided it has no pile or directional pattern.

A circle of 150cm radius would require approximately:

9.3m if the fabric is		91cm wide
7.8m	"	112cm wide
7.4m	"	122cm wide
6.5m	"	137cm wide
5.7m	"	150cm wide

This would make a cloak 143cm long (allowing 14cm for the diameter of the neck).

A circle of 60" radius would require approximately:

10½ yards if the fabric is		36" wide
8⅞ yards	"	44" wide
8⅜ yards	"	48" wide
7½ yards	"	54" wide
6⅜ yards	"	60" wide

This would make a cloak 57" long (allowing 6" for the diameter of the neck).

SIMPLE TROUSERS

Sheet of paper:

½ seat measurement + three times the front crutch width measurement + 5cm (2") ease

x

Outside leg measurement + front crutch width measurement

Note. The front crutch width measurement is used for convenience; with such simple, baggy trousers the measurement is not critical.

SIMPLE TROUSERS

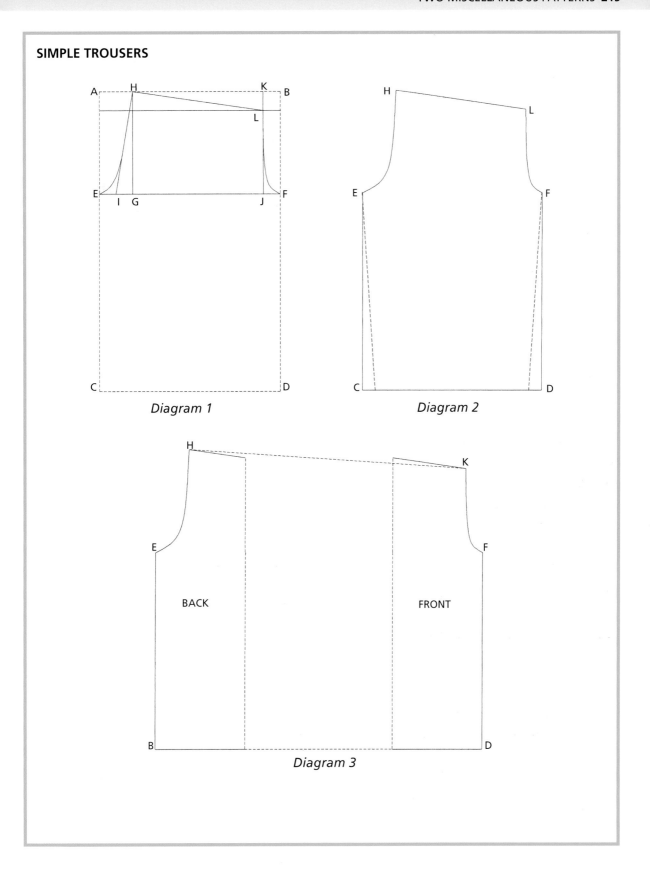

Diagram 1

Diagram 2

Diagram 3

Diagram 1

1 Mark the corners of the paper A, B, C, D as diagram.

2 From C measure up C–E = inside leg measurement minus 5cm (2").

3 Square out E–F right across the paper.

4 From E measure out E–G = twice front crutch width measurement.

5 From G square up to meet A–B at H.

6 I is midway between E–G.

7 Join H–I with a straight line and curve to E as diagram.

8 From F measure out F–J = front crutch width measurement.

9 From J square up to meet A–B at K.

10 From J measure down J–L = front crutch width measurement.

11 Join H–L.

12 Join L–F with a curve as diagram.

13 Cut off surplus paper to complete the pattern as Diagram 2.

Note. If a casing for a drawstring is required, add 5cm (2") to the top of the pattern parallel to H–L.

The legs can be tapered by moving the inside leg seam 5–10cm (2–4") as indicated in red.

Diagram 3

The pattern can be widened by cutting down the centre and spreading the back and front sections. It would be unnecessary to cut an enlarged pattern in paper as the two sections can be placed on the fabric and joined as diagram.

Source material

The illustrations in this book have been selected to show the most characteristic styles of each period but cannot possibly take the place of a dedicated history of costume. A selection of standard works is listed in the bibliography and these can be augmented by collecting a personal archive. Illustrated histories and books on the work of painters and other visual artists are valuable sources of information. Catalogues from exhibitions, magazine articles and even calendars and greetings cards are all worth saving. When looking at portraits, care should be taken to ensure that the sitter is wearing contemporary dress and not costume worn specially for the portrait. The costume worn by John, Marquis of Atholl (1680) would not be confused with general attire but the subject of Gainsborough's painting popularly known as *The Blue Boy* is wearing less extraordinary clothes that are in fact an 18th-century approximation of second quarter of the 17th-century costume. In the 17th-century, sitters often wore loose, informal clothes as it was thought that the portrait would not date so much as if they were wearing the latest fashion.

Three-dimensional resource materials – statues, effigies, memorials and porcelain figurines – are particularly useful as, unlike paintings and drawings, the costume can be seen from all angles. Reference for early costume has to be from paintings and sculpture but it is possible to examine actual garments for later periods. Museums with costume collections have far more items than can be displayed at any one time and there are usually facilities where students can examine specimens from the reserve collection. When seeking permission to see such garments, students should contact the curator in writing (enclosing a stamped, addressed envelope) and be specific about what they would like to see. Interesting costumes should be photographed as comprehensively as possible. It is worth while investing in a digital camera and a tripod.

Small regional museums often have collections of costumes donated by local people, sometimes via the local amateur dramatic society. These may have been altered either to fit a different size or to be used for a purpose other than that originally intended. The alterations are usually easy to recognise by the experienced eye but caution should be exercised by the novice. One common clue is inferior workmanship; if the garment was altered because the original owner lost or gained weight, the alteration is generally neatly done; but alterations for fancy dress or theatrical use are likely to be less well done. The usual alterations to look out for are seams let out or taken in, and extra decoration of inferior quality. Sometimes a man's coat, especially a very beautiful dress coat, may have been adapted to be worn by a woman as fancy dress. Even if the garment has been altered, it is always worth while handling old costumes to examine the cut, fabrics and method of construction.

You may be shown family heirlooms that are associated with an historical event, such as a suit worn by an ancestor on a famous occasion or worn by a famous person. Treat these stories with caution: they may be true or patently untrue or perhaps the suit did belong to an ancestor who was at that event but he did not buy it until many years later.

Museums of rural life or exhibitions connected to industrial sites such as a coal mine or factory may not have costume collections but they usually have clothed figures to illustrate various occupations. It is worth examining these figures as they may well be wearing garments of interest. It is unusual to find old trousers as these would have been worn until they fell apart, but coats can last until they are too old fashioned to be worn or the owner dies and they often turn up on lay figures in modest collections. Very often these collections are only open in the summer months, but permission can be obtained for garments to be examined out of season.

All the sources mentioned are valuable but there are many times when they are not available or there may not be time to make a special journey to see a particular exhibition. It is always worth while collecting a personal archive of reference material whether or not it is relevant to your work in hand. Items should be carefully filed with their relevant information, in particular the date and whereabouts. As well as cuttings from magazines, postcards etc, it is good practice to keep a record of interesting items seen in costume collections, art galleries, stately homes and similar places. These may come in useful in the future and the very process of collecting a wide variety of costume-related data will your increase knowledge and understanding of the subject.

BIBLIOGRAPHY

General works
Arnold, Janet, *A Handbook of Costume*, Macmillan, Basingstoke, 1973.
Black, J. Anderson and Garland Madge, *A History of Fashion*, Orbis Publishers, London, 1975.
Boucher, François, *A History of Costume in the West*, Thames & Hudson, London, 1996.
Byrde, Penelope, *The Male Image: Men's Fashion in Britain, 1300–1970*, Batsford, London, 1979.
Cunnington, C.W. & P.E. and Beard, Charles, *A Dictionary of English Costume 900–1900*, A & C Black,
    London, 1965.
de Marly, Diana, *Fashion for Men*, Batsford, London, 1985.
de Marley, Diana, *Working Dress*, Batsford, London, 1986.
Ewing, Elizabeth, *Everyday Dress 1650–1900*, Batsford, London, 1984.
Köhler, Carl, *A History of Costume*, Dover Publications Inc. Mineola, NY, 2000.
Laver, James, *Costume and Fashion: A Concise History of Costume*, Thames & Hudson, 2002.
Millia, Davenport, *The Book of Costume*, Crown Publishers Inc., New York, 1972.
Ribeiro, Aileen, *The Gallery of Fashion*, National Portrait Gallery, London, 2000.
Styles, John, *Dress of the People*, Yale University Press, London, 2008.
Waugh, Norah, *The Cut of Men's Clothes 1600–1900*, Routledge, 1987.

16th and 17th centuries
Arnold, Janet, *Patterns of Fashion: The cut and construction of clothes for men and women c. 1560–1620*
    Macmillan, Basingstoke, 1985.
Art Classics, *Velázquez*, Series Editor: Eileen Romano, Rizzoli International Publications, New York, 2003.
Brown, Christopher, *Van Dyck*, Rizzoli International Publications, New York, 1999.
Hagen, Rose-Marie and Rainer, *Pieter Bruegel the Elder c. 1525–1569: peasants, fools and demons*,
    Taschen, Cologne, 2000.
Hearn, Karen (ed), *Dynasties, Painting in Tudor and Jacobean England 1530–1630*, Tate Publishing,
    London, 1995.
Mettra, Claude, *Bruegel, the man and his painting*, Ferndale Editions, London, 1980.
Franits, Wayne, *Dutch Seventeenth-century Genre Painting*, Yale University Press, London, 2008.
Kuznetsov, Yury and Linnik, Irene, *Dutch Painting in Soviet Museums*, Harry N. Abrams, New York, 1982.
Latham, Robert (selected and edited), *The Illustrated Pepys*, Bell & Hyman, London, 1978.
Moir, Alfred, *Van Dyck*, Thames & Hudson, London, 1994.
Roberts, Keith, *Bruege*, Phaidon, London, 1982.

18th and 19th centuries
Baumgarten, Linda, *What Clothes Reveal: the language of clothing in colonial and federal America*, The
    Colonial Williamsburg Foundation in association with Yale University Press, Williamsburg, 2002.
Bindman, David, *Hogarth*, Thames & Hudson, London, 1981.
Cobb, Richard (General Editor) – *The French Revolution*, Simon & Schuster, 1988
Craske, Matthew, *William Hogarth*, Princeton University Press, Princeton, 2001.
Einberg, Elizabeth, *Hogarth the Painter*, exhibition catalogue, Tate Gallery Publishing, 1997
Morrison, Venetia, *The Art of George Stubbs*, Quantum Publishing Ltd, London, 2003.
Pyne, W.H., *Picturesque Views of Rural Occupations in Early Nineteenth Century England*, Dover
    Publications Inc. Mineola, NY, 1977.
Rosenthal, Michael, *The Art of Thomas Gainsborough*, Yale University Press, London 1999.
Tozier, Jane and Levitt, Sarah, *Fabric of Society: A Century of People and their Clothes 1770–1870*, Laura
    Ashley, Wales, 1983.
Walker, George, *The Costume of Yorkshire*, Caliban Books, 1978.
Webster, Mary, *Hogarth*, Studio Vista, London, 1978.

Relevant articles in *Costume, The Journal of the Costume Society*

Arnold, Janet, *A Study of Three Jerkins*	Number 5
Swain, Margaret H., *Nightgown into Dressing Gown*	Number 6
Taylor, Lou, *An Eighteenth Century Boy's Suit*	Number 7
Dalton, June, *Fabrics and Thread in a Man's Coat of 1735*	Number 11
Tarrant, Naomi E.A., *Lord Sheffield's Banyan*	Number 11
Strong, Roy, *Charles I's clothes for the years 1633–1635*	Number 14
Murdock, William and Company, John, *An Eighteenth-century Militia Uniform*	Number 17
Edwards, Lesley, *'Dres't Like a May-pole' A study of two suits of c. 1660–62*	Number 19
Wilcox, David, *Cut and Construction of a Late Eighteenth-century Coat*	Number 33

ILLUSTRATION CREDITS